The Buccaneer King

This book is dedicated to the all the heroes and adventurers in the world and to those people who strive for the impossible and achieve it.

The Buccaneer King

The Story of Captain Henry Morgan

Graham A. Thomas

Pen & Sword
MARITIME

First published in Great Britain in 2014 by
Pen & Sword Maritime
an imprint of
Pen & Sword Books Ltd
47 Church Street
Barnsley
South Yorkshire
S70 2AS

Copyright © Graham A. Thomas 2014

ISBN 978 1 84884 840 5

A CIP catalogue record for this book is available from
the British Library

Typeset in Ehrhardt by
Mac Style, Driffield, East Yorkshire
Printed and bound in the UK by CPI Group (UK) Ltd, Croydon,
CRO 4YY

Pen & Sword Books Ltd incorporates the imprints of Pen & Sword
Archaeology, Atlas, Aviation, Battleground, Discovery, Family
History, History, Maritime, Military, Naval, Politics, Railways, Select,
Transport, True Crime, and Fiction, Frontline Books, Leo Cooper,
Praetorian Press, Seaforth Publishing and Wharncliffe.

For a complete list of Pen & Sword titles please contact
PEN & SWORD BOOKS LIMITED
47 Church Street, Barnsley, South Yorkshire S70 2AS, England
E-mail: enquiries@pen-and-sword.co.uk
Website: www.pen-and-sword.co.uk

Contents

List of Plates

1. Morgan at Porto Bello.
2. Puerto del Príncipe (now Camagüey) being sacked in 1668 by Morgan.
3. Henry Morgan recruiting for the attack.
4. Henry Morgan destroys the Spanish fleet at Lake Maracaibo, Venezuela.
5. Map showing Chagres Castle.
6. Submerged palms and battery casemates of Old Port Royal.
7. A drawing of Port Royal before the earthquake that destroyed it.
8. A closer view of the submerged remains of Port Royal.
9. San Lorenzo Fort as it is today.
10. King's Square, St Jago de la Vega (Spanish Town), 1820–24.
11. The Golden Vale, Portland Jamaica, circa 1820–24.
12. Harbour Street Kingston Jamaica, circa 1820–24.
13. Bryan Castle, Great House, Trelawny, Jamaica, circa 1820–24.
14. The Bog Walk, circa 1820–24.
15. The Bridge over the White River, St Mary's, Jamaica, circa 1820–24.
16. Kingston and Port Royal from Windsor Farm, Jamaica, circa 1820–24.
17. Spring Garden Estate, St George's, Jamaica, circa 1820–24.
18. Bridge over the Rio Cobre, Spanish Town, Jamaica, circa 1820–24.
19. The Capture of Puerto Bello. This painting is based on an engraving from a panoramic painting by Samuel Scott. In the summer of 1739, during a debate in the House of Commons relating to the deteriorating situation with Spain in the West Indies, Captain Edward Vernon claimed he could take the Spanish town of Puerto Bello, Panama, on the north side of the Isthmus of Darien with six ships of the line. He was taken at his word, promoted to vice admiral and given six ships to redeem his pledge. The war became known as the War of Jenkins' Ear.
20. Map of Mexico, Florida and the West Indies, by Balthasar Ruyter. This is an extremely rare and unusual map of 1747, showing Mexico, the Caribbean, the West Indies and Florida from roughly Michoacán Mexico, west to Surinam, north as far as modern-day Virginia and south as far as modern-day Ecuador.

Acknowledgements

I would like to thank those authors and researchers who have come before me, such as Dudley Pope, Stephen Talty and Terry Breverton, but I would mostly like to thank the people at British History Online, who have placed a huge number of historical documents online for everyone to access. Without them, the vast amount of information in this book – the letters, the minutes, the reports – would have been much harder to access. They are doing a terrific job!

Preface

When I was researching a book about Blackbeard, the pirate, another name kept cropping up that I could not account for. That name was Sir Henry Morgan. Now, these two men didn't live at the same time (Blackbeard came several decades after Morgan) but scholars and researchers tended to either compare them, or when they named Blackbeard as the most famous pirate who ever lived they would add that Morgan was probably the most famous buccaneer who ever lived.

Intrigued, I had to discover for myself just who this Morgan was. Once I started digging I have to admit I was greatly surprised. The achievements of Morgan – sacking Panama, for example – far outweighed those of Blackbeard, or even Bartholomew Roberts, who took more than 400 ships during his brief career as king of the pirates.

Morgan was a cut above these two men – far above, in my opinion. Unlike the pirates, Morgan was driven by more than just the lure of gold. He was a patriot, loyal to the King and his country; in particular, Jamaica. He realized that pillage and plunder was the way to not only make his own fortune but to build the wealth and prosperity of the island. He never attacked without a commission or letter of marque from the Jamaican government, and all his exploits were against the Spanish, England's enemy at the time. He helped to expand England's influence within the West Indies.

There are many myths that surround Morgan, which some scholars and historians have attempted to dispel. Supposedly, he or his men committed torture and other brutal acts on their Spanish prisoners ... or did they? As we look into the life of Henry Morgan, we shall see.

There was an eyewitness to many of Morgan's campaigns – Alexander O. Esquemeling, who sailed with the buccaneers as a surgeon. Most of the sources of research used for this book call him John Esquemeling, and it is this name that we will use. Knowledge of this man is incomplete although there are many who 'believe that John Esquemeling was a pseudonym for Hendrik Barentzoon Smeeks, a surgeon who left his hometown of Zwolle in central Holland to serve aboard a merchant ship with the Dutch East India Company.'[1] He wrote an account of his voyages in the West Indies and some of the campaigns led by Morgan in which he was involved. It is on his account that scholars have since based their work.

But is it accurate? Esquemeling is the one who tells us that torture was used on prisoners in order for the buccaneers to find out where treasure was hidden. However, if, as Dudley Pope tells us in his book about Morgan, *Harry Morgan's Way*, Esquemeling's account is exaggerated, then what do we believe?

It is highly likely that the truth lies somewhere in the middle. Every writer embellishes his or her own work in order to excite the reader and sell as many books as possible. The accusation that Esquemeling exaggerated his accounts for this purpose is probably justified to some degree, but the authors who claim he was exaggerating are very likely themselves doing this in order to make their arguments more convincing.

While this book touches upon the allegations that Morgan and/or his men tortured prisoners for profit, it is more concerned with the man himself and the times in which he lived. The times were hard; they were rough and brutal.

Wherever possible we will be using official letters and documents to establish the facts but first and foremost this is a story of daring and courage, of an extraordinary man whose actions were akin to empire building. Like all of us, he was flawed, but England has not seen the likes of him for a long, long time and probably never will again. That's what makes this tale so compelling.

Graham A. Thomas
Warminster, April 2013

Marching with Morgan

The commander marched ahead of his men, their colours flying in the hot breeze. Ahead lay the prize and spoils for those who had the courage to take them. He did and so did the 750 men marching with him.

Already the Spanish had tried to outwit him by felling trees along the road. But he had seen this ruse before and so ordered his men to march through the jungle. It was hard going for the heat was stifling, the undergrowth was thick and the men had to hack their way through it. But he knew the town wasn't far and in the town there were riches, wine, food and women.

He smiled at the Spanish attempts to stop him. They had thrown up ambuscades and mounted cannon facing the road to destroy his forces. They hadn't thought that he would go through the dense woods. His men had spotted the Spanish troops waiting with their cannon and musketry at the ambuscades and reported back to him.

But time was short. The blocked roads meant that the Spanish knew they were coming and so would be feverishly hiding their wealth in the surrounding countryside. Once they were past the blockades he spurred his men on.

Finally, they emerged from the woods onto the savannah and could see the town in the distance. The commander urged his men forward, drawing closer and closer to the town. As they came within sight of the entrance he could see the proud Spanish governor on his fine horse behind his foot soldiers and in the middle of his cavalry waiting for them. They were facing the wrong way.

The commander ordered his men to spread out from the rank and file formation into a semi-circle. He ordered the drums to beat, the men to quicken their step, muskets at the ready and the colours to fly.

Alarmed, the Spanish governor turned to face them, leading his mounted troops towards the buccaneers now marching towards the town. The Spanish horses charged but the commander expected this and had put his best shots at the front of his semi-circle formation. As the Spanish rode in, they were cut down from three sides by accurate musket fire. Regrouping, the Spanish charged again and again each time they met a hail of musket balls. Horses reared, men fell, their flesh torn by hot iron balls ripping into them.

The commander fired at approaching targets, waiting until the enemy were almost on top of him before pulling the trigger. More Spanish fell from their horses, shot through with musket balls. A musket ball ripped into the Spanish governor, throwing him from his horse, his blood flowing freely. Seeing the death of their leader those remaining Spanish still mounted headed for the woods for protection but even they were cut down by a rearguard the commander had placed behind his main formation.

As the Spanish mounted troops fled, the commander raised his sword and called for his men to surge forward. Shouting and screaming the men charged towards the town and met the Spanish foot soldiers. They quickly cut through them with swords and musket fire. The Spanish, seeing that their governor was dead and that the marauders held the upper hand, retreated, some heading back into the town while others headed across the open savannah towards the woods but were cut down long before they reached safety.

Those that retreated back into the town immediately shut themselves into houses with the inhabitants to continue the fight. They hid in windows and behind doors, waiting for the chance to fire on the invaders.

They didn't wait long.

The commander ordered the men to enter the town and take it. As they came rushing in the Spanish soldiers fired on them from their hiding places. Some of his men were killed and injured. Musket balls smashed into the walls and cobblestoned streets. His men took cover, returning the fire. But this kind of fighting could go on for days [and] time was not on the commander's side. He ordered runners to take messages to the Spanish saying that he would burn the town to the ground and kill everyone in it, including women and children, if the Spanish continued to resist.

The firing stopped. After a while a white flag appeared and the last elements of resistance surrendered. Immediately, the commander ordered his men to spread throughout the town, taking any prisoners and locking them into the churches. As they spread out the men grabbed what loot was still left and corralled the prisoners.

With the town secure, the commander sent expedition parties into the surrounding countryside to search for wealth that had been hidden.

Over the time of the occupation more and more prisoners would be brought into the town to be tortured and punished until they told the marauders where their wealth was hidden as ransom for their lives. Indeed, four prisoners had been freed by the occupiers to go out into the country and raise the ransom they wanted. These four prisoners returned with nothing, saying they needed more time.

But the Spanish stalling tactics would work against them and many died of starvation.

So the account goes.

Who were they and who was their commander? He was Captain Henry Morgan and he was to become 'the greatest and most renowned of all the buccaneers'.[1]

The year was 1668 and the town that Morgan attacked and occupied was Puerto del Príncipe. The men who followed him were hard men, pirates and privateers out for loot and glory. They were largely English and French and they hated the Spanish. When these men heard of the expedition against Spanish-held Cuba and that it was to be commanded by Morgan, they flocked to join him for they were sure of victory. His reputation and his deeds were already known far and wide.

> He was, in his way, a military genius, a truly remarkable leader of irregular troops whose skill in planning attacks, implementing them with secrecy and dash, and in maintaining throughout amazing discipline over his men commands admiration.[2]

Henry Morgan is best known as the man who sacked Panama City. His reign as a privateer lasted only four years but his career in Jamaica lasted much longer. Prior to him and his crew setting sail in 1670 for the Panama expedition the mood in the English colony of Jamaica had changed. Peace with Spain was being negotiated and became a reality with the signing of the Treaty of Madrid the same year. But before official news of the treaty arrived in Jamaica, Sir Thomas Modyford, the governor of the island, gave the go-ahead for the expedition. As this story unfolds the justifying circumstances of the mounting of this operation will be revealed.

After the Panama affair, Morgan and Modyford were sent to London to be punished for ignoring the treaty. Morgan was the toast of the town and was knighted. However, Modyford was imprisoned in the Tower of London. Morgan returned to Jamaica as Lieutenant Governor, with instructions to suppress the buccaneers, many of whom were his old shipmates. He died a rich man in 1688.

History has seen no other commander like Morgan, certainly no British commander. He would lead most of the attacks himself, often at the head of hundreds or, in the case of Panama, more than a thousand men. He was a product of his time. Perhaps Nelson is the closest to rival the deeds of Morgan than any other British commander. Although he had the title of captain or admiral he was a military man – a brilliant tactician and strategist in land warfare. One big difference between Morgan and other privateers/priates of history is that he always made sure he had commissions from the governor for his expeditions.

The truth about allegations of the use of torture against prisoners taken by Morgan's men, and whether he ordered or condoned this, is shrouded in the mists of time. For us to understand the man we need to take a detailed look at his battles, the actions that made him famous, and for this there are letters, some eyewitness reports, Spanish reports of the events and the work of John Esquemeling, who published his experiences on Morgan's expeditions in a book entitled *The Buccaneers of America*. As with any eyewitness account the accuracy and reliability of the detail must be not be taken for granted; we need also to use a wide variety of other sources.

This is the story of Sir Henry Morgan, buccaneer, family man, politician and a great leader.

Part I

The Buccaneer

Chapter 1

First Moves

Captain Henry Morgan was different to his contemporaries as well as to the pirates and buccaneers that came after him. For a start, he was successful. He was married to the same woman for twenty years. Despite the atrocities he is alleged to have committed or that were committed in his name upon the Spanish he was never punished for them; instead he was made a hero and knighted by the English. He was appointed as Lieutenant Governor of Jamaica and then was relieved of his position by a vindictive and rather paranoid governor who believed that Morgan was at the heart of everything wrong in Jamaica. Nothing was further from the truth and we will look into this in detail later in this book.

Perhaps one of the chief differences between Morgan and pirates like Roberts, Vane, Blackbeard and many others is that he did his fighting on land and did not take ship after ship. He rarely got involved in great sea battles. While he was elected as admiral by the men who served with him, he was more of a general than an admiral.

Of course there is a lot of other material that has been written about Morgan. This book attempts to look at the different sides of the man. How do we marry the ruthless man capable of bringing so much misery and misfortune to his enemies with the man who was devoted to his wife and family and who was given one of the highest offices in the thriving colony of Jamaica? To the civilized twenty-first-century mind this can be hard to reconcile. Was he just a butcher, a monster, a man driven by greed and power, or was he driven by patriotism? Was he truly responsible for the torture and murder of Spanish prisoners? Some scholars say yes, others disagree.

The only way for us to find answers to these questions is to put the man into context, look at his actions, at the times in which he lived, at his letters and the people who influenced him the most. One key point is that Morgan always thought of himself as a privateer. He never embarked on an expedition without a commission from the government of Jamaica, no matter how tenuous that commission might be. History labels him a buccaneer, or a pirate in some cases, but he was, technically, a privateer. 'The one label we can give him is that of buccaneer, that romantic-sounding word that applied to several generations of fortune hunters who roamed the Caribbean looking for plunder.'[1]

What do we know of Morgan? Certainly we don't know what he looked like as there is no physical description of him, save for the one given by the physician attending him in the last months of life. By then, the power and might of the man had gone out of him and he was reduced to a sallow, lean and gaunt figure with a swollen belly. But to lead hundreds of men – who were not military men but largely buccaneers, privateers and fortune hunters – on expeditions against the Spanish, and be able to instil enough discipline in them to successfully carry out his military plans, takes a man of considerable power, discipline, strength and self-confidence. As we have seen in the introduction, Morgan was able to improvise in the middle of an operation by skirting blocked roads and marching his men through thick, humid rain forest. For this to work the improvisation had to go all the way down the line from Morgan's commanders at the top to the men at the bottom.

Many writers suggest that Morgan was born around 1635 to a good Welsh family from the county of Monmouth. His father was Robert Morgan, a farmer living in Llanrhymni. This branch of the family was related to the Tredegar House Morgans, who lived just a few miles away to the east. Robert had a brother, William, of Llanrhymni Hall, in the same area. Inside the Church of St Mellons, not far from Llanrhymni, there are many memorials to the Morgans. Indeed, during this time in the counties of Monmouthshire and Glamorgan there were a handful of other 'great families', such as Herbert, Stradling and Matthews.

Henry had two distinguished uncles, both brothers of his father: Edward, who was a colonel in the Cavaliers during the Civil War fighting for the Royalist cause; and Thomas, who also fought in the Civil War but on the side of the Parliamentarians under Cromwell. Edward was later to become Lieutenant Governor of Jamaica, a post that Morgan himself would hold.

> One thing is certain about Morgan – he was the product of his time. He could not have flourished as the greatest of the buccaneers had he been born twenty years earlier or twenty years later.[2]

Henry Morgan married the daughter of Edward Morgan in Jamaica. Deciding to follow in the footsteps of his uncles, Henry joined an expeditionary force that left Britain in 1654 under the command of General Venables and Admiral Penn, with the objective of taking the islands of Hispaniola and Cuba from the Spanish. The force arrived in Barbados on 29 January 1655, when Morgan was just twenty years old. Venables needed men, so from the islands of

St Kitts and Nevis he recruited 1,200 men, and then once in Barbados took on another 3,500. It didn't matter that they were barely trained for the task in hand.

Arriving at Hispaniola they headed for the south side of the island, landing at Santo Domingo, where Penn and Venables sent 7,000 men ashore to capture the town and the rest of the island according to the original plan. But things went badly for the English force. The men were affected by tropical disease and this, combined with incompetent leadership, left the expedition in chaos and more than 2,000 men died, not from battle, but from sickness. The English were forced to withdraw.

Undaunted, Penn and Venables turned their attention to another Spanish settlement that was lightly defended – Jamaica. Had the defences been much stronger the poor leadership could have spelt disaster, but the English had the greater numbers and they overwhelmed the Spanish. However, this was not the end of the matter.

The last Spanish governor of the island, Don Cristoble Arnalso de Ysassi, fled to the hills, where he commanded an effective guerrilla war against the English. But two expeditions from Cuba sent to reinforce the courageous Don were met off the north coast of the island and defeated while the Don and his forces were defeated in 1657 near Ocho Rios. By 1660 the Don's forces were few; the slave allies (known as the Maroons) he'd brought with him after fleeing the city deserted and before the year was over he and what was left of his guerrilla force escaped under the cover of darkness, rowing in canoes to the safety of Cuba.[3]

At that time, the war in Europe against Spain was officially over but in the West Indies the situation was much more fluid. The Spanish continued to capture English ships cruising off the Spanish Main[4] and considered all English ships as pirate ships and treated them accordingly.

By early 1660 Morgan was heavily involved in the skirmishing that continued as the former Spanish governor did his best to hang on. When Morgan was not involved in expeditions against the guerrillas he was a privateer operating under the command of Commodore Christopher Myngs. The main port was called Cagway, or Caguaya, and the English built a fort there to protect the natural harbour. Hearing of the regular expeditions of Myngs's fleet against the Spanish, privateers began to flock to the new settlement.

The young Morgan proved to be popular and soon made friends amongst the privateers. As a captain he distinguished himself by taking three ships on a single raid. 'Captain John Morris, a friend of Morgan's, bought one and renamed it the *Dolphin*.'[5] Captain Robert Serle bought another, the largest of the three, which had eight cannon and weighed more than 80 tons. He named this ship the *Cagway*. Along with Captain John Lawrence, who renamed his ship the *Pearl*, these four men became fast friends and the most popular and daring of all the Cagway privateers.

News arrived from England in August 1660 when the *Convertine* sailed into the harbour. Charles II was back on the English throne having been restored to it by General Monck. Peace had been declared now between England, France and Spain, while Monck was made Earl of Albemarle for his help in getting Charles II back on the throne. However, Jamaica was not returned to the Spanish in the peace deal.

Colonel D'Oyley as the first governor of Jamaica was tasked with defending the new English settlement. He had a twelve-man council to assist him and one of its members included a close friend of Henry Morgan, Henry Archbald, who had arrived on the *Convertine*. Another friend, Thomas Ballard, was also elected to the council. The task of defending Jamaica was a daunting one as there were no resources other than the privateers and any help from England was months away. After less than a year in office, D'Oyley, who had proved to be an unpopular governor, decided he couldn't cope and asked to be relieved.

His replacement, Lord Windsor, immediately began to make changes upon his arrival in Jamaica. To honour the newly restored king, Port Royal became the new name for Cagway and the fort was given a new battery of cannon and renamed Fort Charles. Lord Windsor then created a militia that was made up of five regiments and Henry Morgan was given a commission in the Port Royal Regiment for his work in fighting the Spanish guerrillas under the hapless Don. But there was a thorn in the side of the young colony. The Spanish rebels had been supplied by the Spaniards in Cuba from the closest settlement to Jamaica, Santiago de Cuba, on the island of Cuba, only 150 miles away from Jamaica. Lord Windsor believed this would be a perfect place for the Spanish to launch their invasion of Jamaica. Even though there was peace between England and Spain in Europe, the council in Jamaica voted to send an expedition to destroy Santiago de Cuba.

Myngs led the fleet towards Cuba and, once again, Morgan was commanding his own ship as captain, along with his friend Robert Serle in command of the *Cagway*. Myngs's flagship, the *Centurion*, was a forty-six-gun vessel and sailed at the head of the fleet.

On 5 October 1660 they sighted Santiago de Cuba and having obtained information from former prisoners of the Spanish who knew the town, they realized that a frontal assault would be a disaster because of the Spanish cannon protecting the narrow entrance to the huge harbour. Instead, they landed 2 miles down the coast, near the mouth of the San Juan River, and began landing men and supplies. They marched and hacked their way through the dense forest heading for the town in an assault from the rear.

The following morning, Myngs's forces reached the town, having cut through 9 miles of forest, and attacked. The Spanish were taken by surprise and fled, leaving riches behind them. The privateers began a systematic looting, which ended when they blew up the town and the fort with 700 casks of Spanish gunpowder they'd seized.

On 22 October, Myngs returned with the rest of the fleet and vast amounts of plunder taken from the town including 'six ships, cannon, wine, silver plate, church bells, hide and more. Just six buccaneers were killed and twenty went missing.'[6]

By 1662 Lord Windsor had stepped down as governor due to ill health and Sir Charles Lyttleton, who had been Windsor's lieutenant governor, was now temporarily in charge. But Lyttleton was a man of peace and refused to attack the Spanish. Since the end of the war in Europe, envoys had been sent from Jamaica to the Spanish Main to negotiate peaceful trade. However, the Spanish flatly refused to allow trade with the new English colony. Concessions and diplomacy weren't working. To make matters worse, when Windsor had been governor, he'd received instructions from King Charles II to force trade, if necessary.

Since the attack on Cuba the privateers had been idle and there was no pay for them while they sat and waited for Lyttleton to issue the necessary papers enabling them to go out and plunder the Spanish.

Myngs was impatient. He knew that the privateers could turn to piracy if they didn't have some direction. He also knew that on the coast of Mexico there were English log cutters who had great difficulty getting their wood from the coast to England via Jamaica because of the Spanish. It was these log cutters that Myngs wanted to protect and ensure their trade routes were secure. Day after day he approached Lyttleton, slowly wearing the man down until, finally, on Christmas Day 1662, Lyttleton relented and letters of marque were issued to the privateers to attack the Mexican coastline, specifically a prosperous town built on a Mayan site known as Campeche. Its full title was San Francisco de Campeche and it was called Campeachy by the English.

It would not be an easy victory. To the north and south the town and its harbour were guarded by two fortresses, the Castillo San Jose, 2 miles north of the town, and the Castillo San Miguel, 2 miles south. Both these fortresses stood at the tops of hills overlooking the town. There were also 'three batteries of cannon between the fortresses, protecting the town and the port'.[7]

In Jamaica preparations were under way for the expedition against the Spanish. Myngs chose his captains, giving each of them letters of marque.

Those captains included 27-year-old Henry Morgan, his two friends, Captain John Morris and Captain Jackman, along with Captain Abraham Blauveldt and Captain Edward Mansveldt – the latter an experienced and famous Dutch buccaneer more usually known as Mansfield. The fleet Myngs assembled included fourteen ships from Port Royal, three French ships from Tortuga and three Dutch privateers, along with more than 1,100 men. Leading the fleet in the *Centurion*, Myngs raised his sails and hoisted his anchor, setting sail from Port Royal in January 1663.

Along the way, one ship was lost in a storm and three more were separated from the fleet. They sailed for days, crossing more than a thousand miles of ocean. By 9 February 1663 they anchored a mile down the coast from Campeche and began landing their men.

While they did this, Myngs sent a boat to the governor asking for his surrender. He waited for the response.

Realizing that the Spanish were stalling, he decided not to give them time to move or hide their valuables and prepare for a fight so he attacked the town, his men only armed with pikes, swords and pistols against the cannon. The fighting was intense.

For almost an entire day they fought. The buccaneers had to take the stone houses one by one while being shot at by Spanish snipers and soldiers. Shot whizzed around, bouncing off cobblestone, embedding into stone walls, tearing through clothing and ripping into flesh and bone. Men shouted as they attacked. Spanish soldiers were impaled by pikes. In close combat men were cut down by pistol shot and swords. Shards of wood, stone and metal flew in all directions from pistol and cannon shot.

Myngs was wounded three times but by the end of the day, the buccaneers were successful. In the harbour they captured fourteen vessels, and crews were chosen to take them back to Port Royal. 'The Spanish counted their losses at 150,000 pieces of eight, and the damage done to the town and the fort costing another 500,000 to repair.'[8]

Myngs and the rest of the fleet left Campeche on 23 February but did not arrive in Port Royal, Jamaica, until 13 April. In his book *Admiral Sir Henry Morgan*, Terry Breverton suggests that the delay was down to the fleet spending some time sharing out the loot they had plundered from the Spanish 'rather than bring it back to Jamaica for the English royal family and assorted ship owners to take their commission.'

But what of Henry Morgan? The captains and crews that sailed with Myngs and sacked Campeche had made a considerable amount from that action.

Morgan and three other captains – John Morris, William Jackman and David Marteen – set sail from Port Royal in December 1663. They told no one where they were going. Their letters of marque were still valid. Their little fleet had been prepared and supplied, and more than 200 men signed on … but for what purpose no one knew. They effectively vanished for almost two years. The question is, where did they go?

Chapter 2

The Rise of Port Royal

In late 1663 Morgan and the other captains set sail on what would be a twenty-two-month voyage.

While Henry was away things had changed in Jamaica. A new governor, Sir Thomas Modyford, had arrived and with him came more than a thousand settlers. Having been the governor of Barbados previously, and a planter on that island, Modyford realized how important the buccaneers were to Jamaica. The riches they gained from their expeditions they spent in Port Royal. This helped to develop the town, as well as the sugar and cocoa plantations, and encourage further agriculture. Modyford knew that the really wealthy privateers who had made Jamaica their home would be developing their land assets further.

Modyford's deputy was Colonel Sir Edward Morgan, Henry Morgan's uncle, who had been given the position as a reward for his Royalist support during the English Civil War. On the crossing from Britain, his wife and eldest daughter had died. However, in addition to Henry Morgan there was a distant cousin, Bledri Morgan, who had arrived earlier on the island, back in 1662.

When the colonel arrived with his surviving daughters there was no news of Henry; indeed, no one knew where he'd gone.

One of Modyford's first deeds was to move the capital of Jamaica from Port Royal a little further inland, to St Jago. Developing the plantations and convincing the settlers to grow crops was Modyford's top priority along with ensuring the island's security and rule of law. News of Myngs's attack on Campeche had spread far and wide, so much so that in September a letter arrived from King Charles II asking the governor to revoke the letters of marque for attacking the Spanish Main.

While the council agreed with Modyford that the aggression towards the Spanish should be stopped, Modyford knew that it would not go down well with the buccaneers and privateers on the island. They were already a rough and tough bunch and the new governor knew he had to make his authority on the island known. He was able to set an example when Captain Munro turned to piracy after his letter of marque had been revoked. Munro and his crew began capturing several English ships so Modyford himself went out and captured Munro. The pirate and his crew were hung in Port Royal.

But Modyford still had the problem of revoking the privateers' commissions. Many were plundering the Spanish Main and once they returned to Port Royal would be stripped of their commissions. They should also have had their booty taken from them if Modyford was adhering to the full letter of the law, but he knew they were the main defence for the island and if he took their ill-gotten gains away they would leave and possibly join up with the French at Tortuga, where they would be able to keep their wealth. He came up with a plan whereby they could keep their plunders and be given plantations so, instead of going back to sea, they could become the bedrock for Modyford's agricultural development.

By early 1665 the threat of war with Holland was very real. Myngs had been recalled to England because of it. Modyford had only the privateers on Jamaica, those operating out of Hispaniola and Tortuga, that he could rely on for defending the island.

A decision was made to take the fight to the Dutch by attacking their possessions of Saba and St Eustatius in the Leeward Islands, as well as Bonaire and Curaçao off the coast of Venezuela. The man to lead this expedition was Colonel Edward Morgan. By the time the fleet was ready to sail, England had declared war on Holland. Ten ships with more than 650 men had been put under Colonel Morgan's command. Morgan, a man with more than forty years of military experience, made a new will on the night before they sailed: he left his plantation to his two sons and a claim on the Llanrhymni estate back in Wales to his surviving eldest daughter, Mary Elizabeth, whom Henry Morgan would later marry.[1]

The plan of attack had been worked out by Modyford. The expedition was to attack the Dutch fleet at St Kitts, take the Dutch settlements of St Eustatius, Saba and Curaçao and then attack the French on the return journey at both Hispaniola and Tortuga.

However, things did not go entirely to plan. East of the Virgin Islands the fleet attacked St Eustatius:

whereon Col Morgan with 319 men landed, and after small opposition took the place, the good old Colonel leaping out of the boat, and being a corpulent man got a strain, and his spirit being great he pursued over earnestly the enemy on a hot day, so that he surfeited and suddenly died, to almost the loss of the whole design.[2]

In order to secure or partially secure the services of the buccaneers, Morgan had agreed to the men sharing equally in the plunder. But once the fort had been stormed and the governor of the little island surrendered, there was precious little plunder to be found. What there was – around 900 Negro and Indian slaves, cotton and guns – the buccaneers argued over how they were to be shared. Another group of buccaneers set sail for a different island only a few leagues away and forced the inhabitants and the governor there to surrender. This island was Nevis. Because of the arguing and such a poor showing in terms of plunder the expedition returned to Port Royal. When Colonel Morgan died the expedition was taken over by Colonel Carey.

> Col Carey succeeded him, and about three weeks after sent Maj Rich Stevens with a small party and took Saba also. Besides other plunder they had 900 slaves, 500 are arrived at Jamaica, with many coppers and stills, to the great furtherance of this colony, being very brave knowing blacks. The distractions caused by the loss of Col Morgan and the too easy disposition of Col Carey, to whose more large relation he refers his Lordship. Was much troubled that the main design against Curaçao was thus frustrated, and sent for the leading men of the privateers lately come in from Spanish quarters, whom he had obliged by not questioning them, and caused Major Byndloss to hold correspondence with the old privateer, Capt Mansfield, and to appoint a rendezvous at Blue Fields Bay, where it is calculated will be no less than 600 privateers, and they will forward the design of Curaçao, which he hopes will be the King's before this letter is in his hands.[3]

In the preceding letter by Modyford he recommends that the plantations taken on Eustatia and Sabia (Nevis) be sold to the English at St Christopher's and goes on to say that in addition to Carey's easy temperament he believed the reason for the loss 'of the design of Curaçao' was the 'covetousness of some of the officers and soldiers'.

> Please consider the militia is under no pay and the soldiers all but paper commissions, whereas in the actions of St Jago de Cuba and Campeachy they had the countenance of the King's ships.

Modyford stated that the Spanish prizes taken in the Campeachy raids had been sold but that the privateers 'plunder them and hide the goods in holes and creeks, so that the present orders little avail the Spaniard, but much prejudice His Majesty and His Royal Highness in the tenths and fifteenths of prizes.'

Indicating the trouble he was having with the lawlessness of the privateers he wrote, 'Some of the privateers are well bred and with good handling we hope to bring them to more humanity and good order, which once obtained His Majesty hath 1,500 of the best men in the world belonging to this island.'

Still there was no word from Henry Morgan and the other three captains. Indeed, Morgan had no idea that his relative Colonel Edward Morgan had died, nor did he know that Holland and England were at war.

Finally some news did come, in July 1665, when a Dutch captain who was also not aware of the war sailed into Port Royal. He had news of Morgan. This captain's name was David Marteen and he told the people of Port Royal that captains Morgan, Morris and Jackman would soon be arriving there, their holds stuffed with treasures taken from three major towns they'd attacked and plundered.

When they sailed in, they arrived as rich men and as heroes. There was little Modyford could do. As they had been away for almost two years they'd no idea that there was peace of sorts between Spain and England.

Morgan was now thirty years old, fit and tanned, a man celebrated across the island who must have seemed larger than life, especially when the news of his exploits got out. But there was sadness as well. Once he was back in Jamaica he found the two sons of Colonel Edward Morgan working on the plantation left to them by their father. Morgan also discovered that the old colonel had left behind three daughters. Colonel Edward Morgan had died a poor man and in his letter to Lord Arlington Modyford asked for assistance for the Colonel's family, pointing out that he was still owed money by the King.

Around the same time that Henry married Mary Elizabeth, the eldest surviving daughter of Colonel Edward Morgan, his friend Major Robert Byndloss married Edward Morgan's second daughter, Anna.[4]

While Morgan and the other three captains had returned to Port Royal in triumph, the question on everyone's lips was, what had they done on their long voyage of twenty-two months?

Chapter 3

Granada Sacked

In a letter dated 1 March 1666, Governor Sir Thomas Modyford wrote to the Duke of Albemarle detailing Morgan's exploits during this voyage. In late 1663 Morgan had left Jamaica with a fleet of five ships and more than 200 men, sailing past Cuba towards the Yucatán Peninsula.

Rounding the peninsula they sailed into the Gulf of Mexico, hugging the shoreline. For more than 150 miles, the little fleet cruised along the ragged, rough coast filled with reefs, shoals and bays, searching for the appropriate river to take them inland.

> Every action gives new encouragement to attempt the Spaniard, finding them in all places very weak and very wealthy. Two or three hundred privateers lately on the coast of Cuba, being denied provisions for money, marched 42 miles into the country, took and fired the town of Santo Spirito, routed a body of 200 horse, carried their prisoners to their ships, and for their ransom had 300 fat beeves [cattle] sent down. Many of their blacks would not go back, but stay with our men, and are willingly kept for guides.[1]

Using sounding lines to test the depths of the waters the ships sailed into the Bay of Campeche and finally anchored in the mouth of the Grijala River. This was the river that would take them to their objective. Before they could continue they needed water, food and, above all, information. From the anchored ships they disembarked 107 men and slowly rowed 3 miles inland along the river, where they came to the small village of Frontera. Unsure of the reception they would receive from the local inhabitants they were surprised to find the Indians hated the Spanish and were more than happy to help these English privateers attack Spanish towns further down the river.

Their objective was to attack Villa de Mosa, or Villahermosa, the capital of Tabasco province, which had been founded by the Spaniards in 1596 and was some 40 miles inland.[2] But the four captains wanted the element of surprise on their side, which meant that rowing down the river to the town was out of the question; they could not take the chance of being spotted by any Spanish settlements, guards or lookouts along the river who could then raise the alarm before they reached the town. Nor could they simply walk along the riverbank and hide in the woods as they approached for the banks were thick with jungle and swamps. The only way to reach the town was to march inland, avoiding the swamps and jungle. The buccaneers set off 'and guided by Indians marched with 107 men, 300 miles to avoid discovery to Vildemos, which they took and plundered.' The town's defences were poor but without the benefit of the Indians guiding them over the 300-mile journey, beyond the swamps, beyond any Spanish farms or settlements so as to avoid detection, they could not have achieved what they did. Indeed, the Spanish were complacent and believed they were safe from any attack. After all, the closest English territory to them was several hundred miles away in Jamaica.

They were wrong.

The four captains burst into the town square, taking the Spaniards completely by surprise. Shots broke the still quiet air and the Spanish, overwhelmed, quickly acquiesced. The buccaneers searched every house and building, gathering whatever plunder they could find, as well a few hundred prisoners.

The alarm must have been raised as the buccaneers plundered the town for when they headed back to their ships they would have been dismayed by what they found.

> But on returning to the mouth of the river they found that their ships had been taken by the Spaniards, who soon after attacked them with ships and 300 men. The Spaniards were beaten off without loss of a man.[3]

With their ships taken by the Spanish there was no way of escape as the Spanish soldiers attacked. They could go back up the river to the town but by this time the alarm had been raised and no doubt the Spanish would be rushing as many men to the river as they could. There was nothing for it but to stand and fight.

It was to be a one-sided skirmish. The buccaneers had superior muskets and musketry, and better experience. One by one, the Spanish soldiers fell from the firepower of the buccaneers until they retreated and sailed away.[4] Morgan now faced the problem of not having any ships with which he could continue his voyage. Modyford takes up the account in his letter:

> They then fitted up two barques and four canoes, took Rio Garta with thirty men and stormed a breastwork there killing fifteen and taking the rest prisoners, crossed the Bay of Honduras, watering at the Isle of Rattan, took the town of Truxillo and a vessel in the road, and came to the Mosquitos, where the Indians

are hostile to the Spaniards, and nine of them willingly came with them. They then anchored in Monkey Bay near Nicaragua River, up which they went in canoes, passing three falls, for a distance of 37 leagues, where began the entrance to a fair laguna or lake, judged to be 50 leagues by 30, of sweet water, full of excellent fish with its banks full of brave pastures and savannahs covered with horses and cattle, where they had as good beef and mutton as any in England. Riding by day under keys and islands and rowing all night, on the fifth night by the advice of their Indian guide, they landed near the city of Gran Granada.[5]

Centuries before, Columbus had taken the same route and he reported that during the rainy season the mist, the sky and the water would merge together in one colour, making navigation difficult and the horizon all but impossible to distinguish. Columbus's progress along this coast had been slow. Morgan's wasn't, and as they arrived in the mouth of the San Juan River, the four captains prepared to row ashore and meet the Indians.[6]

Once again, the Indians proved to be invaluable as their hatred for the Spanish was intense enough for them to readily agree to help the English buccaneers. They told the four captains that the river fed into Lake Nicaragua and at the far end of this giant lake lay Granada, a grand city with two colleges and seven churches and monasteries. The city was said to be impregnable. The captains – Morgan, Jackman, Morris and Marteen – would show that it was not.

Hiding by day under keys and islands and rowing all night, on the fifth night by the advice of their Indian guide, they landed near the city of Gran Granada, marched undiscovered into the centre of the city, fired a volley, overturned eighteen great guns in the Parada Place, took the sergeant major's house, wherein were all their arms and ammunition, secured in the Great Church 300 of the best men prisoners, 'abundance of which were churchmen', plundered for sixteen hours, discharged the prisoners, sunk all the boats, and so came away. This town is twice bigger than Portsmouth, with seven churches and a very fair cathedral, besides divers[e] colleges and monasteries, all built of freestone, as also are most of their houses. They have six companies of horse and foot besides Indians and slaves in abundance.[7]

The Spanish were completely unprepared for the buccaneers. They'd heard the stories of the buccaneers and pirates from the English settlements but, like the people of Villahermosa, they believed they were safe, hundreds of miles from any English enemy. Yet, quite suddenly, the stories had turned into reality as the heavily armed buccaneers marched into the town with hundreds of Indians who joined in the plundering.

Prisoners were rounded up and locked into the Great Church as the plundering continued. Many Indians wanted to execute the prisoners there and then, especially the religious leaders who had ruled so harshly over them. However, once Morgan and his fellow captains explained that the English were not going to stay and rule in the town, the Indians reluctantly agreed to spare the lives of the prisoners. But rather than staying in the city and enduring the wrath of the Spanish, most of the Indians moved into the mountains while others returned with the buccaneers aboard Marteen's ship.

More than 3,000 Spanish fled the city as the invaders took everything of value they could find: gold, silver plate, jewels, coins – anything they could get their hands on. While plundering, Morgan ensured the Spanish guns were either destroyed or also taken and all their vessels sunk.

> At the end of the lagoon they took a vessel of 100 tons, and an island as large as Barbadoes called Lida, with a fine neat town which they plundered. The air here is very cool and wholesome, producing as the inhabitants told them all sorts of European grains, herbs, and fruits in great plenty, that five leagues from the head of the lagoon is a port town on the South Sea called Realleyo, where the King [of Spain] has ships built for trading between Panama and Peru, and that there is a better passage to the lake by Bluefields river to the north-east, and another to the south-east through Costa Rica, almost to Portobello, a country inhabited by Creolians, mulattos, and Indians, whom the Spaniards dare not trust with arms.[8]

The plundering of Granada was an audacious act and set the stage for future attacks on the Spanish by the English buccaneers operating out of Jamaica. Indeed, it was the most ambitious and startling venture of the time in the West Indies.[9] For a start, Morgan had sailed over hundreds of miles in waters where few detailed maps existed. Sailing entirely into the unknown, he'd no idea how the Indians would have received them, or if they would have been hostile to the English. As it turned out he was able to build alliances with them using the information and intelligence they provided as the backbone for his raids and attacks on the Spanish. Even though he lost his original ships, he'd improvised and used lesser vessels to continue the voyage. The vast majority of his men came back to Jamaica with him safely, and much richer. Staying away from the heavily fortified main centres of Spanish military might – Havana, Cartagena and Panama – the buccaneers had plundered throughout the vast area of Central America and the West Indies, attacking the vulnerable and poorly defended towns and villages. They had no navigation systems, no satellite systems, no onboard computers and no powerful engines to rely on.

They lived off the land, as we can see from Modyford's letter, shooting cattle and catching fish at the mouth of the Nicaragua River.[10]

Throughout the voyage they'd encountered Indians hostile to the Spanish and the Spanish Empire. Indeed, during the plundering of Granada, the Indians told them of Spanish towns and cities of great wealth beyond Granada that Modyford outlined in his letter to the Duke of Albemarle:

> The Indians are driven to rebellion by cruelty and there is no reconciling them. They told them also of a city called Legovia, where there are many sheep with excellent fine wool. By comparing this relation with maps and histories it appears that this country is in the middle of the Spanish dominions in America, dividing Peru from Mexico, both lying very convenient to infest by sea, but being environed with impassable hills, rocks, and mountains, very difficult if not impossible to be attacked by land. The wealth of the place is such that the first plunder will pay the adventure, being well supplied with commodities and food and free from vermin; the assistance of the Indian and negro slaves if well handled will be very considerable; the Creolians will not be long obstinate, when they feel the freedom and ease of His Majesty's Government; 2,000 men, some say 500, may easily conquer all this quarter; the Spaniards in their large dominions being so far asunder they are the easier subdued. This place can be reached in eight or ten days' sail; the proper time to attempt is between March and August, the rest being rainy months when the rivers are high and the strength of their streams not to be stemmed. Has represented this matter to His Grace, being convinced that if ever the reason of state at home require any attempt on the Spanish Indies, this is the properest place and most probable to lay a foundation for the conquest of the whole.[11]

When the four captains returned to Port Royal, Modyford faced a dilemma. Morgan and his fellow captains had left Jamaica with old letters of marque signed by Governor Windsor, Modyford's predecessor, so technically they were in the right. The four captains and their crews sailed into Port Royal as wealthy men. Modyford realized he had to walk a thin line. He couldn't take away their riches because he couldn't afford to alienate them. Instead, he could encourage them to use their wealth to buy land in Jamaica and turn towards agriculture.

He wrote to Lord Albemarle, telling him of the riches available in the Spanish territories of Central America and warning of the French build-up of forces at Tortuga. Modyford then approved another expedition, this time to Dutch Curaçao, which would be led by the experienced privateer Edward Mansfield.[12]

Chapter 4

The Cartago Fiasco

Receiving advice that the French forces are very much increasing at Tortuga and the south-west of Hispaniola, thought it high time to send a declaration thither, importing his intentions to grant commissions against the Spaniard, which the old privateers assure him will undoubtedly bring back the English and most of the Dutch and French to this port, where they have a better market for their goods.[1]

The Spanish were furious with Morgan's actions at Granada. He had attacked and plundered the heart of the Spanish Main – towns and cities that hitherto the Spanish thought had been safe from the buccaneers. Now they knew differently. The Spanish began to liken his exploits to those of Francis Drake a century before. Indeed, Stephen Talty, in his book *Empire of Blue Water*, suggests that Morgan had acquired the nickname 'El Draque' by the Spanish.[2]

However, as we have seen, the world had moved on by the time the four captains returned wealthy heroes from their voyage. War with France and the Dutch was brewing and so King Charles II of England had turned to the Spanish to form an alliance. As a result he'd issued a proclamation for reigning in the privateers in Jamaica and stopping their raids against the Spanish. The trouble was, the Spanish empire of the West Indies was rich with treasure and every privateer and pirate knew it. If the English authorities in Jamaica would not give the buccaneers (privateers) commissions to attack Spain, the privateers knew that the French authorities at Tortuga would, so many headed for that island.

For most buccaneers it didn't matter where they got their commissions or letters of marque from as long as they came from a legitimate government. For example, English privateers could have French or Dutch commissions to sail against the Spanish, while French and Dutch privateers could carry English commissions for attacking the Spanish, or each other, depending on the fickle political situation in Europe.

So by the time Morgan returned, the situation was much different. Now there were more than 1,500 buccaneers and privateers in Port Royal. Known as the Brethren of the Coast, the privateers were out of work. These were men of action and adventure and being stuck in a town with nothing to do could easily lead to lawlessness.

While many privateers moved to Tortuga to gain commissions against the Spanish, many others remained in Port Royal, causing the merchants to worry for their safety. But their fears were unfounded as the vast majority of privateers slowly left Port Royal, seeking commissions elsewhere. Yet the King's orders to reign in the Brethren did not call for any reinforcements to Jamaica's militia, nor did it provide for any Royal Navy warships. The only thing that kept the island safe was the privateers, and now they were leaving. A continual thorn in the side of the Spanish, Jamaica was wide open to attack, not just from the Spanish but from the French, the Dutch and from pirates.

Some locals decided to turn to privateering without permission and these were rounded up by Modyford and hung as an example. To make matters worse, his letters to the secretary of state in London, Lord Arlington, went unanswered. While he had permission to act in the best interests of the King and of the island, he knew very well that the instructions from the King regarding no attacks on Spanish holdings meant he could not allow Morgan to lead any expeditions against the Spanish Main.[3] But something had to be done.

Modyford finally moved. On 22 February he called an emergency meeting of the council. He placed Morgan in charge of the local militia. That council meeting was extraordinary in one respect – it went directly against the King's orders. The fine frightened men of the Council of Jamaica decided to start granting commissions against the Spanish. They concluded that doing this would provide safety for the colony, which would help the merchants and farmers that supplied and provisioned the Brethren on their expeditions. Granting commissions would also stimulate trade, enable the growth of the plantations and act as a deterrent or even revenge against the Spanish, who were continuing to commit hostile acts against Jamaica.[4]

Modyford decided to play it safe. Instead of attacking the Spanish, he granted a commission to attack the Dutch colony at Curaçao, more than a thousand miles away. In charge of this expedition was the experienced privateer Edward Mansfield (ironically, he was Dutch). According to some sources, Morgan was to remain behind and continue to build Fort Charles, a huge stronghold at the mouth of the entrance to the harbour at Port Royal.

The mission went wrong shortly after the fleet set sail from Jamaica. The Brethren decided that attacking Curaçao would not provide them with the riches they were after. The Dutch were fellow Protestants and they were nowhere near as wealthy as the Spanish, so they switched their target from Curaçao to Cartago, the Costa Rican capital.

The private soldiers aboard the *Admiral* were against it, averring publicly that there was more profit with less hazard to be gotten against the Spaniard, which was their only interest. Two of their fleet are gone to Tortuga, and the other four joining with two French rovers are gone to attempt the retaking [of] the island of Providence, where they intend to set up for themselves.[5]

The reason for switching targets was partly due to the intelligence the Brethren received from a man who had been a prisoner aboard a Spanish ship taken as a prize. This individual told of the riches to be had in the provincial capital of Cartago, which was, according to this person, virtually undefended and had never been attacked. The same prisoner told Mansfield and his captains that he could guide them to Cartago from Almirante Bay, a safe harbour where Mansfield could leave his ships at anchor.[6]

So they switched targets but it made little difference to the success of the mission. Arriving in Almirante Bay the fleet landed at Cape Blanco, where they disembarked more than 600 men who immediately began their long march inland to take the town. The invaders plundered small towns and villages for food as they marched towards Cartago. For almost 75 miles, the going was relatively easy before they turned west and began to cross the mountains to reach their target. On either side, peaks rose thousands of feet into the air while the buccaneers could only march through a narrow pass. Desperate to keep the element of surprise, they pressed on. The idea was that they would surprise the city, plunder it and leave wealthy men. However, this didn't happen. An Indian woman raised the alarm and the Governor of Cartago roused the Spanish militia, who were ready and waiting for the Buccaneers when they arrived. In a letter to the Duke of Albemarle, Modyford states: 'Understanding that the inhabitants had carried away their wealth, they returned to their ships without being challenged.'

According to Philip Lindsay, in his book *The Great Buccaneer*, they reached Cartago only to find that most of the inhabitants had fled the town with their wealth. To make matters worse, they now had to contend with the Spanish militia. In the town they:

destroyed whatever they could lay their hands on, wantonly killing the inhabitants and hamstringing the cattle. Then they enjoyed their favourite sport of smashing the images in the church before setting fire to what remained and turning their backs on a futile expedition.[7]

But the march back to their ships was a starvation march for they were not only without plunder but also without supplies. They'd sustained casualties in a fight against the Spanish, where they were soundly beaten.[8]

The details of the expedition are somewhat sketchy and some scholars believe that Morgan sailed on this ill-fated venture. Indeed, Philip Lindsay states: 'There is every reason to believe that Morgan sailed with the fleet. It is unfortunate that he was not in command for Mansfield was growing old, and he dallied, not wishing to attack well-fortified Curaçao.'[9] Breverton supports this idea in his book but goes even further by saying that 'Morgan captained a ship under Admiral Mansvelt, and was made vice admiral because of his attack on Granada.'[10]

Not every scholar or historian believes that Morgan was involved in this mission. In his book *Harry Morgan's Way*, Dudley Pope states: 'Morgan is likely to have stayed behind in Port Royal when Mansfield went off to Curaçao because, better than most, he could organize the militia.'[11] We can take this statement one step further because Morgan's name did not appear on the list 'of men recruited for the mission. Modyford had put him in charge of the militia and the defence of Jamaica.'[12]

The most heavily used source of information on Morgan, other than official letters and documents written by Modyford and others, is that of Esquemeling, who sailed on some of Morgan's voyages and so was an eyewitness to the actions and exploits of the buccaneers. However, it is difficult to tell what is truth and what is embellishment in Esquemeling's book, which was published in 1678. He states that Morgan did sail on the expedition and was made a vice admiral so it is likely that the proponents of this theory based their information on his book.

Every source agrees that the Mansfield attack on Cartago was a disaster that weighed heavily on Mansfield. To make amends he decided to attack the island of Old Providence.

On 12th inst arrived Capt Mansfield and one other ship, and complains that the disobedience of several officers and soldiers was the cause of their not proceeding on the design of Curaçao.[13]

Chapter 5

The Providence Affair

Sitting off the eastern coast of Nicaragua lies an island that had already changed hands more than once. A group of Puritans had settled it in Cromwell's time, only to be driven out by the Spaniards some years later. This island is rugged and rocky, with barrier reefs all around it and a harbour deep enough to hold several ships. The island is Old Providence, and attached to it on the westward side is a smaller island known as Santa Catalina. In Morgan's time it lay in Spanish hands.

Stinging from the fiasco of Cartago, Mansfield wanted to take this island to repair his reputation. If he could build a heavily armed fortress there, its guns aimed at the Spanish as they sailed by, 'the Peruvian trade with Spain could be ruined, the treasure ships taken with ease and the galleons from home with cargoes of provisions and clothing and other necessities plundered before they neared the shore.'[1]

It should have been an easy place to defend; its mountains made natural battlements and the narrow passes between them were perfect for ambushing invading forces. Indeed, entering the harbour would have been difficult as only one ship at a time could pass through the narrow, difficult channel before reaching the wider open water of the harbour. The high ridges around the harbour entrance would have made any invading ship trying to reach the anchorage open to ambush.

It was perfect for Mansfield. He had a vision of turning the island into a permanent base for the Brethren – a privateers' haven. It was perfectly positioned for such a purpose, being close to the Spanish Main making it much easier for privateers from Jamaica to attack Spanish shipping. Jamaica lies more than 400 miles to the north of the island while to the south is Portobello, a ripe and juicy target only 300 miles away instead of the long 625 miles from Jamaica.

Mansfield was also motivated to take the island because he wanted to rebuild his stature with the Brethren. The Curaçao and Cartago failure weighed heavily on the old man and he knew that he had to do something to make amends. More than half of the fleet that set sail to attack Curaçao had left because of what had happened at Cartago. If he failed to take Old

Providence – well, that just didn't bear thinking about. With no more than half a dozen ships, Mansfield set sail.

> The old fellow was resolved (as he tells me) never to see my face until he had done some service to His Majesty, and therefore with 200 men which were all were left him and about eighty of them French, he resolved to attempt the island of Providence, which was formerly English, and by the Spaniards' whole armada taken from us in 1641, and ever since carefully garrisoned. In order to this he set sail, and being an excellent coaster, which is his chief if not only virtue, in the night he came within half a mile of it by an unusual passage among rocks, where they say ships never came, and in the morning early landed, marched four leagues, and surprised the Governor, who was taken prisoner. The soldiers got into the fort being about 200, but on conditions to be landed on the main they yielded twenty-seven pieces of ordnance, 100 double jars of powder, shot, and all things necessary were found, and the fort very strongly built; they acknowledge but very little plunder, only 150 negroes; they brought off 100, and left thirty-five men and Capt Hattsell keeper of the magazine; they say many of the guns have Queen Elizabeth's arms engraven on them.[2]

With the island now in English hands, Mansfield was determined it should remain so. Leaving behind a small garrison Mansfield immediately set sail for Jamaica to get more reinforcements, which would ensure any Spanish invasion would be soundly repelled. But Mansfield was to be disappointed. In Jamaica, the rules regarding attacks by privateers on Spanish vessels and settlements still held, which meant that he could not raise the reinforcements he'd hoped for and that he knew the island needed. He had acted outside of Modyford's original instructions, which had put the Jamaican governor in a difficult situation.

> Has yet only reproved Mansfield for doing it without orders, and really he dare not go further than rebukes without His Majesty's express orders, lest he should drive them from that allegiance which they make great profession of now more than ever. Neither would he without manifest imprudence but accept the tender of it in His Majesty's behalf, and considering its good situation for favouring any design on the rich main, lying near the river which leads to the lake [Nicaragua], holds it his duty to reinforce that garrison, and to send down some able person to command it. Meantime they are increasing apace in ships and men, privateers daily coming in and submitting to the strictness of the commissions and instructions he puts on them for His Majesty's service.[3]

Disgusted, Mansfield left Jamaica and headed for Tortuga to raise the men he needed to reinforce Old Providence. He knew that time was of the essence. Sadly, by this time, age had caught up with him and he died there.

His death left a gap in the structure of the Brethren that needed to be filled. Morgan would be the one to take over from Mansfield as Admiral of the Brethren but this had not yet taken place. There was still the question of Old Providence. Modyford was no fool and he realized the island needed a strong garrison if it was to be held by the English. However, the only way he could raise a force to keep it was by asking for volunteers; none of the militia on Jamaica could be spared. The first volunteer to come forward was Thomas Whetstone, a privateer captain in his own right who had been Speaker of the House of Assembly for almost two years.[4] Whetstone offered his ship and the command of the rest of the volunteers was given to Major Samuel Smith, an experienced army man. The rest of the volunteers numbered thirty-three and so this small force set off for Old Providence. Smith was to be the new English governor representing the King.

Jamaica would not hear from Smith and Whetstone for two years. In the meantime, Modyford was desperately trying to follow the ruling from London about keeping the peace with Spain, which meant curtailing the activities of the Brethren – an almost impossible task.

Not since March had Modyford given out any commissions to privateers to attack Spanish ships or settlements. The result of this had a profound effect on the security and prosperity of Port Royal and the rest of the island. Modyford did have the power[5] to grant commissions but according to his letter to Lord Arlington dated 21 August 1666,[6] he 'was glad of this power, but resolved not to use it unless necessity drives me to it.' And necessity did.

In Port Royal the Treaty of Madrid had not given the merchants the legal right to sell their goods to the Spanish, while the privateers could do as they chose. The traders who ran the slave trade complained there was no contract that gave them a fair advantage with the Spanish, while the planters were furious because many of their able-bodied men left the fields to become privateers and had largely gone to Tortuga.[7]

And when he saw how poor the fleets returning from Statia were, so that vessels were broken up and the men disposed of for the coast of Cuba to get a livelihood, and so be wholly alienated from us. Many stayed at the Windward Isles, having not enough to pay their engagements, and at Tortuga and among the French buccaneers.[8]

Finally, Modyford called a meeting of the council, where they agreed to start providing commissions against the Spanish to the privateers. This about-turn was largely, as Modyford wrote in his letter, because the guards at Port Royal, which before the treaty had been signed numbered as many as 600, were now around 135 as the men flocked to Tortuga for privateering commissions. Port Royal needed men who could fight and wanted to fight, and the only way to fill the place with those men, the council believed, was to grant commissions against the Spanish. Added to this were the rumours of war with France, so Modyford issued a declaration of his intent to grant commissions to privateers against the Spanish.

As the privateers poured in the change was palpable.

His Lordship cannot imagine what a universal change there was on the faces of men and things, ships repairing, great resort of workmen and labourers to Port Royal, many returning, many debtors released out of prison, and the ships from the Curaçao voyage, not daring to come in for fear of creditors, brought in and fitted out again, so that the regimental forces at Port Royal are near 400. Had it not been for that seasonable action, he could not have kept this place against French buccaneers, who would have ruined all the seaside plantations at least; whereas he now draws from them mainly, and lately David Marteen, the best man of Tortuga, that has two frigates at sea, has promised to bring in both.[9]

By Christmas of 1666, Modyford knew that Old Providence had been lost to the Spanish but he did not know the details until August 1668, when two men, virtual skeletons covered in sores and heavily scarred, sailed into Port Royal. They had been prisoners of the Spanish after being enslaved and kept in irons for almost two years. The two men were Major Samuel Smith, the man who was to have been the governor of Old Providence, and Captain Henry Wasey, the master of the *Concord*, a merchant vessel. Three more men of the ill-fated mission to establish a garrison on Old Providence arrived in Port Royal a few days later. The rest remained slaves of the Spanish, but the few survivors who arrived in Port Royal had a terrible story to tell.

When Mansfield had taken Old Providence after the surrender of the Spanish garrison, he'd ordered the prisoners, who also included the Spanish governor, Don Esteban del Campo, to be transported to the Spanish Main. The arrival of the ship in Portobello carrying the men from the Old Providence garrison and the ex-governor, Don Esteban, was the first thing that alerted the Spanish Main to the fall of the island.

Determined to take Old Providence back, the governor of Panama, Don Juan Pérez de Guzmán, quickly swung into action, ordering the militia at Portobello – along with the recently arrived Old Providence garrison who had sailed into Portobello under the flag of truce ordered by Mansfield – to be mobilized to take the island back. The man in charge of this Spanish mission to retake the island was the mayor of Portobello, Jose Sanchez Ximenez. In the harbour at Portobello were two large ships ideal for this expedition and one of them was the merchant vessel *Concord*, commanded by Captain Henry Wasey. The moment he'd heard of the capture of Old Providence, Sanchez had ordered the arrest of Captain Wasey.

> That on 25 May 1666 he was seized with his said ship lying at anchor in Portobello, and put in irons on pretence of being a spy, although registered and licensed, and was forced to send to Panama for an attestation that the Spaniards manned his said ship and sailed her to Providence to retake said island.[10]

Clapped in irons, Wasey was marched from the ship to the city jail, where he was thrown into the dungeon to rot.[11]

The year was 1666 and the Spanish expedition to retake Old Providence, with more than 500 fighting men, set sail on 2 August. Against this attacking force Smith had a total of seventy-two men on the island, with only fifty-one fit enough to fight. They were doomed from the start but it was not the walkover that the numbers might imply. It took the Spanish three days of hard fighting to take the island. According to Major Smith's deposition, he was, on '19 August 1666, by three Spanish vessels, a New England ketch taken from the English by the Spaniards, and an English ship, the *Concord*, thirty guns, of which Henry Wasey was commander, manned by Spaniards, summoned to surrender.'

Smith refused.

> Whereupon the enemy landed, and after three days' siege he was forced to surrender upon articles for good quarter, which the Spaniards did not in the least perform, for the English, about forty, were immediately made prisoners, and all, except Sir Thos Whetstone, this deponent, and Capt Stanley, who were commanders, forced to work in irons and chains at the Spaniards' forts, with many stripes, and many are since dead through want and ill-usage. Said three commanders were sent to Panama, where they were cast into a dungeon and bound in irons for seventeen months. At length being released this deponent arrived at the Havannah, 'his company being lost', where he was clapped into gaol.[12]

Having betrayed the English by not accepting their surrender honourably, as they said they would, the Spanish sent the prisoners to Portobello. We know this from Captain Wasey, who said that he saw 'prisoners taken in Providence made slaves in Portobello and thirteen more slaves in Cartagena'.[13]

In Europe, England and Spain were at peace but in Jamaica the peace meant nothing as Modyford referred to 'the cruelty and false dealings of our neighbours' in a letter to the Duke of Albemarle regarding the capture of Old Providence, which, he stated, was 'a violation of the peace which they so much pretend to in these parts'.[14]

Hearing about the savagery with which the Spanish treated their English prisoners from Old Providence, especially after they'd agreed to an honourable surrender, the people of Jamaica demanded vengeance. It was a difficult story to hear. Once the English prisoners had laid down their weapons:

> on condition of having a small barque to transport them to Jamaica. But when they had laid down their arms the Spaniards refused them the barque, and carried them slaves to Portobello, where they were chained to the ground in a dungeon 12 foot by 10, in which were thirty-three prisoners. They were forced to work in the water from five in the morning till seven at night, and at such a rate that the Spaniards confessed they made one of them do more work than any three negroes, yet when weak with want of victuals and sleep they were knocked down and beaten with cudgels, and four or five died. Having no clothes, their backs were blistered with the sun, their heads scorched, their necks, shoulders, and hands raw with carrying stones and mortar, their feet chopped, and their legs bruised and battered with the irons, and their corpses were noisome one to another. The daily abuses of their religion and their king, and the continual trouble they had with friars, would be tedious to mention.[15]

This news stoked hatred of the Spanish in Jamaica and the demand of retribution grew as news that the Spanish, buoyed by their success at Old Providence, were assembling a fleet to attack Jamaica. Something had to be done. The 'something' would fall on Morgan's shoulders and it would be carried out in a spectacular way.

Chapter 6

Morgan Prepares

About the middle of August last of the fleet of privateers returned from taking Portobello: hears it thus, that six captains with 500 men took the town and three castles and kept them thirty days, and redelivered them for 100,000 pieces of eight, besides what they plundered the town of, which was very rich. They are all gone out again, on what design he cannot tell, but one Capt Morgan is their admiral.[1]

In January 1667, France declared war on England and now Modyford faced a threat from the Dutch and French privateers operating out of Tortuga and other bases. The number of buccaneers in Port Royal was substantially reduced, which made Jamaica seem a relatively easy target.

The promise of HMS *Oxford* being despatched from home for its protection could have brought little hope to him when he looked at the map and saw how small, how vulnerable was his island in a sea of enemies.[2]

Worse still were the persistent rumours that the Spanish were amassing a fleet to attack and take Jamaica after their success taking Old Providence. All that stood in the way of the Spaniards were the Brethren.

After his daring attack on Granada Henry Morgan had become a rich man. He was also a powerful man. From the spoils of his Granada adventure, Morgan had purchased his first plantation. He moved in the same circles as the other plantation owners and shared their same concerns. He was known to Modyford because he was the nephew of the late Edward Morgan. Indeed, Modyford saw in Morgan a true leader, someone who the colony could rely on when things seemed at their bleakest. At the age of thirty Morgan was tanned and muscular, with a strong will, quick brain and dynamic personality. He was brave and had that special quality that made men of all nationalities, with different languages, cultures and backgrounds, follow him over some of the harshest terrain, over hundreds of miles, and then return to boast in the taverns and bars about how they had followed Admiral Henry Morgan. He was the kind of man who in any society, right up to the present day, would be a hero.

With Mansfield now gone, Morgan's hour had arrived.

Modyford had put him in charge of the militia – the Port Royal Volunteers – and the rebuilding of Fort Charles. He'd been made colonel of the militia and increased the numbers of volunteers four-fold. His brother-in-law, Major Byndloss, had been put in command of the fort, which was now completed to Henry's satisfaction. The influence that Morgan had on Jamaican society was growing and he became a regular visitor to Modyford's official residence.[3]

It's not surprising then that the one person the colony turned to for discovering the truth about the rumours of imminent invasion was Henry Morgan. Governor Modyford signed a commission that gave Morgan the rank of admiral – the commander-in-chief of the Jamaican forces. The commission was for Morgan 'to draw together the English privateers, and take prisoners of the Spanish nation, whereby he might inform of the intentions of that enemy to invade Jamaica, of which Sir Thomas had frequent and strong advice.'[4]

Morgan began to prepare his fleet. Word went out that preparations were under way and privateers from 'the coves of Tortuga and the bars of Port Royal'[5] appeared to sign on under Morgan's command. Indeed, Morgan's old friend John Morris, who had sailed with him on his first expedition, now joined him and would be invaluable to the admiral. In order to gain as much secrecy as they could an expedition of this nature was rarely planned in port, according to Stephen Talty. Instead the privateers would arrange to meet in a safer, quieter location where they could plan their moves without prying eyes or listening ears. In addition to Morris, Morgan was joined by Captain Edward Collier, and a flotilla of about half a dozen ships left Port Royal bound for a rendezvous point in the South Cays, just off the southern side of Cuba.

Accounts differ as to the size of Morgan's fleet. Some say it was ten ships while Phillip Lindsay states that Morgan sailed his already assembled fleet of ten ships 'to the Isle of Pines where he was joined by two more ships and 200 men.' However, as both Lindsay and Pope indicate that he had a fleet of twelve ships and roughly 700 men, we will make the assumption that this is the case.

One of the individuals on the two privateer ships that joined Morgan's fleet while they waited at the Isle of Pines was a man who wrote the narrative of Morgan's exploits and is the major source of our information for this period of Morgan's life. That man was Alexander Esquemeling.[6] In our case, we are using a book by another pseudonym – John Esquemeling.

As has been established, there are parts of Esquemeling's book, *The Buccaneers of America*, that most scholars believe are embellished or possibly even fictional. While this may be the case, Talty states that 'key passages are verified by Spanish accounts, Morgan's reports and other sources.' Indeed,

Dudley Pope states that Esquemeling's account of the raid on Panama matches the Spanish accounts and so can be taken as reasonably accurate. However, as it is the only eyewitness account we have to help tell Morgan's story, it is a key piece of the puzzle.

> The recital coming from his own pen might be questioned, and indeed has been questioned, but there seems little reason for Esquemeling to have lied.[7]
>
> We will give him the benefit of a large doubt, and accept him on his own terms as a highly honest, honourable surgeon, a virtuous, industrious, skilful 'excellent good fellow', to use his own commendation, one who never cut a throat or drank out of a bottle.[8]

If we are going to use Esquemeling as our main source for the next few chapters it is worth looking at what detail there is of his life. For that we can turn to Philip Lindsey, who provides some background to Esquemeling's life. Most sources do believe that Esquemeling was Hendrik Barentzoon Smeeks. Lindsey tells us that 'after various adventures including shipwreck on the west coast of Australia, he arrived back in Holland to weave his adventures into a tale called *Krinki Kesmes*,' which was published in 1715. Smeeks also wrote a number of romantic tales, which Lindsey tells us is one of the main reasons why many critics do not take him seriously or have difficulty attributing Smeeks as the same Esquemeling.

If we are to believe Lindsey, Esquemeling's tale is one of misery. He was born around 1643 in Zwolle in Holland and as we have already stated he entered service with the Dutch East India Company in 1657. After his time with the Dutch East India Company he accepted a position as barber/surgeon to the French West India Company and arrived in Tortuga to take up his post. However, the company decided its holding on the island was unprofitable and sold all its property, including its employees. A French buccaneer then purchased Esquemeling's indenture and, unfortunately, this man turned out to be very cruel indeed. Beaten and starving, Esquemeling became very ill and his cruel master sold him to another man who was much more humane. Esquemeling recovered and after serving his new master for a year was set free. So, almost penniless and with few possessions, when the word of Morgan's expedition to attack the Spanish went round, Esquemeling joined.

He provided a detailed look at the preparations the buccaneers would make for each voyage, giving the modern reader an insight into their way of life.

> On the ship, they first discuss where to go and get food supplies. This means meat – for they eat nothing else on their voyages, unless they capture other foodstuffs from the Spaniards.[9]

This meat was usually pork or else it would be turtle meat. Quite often the buccaneers on their voyages would plunder the pens where the Spaniards would keep 'thousands of heads of tame hogs'. If they needed to hunt themselves, the buccaneers would employ 'a hunter of their own nationality who has a pack of hounds, letting him have whatever share of the catch they think fit.'[10]

Esquemeling tells us that often some of the buccaneers would accompany the hunting party to ensure that any meat caught was properly salted and smoked while the rest of the men ensured that the ship was ready to put to sea, 'careening and greasing and doing all that is necessary.'

Once all the meat had been salted and smoked it was then stacked in the hold along with other provisions. The buccaneers had two meals a day of this meat, consisting of only one course. 'The fat is skimmed off the cauldron and put into little calabashes, for dipping the meat in,' writes Esquemeling, 'and often it tastes better than the food on a gentleman's table.'

Once all the preparations were made a council meeting was held to decide where they should go. This decision was by common vote and it was at this meeting that an agreement was drawn up stipulating what the captain or leader of the expedition would get for himself and the for the vessel and what everyone else would get in terms of the loot gained on the expedition. However, for specific tasks some amounts would be deducted from the whole amount of the plunder. For example, the hunter would get '200 pieces of eight. The carpenter, for his work in repairing and fitting out the ship would be paid 100 pieces of eight. The surgeon would receive 200 or 250 for his medical supplies according to the size of the ship.'

Those who were wounded in battle would also be compensated and their amounts would be deducted from the whole. For example, a man who lost his right arm would be compensated with six slaves or 600 pieces of eight, whilst for the loss of the left arm the compensation would be '500 pieces of eight or five slaves'. Compensation for the loss of an eye would garner only 100 pieces of eight or one slave. 'If a man lost the use of an arm, he would get as much as if it had been cut off, and severe internal injury which meant the victim had to have a pipe inserted in his body would earn 500 pieces of eight or five slaves in recompense.'[11]

Once all of these deductions had been made the men then received the rest, with the captain drawing 'four of five men's portions for the use of his ship, perhaps even more, and two portions for himself. The rest of the men share uniformly, and the boys get half a man's share.'

Esquemeling tells us that no one man would keep the plunder gained on the expedition:

Everything taken – money, jewels, precious stones and goods – must be shared among them all, without any man enjoying a penny more than his fare share. To prevent deceit, before the booty is distributed everyone has to swear an oath on the Bible that he has not kept for himself so much as the value of a sixpence, whether in silk, linen, wool, gold, silver, jewels, clothes or shot, from all the capture. And should any man be found to have made a false oath, he would be banished from the rovers and never more be allowed in their company.[12]

With all their preparations made by the end of March 1668, the fleet was ready to sail to attack their first target. Admiral Henry Morgan had a dozen ships in this fleet and more than 700 men of French and English nationalities. However, this was not a fleet of large warships. Indeed, the largest ship was the *Dolphin*, commanded by John Morris, which had been captured from the Spanish and taken as a prize back to Port Royal. Originally the ship had four guns but for this expedition it had eight and was capable of carrying upwards of sixty men. Many of the other ships in the fleet were large, open boats where the forward part of the boat had been decked over to provide shelter for the crew and provisions. Normally, these boats would have a single mast for catching the wind but in calm waters, complex cays and coves could be rowed for more difficult manoeuvring.

Against a fleet of heavily armed Spanish warships, Morgan's fleet would have had no chance but Morgan was not taking this fleet to sea to fight warships. This was a fleet for landing hundreds of men and attacking villages, settlements, towns and even cities. In short, they were a means of getting from point A to point B and were not designed for sea battles as the ships of notorious pirates like Blackbeard or Charles Vane were. Many of the people manning the ships of Morgan's fleet were former soldiers and not sailors. They thought in terms of land battles, marching mile after mile, plundering towns and villages, taking food and water as they went rather than sailing on the open sea to attack enemy vessels.

Finally, with all preparations made, the fleet slipped anchor and headed out to sea to turn the tables on the Spanish and bring some form of retribution upon them.

Chapter 7

Puerto del Príncipe Attacked

Before they left the South Cays, Morgan called a council of war with all his captains to decide on the target to attack. The sun shone and the fleet bobbed at anchor in a beautiful blue sea teaming with wildlife. The trees and vegetation along the shore were vibrant with colour.

And the men talked. There were several proposals for attacking Havana. This proposal was to be a surprise assault by night with the buccaneers plundering the city and taking several priests hostage before any defence could be mounted against them. There were murmurs of approval from some of the men while others who had been imprisoned by the Spaniards in Havana reckoned the buccaneers would need 1,500 men to take the city and make the raid successful. Ultimately, the motion wasn't carried.

Esquemeling tells us that another man spoke up suggesting the buccaneers raid Puerto del Príncipe. 'He had been there, he said, and there was plenty of money in the town, for it was where the Havana merchants came to buy hides. Lying some distance from the sea, the place had never been plundered and so the inhabitants had no fear of the English,' writes Esquemeling.

It is at this point that Morgan made a mistake, which he quickly learned lessons from for his subsequent expeditions. On board the ship where the council meeting was taking place, a Spaniard who was a prisoner of the English overheard their plans. He'd been a prisoner for some time and had managed to pick up enough English to enable him to understand what they were planning. Morgan did not have the Spaniard removed from earshot when the meeting was taking place as he assumed he did not understand English.

This man jumped overboard one night and began swimming for the nearest island. The English at once sprang into their canoes to fish him out again, but he managed to land before they could catch him and hid among the trees, where they could not find him.[1]

The next day the Spaniard managed to reach Puerto del Príncipe and he raised the alarm. Now Morgan's element of surprise was gone. Immediately, the Spaniards began preparing for the coming attack, with many inhabitants hiding themselves and their valuables in the woods near the town. At the same time, the governor of the town began to assemble as many men as he could to defend the place. Mustering about 800 men, he had many trees cut down and hauled across the roads. Ambushes were set up with cannon mounted so that the buccaneers would be hit with shot as they came down the road. These ambushes, or ambuscades, were manned with only the men that the governor thought fit enough, while he had the rest of his forces mustered in an 'open field near the city, whence he could see the enemy's approach from afar.' Esquemeling states that the buccaneers:

> put their men ashore, and finding all the cattle driven up the country and the inhabitants fled, they marched 20 leagues to Porto Principe on the north of the island, and with little resistance possessed themselves of the same.[2]

Instead of using the roads and being ambushed Morgan led his men into the stifling thick forest and began a long march through very difficult terrain that avoided the ambushes and 'after a long, sweaty march the pirates emerged onto a plain, *la Savana*, that lay before the city.'[3] With drums beating and banners flying the buccaneers began advancing, forming into a semi-circle and the governor seeing Morgan's army before him ordered his cavalry to attack the buccaneers from the rear and cut them to pieces. However, things did not turn out the way he'd anticipated.

With the buccaneers now in their semi-circle formation the Spaniards charged them, but the musket fire from the buccaneers was very accurate. Esquemeling takes up the rest of the story:

> The buccaneers never missed their mark, and kept up a continuous fire without pausing in their charge. The defenders' courage began to flag, especially when they saw their governor fall. They began to retreat towards the forest, where they would have a better chance of escape, but most of them were struck down before they reached shelter.

Within an hour Morgan's forces were in the town and had captured it, but some Spaniards still held out, taking pot shots at them. Esquemeling writes:

> Some locked themselves in their houses and fired from windows, but once the buccaneers became aware of this sniping they threatened to burn down the whole town, destroying women and children and all.

The Spanish now had no choice and they quickly surrendered. Morgan had them all locked up in the large churches in the town. The buccaneers then began plundering the empty homes in the town and once this had been done, Morgan sent them out 'on marauding expeditions, every day bringing back fresh booty and prisoners, so time did not lie heavy on their hands.'[4]

Even though Morgan's men were out in the countryside searching for booty, Morgan turned to an old tactic used by pirates – ransoming the prisoners. He released four prisoners and 'sent them into the adjacent woods to find the people who had fled and demand money for the imprisoned families.' In addition, says Esquemeling, Morgan also told the prisoners that the people who had fled would have to pay a ransom for the town or they would burn it to the ground.

A few days later, the four men returned, telling Morgan that they couldn't find anyone and they needed another fifteen days to do the job properly. Morgan agreed to this and while he was negotiating with the prisoners, Esquemeling tells us that 'seven or eight buccaneers, who had been out of town shooting cattle, returned with a Negro prisoner.' This man was carrying letters from the governor of Santiago, the capital city of the adjacent province lying some 160 miles to the east of Puerto del Príncipe. These letters were addressed to some of the prisoners and once Morgan had opened them he discovered they were telling the prisoners 'not to make too much haste to pay any ransom.' The letters also said the governor was building an army and 'would soon be coming to relieve the town.'

We can only imagine how Morgan felt. The Spanish had betrayed him. Calling his captains together, Morgan explained how the Spanish had deceived them and then turned to the prisoners demanding that the ransom for the town be paid the very next day or he would reduce the entire city to ashes. 'The Spanish again answered that it was impossible; their people were scattered here and there, and the money could not be collected in so short a time.'[5]

Not wanting to hang around any longer and knowing that an army was being prepared to intercept and stop him, Morgan realized that getting the ransom would be difficult so instead he told the Spaniards that he would 'forbore to fire the town, or bring away prisoners, but on delivery of 1,000 beeves released all.'[6] He then took six of the leading citizens as hostages, telling the Spanish that they would not be released unless they, the Spanish, killed the cattle, salted the carcasses and carried the meat on board. They agreed.

Esquemeling writes that the next morning the Spanish arrived on the beaches near Morgan's anchored ships with the cattle and demanded their prisoners back. Morgan replied they would only be released once the cattle had been slaughtered and salted and loaded on their ships. However, Dudley Pope writes in his book that it was two days later that the Spanish arrived on the beaches with the cattle.

In order to ensure the speedy release of their fellow countrymen, the Spanish worked with great haste until all the meat had been salted and stowed aboard Morgan's ships. While this was happening an incident occurred that tested Morgan's leadership. Remember, he was leading a force of men from different nations and cultures with different languages, and they all followed him because of his charisma and because they trusted that he would be successful. This incident would now test his mettle in the eyes of the men who followed him. Esquemeling provides the details:

> An Englishman had shot a Frenchman dead on account of a marrow bone. I have recounted earlier how the buccaneers when they killed a beast suck out the marrow and these men did the same thing. The Frenchman had flayed an animal and the Englishman came up and helped himself to the marrow bones. This started the quarrel and they challenged each other to fight it out with muskets. On coming to the duelling place, away from the rest, the Englishman was ready before the other, and shot him through the body from behind. Upon this, the French seized their muskets and wanted to fall on the English, but Morgan thrust himself between the rival groups and promised the French he would do right by them and have the Englishman hanged as soon as they reached Jamaica.

Morgan was as good as his word for as soon as they returned to Jamaica, the man was hanged.

With all the meat and booty aboard, Morgan released the six hostages and before setting sail arranged a rendezvous point back at the South Cays[7] with his captains where they could divvy up the plunder. This was a small cay called Isla de las Vacas (Cow Island, or Île à Vache), just off south-west Hispaniola. 'This was Morgan's favoured rendezvous for dividing booty after expeditions, as some of his captains and crews could not return to Port Royal because there was a price on their heads.'[8]

Once they'd arrived there they discovered the booty they'd pillaged in terms of gold, silver and other goods amounted to 50,000 pieces of eight, which, according to Esquemeling, 'was of little help to them, for it would not even pay the debts they owed in Jamaica.'

In this account of the attack and capture of Puerto del Príncipe by the buccaneers we start to see some discrepancies between the sources. Esquemeling clearly states that the Spanish prisoners were 'given little to eat and every day were pained and plagued by unspeakable tortures to make them say where they had hidden the money or goods.' Esquemeling is referring to the buccaneers torturing the Spanish prisoners.

However, Pope states that 'there was no threat that he would hold a few of the leading citizens over a barbecue pit.' So he believes there was no intention of torture as far as Morgan was concerned. On the other hand, Stephen Talty does not even mention that the prisoners were tortured or treated roughly on this particular raid.

Could this be one of Esquemeling's embellishments, blending fact with fiction in order to make his narrative more sensational?

Chapter 8

A New Target

At this stage it is necessary to make an observation and an assumption. If we assume that, for the most part, Esquemeling's account of the raids Morgan carried out on Puerto del Príncipe, Portobello and Panama City are roughly accurate, does it mean his references to the torture carried out by the buccaneers is also true?

In his book *Harry Morgan's Way*, Dudley Pope states that Esquemeling didn't like Morgan and so his account of his exploits was biased. Esquemeling maintains that in the raid on Portobello, which we will look at in later chapters, the buccaneers locked all the prisoners into one room in one of the castles and 'instantly set fire to the powder (whereof they found great quantity) and blew up the whole castle in the air, with all the Spanish that were within.'[1]

But Pope sites a report from another expedition that took place some ten years later, where the author of the report saw the three castles as being very large and very strong, so this refutes Esquemeling's account. The castles were not blown up. Nor does Morgan himself say this in his report.

With such poor takings from the raid on Puerto del Príncipe, the French who had been with Morgan decided to join forces with the legendary privateer Francois L'Olonais. He was renowned for his cruelty towards his prisoners and was the top privateer operating out of the French port of Tortuga. This departure dramatically reduced Morgan's forces, but his fleet was increased when Captain Jackman arrived after having pillaged Campeachy and they joined forces.

Depending on which source one believes at this stage, Morgan was joined by Jackman while at Cow Island or he had sailed back into Port Royal, where he reported to Modyford and where he met with Jackman and persuaded him to join him to attack the next target. That target would be Portobello. When he set sail he was back up to strength with nine ships and more than 460 men.[2]

Whether they sailed from Port Royal or from Cow Island, before they even raised their sails Morgan had the difficult task of trying to bring the remaining men together. The disappointing raid on Puerto del Príncipe meant that many men decided to try their luck with the French or elsewhere and morale with the remaining English was at a very low ebb. Morgan rose to the challenge and, gathering them all around him, he spoke: 'Morgan put spirit into them, saying he knew of ways of making them rich if only they would follow him. The high hopes Morgan held out made them agree.'[3]

Such was Morgan's oratory skill, his charisma and strength, he managed to bring the men together and they all resolved to follow him, including the Campeachy privateers under Captain Jackman, even though at this juncture they did not know their destination. The lessons he'd learned from the raid on Puerto del Príncipe ensured that no one would know the destination or his plans until the very last minute.

Finally, in May 1668, the fleet set sail and a few days later they came in sight of the coast of Costa Rica. Still Morgan had not revealed his plans to either his captains or his men. They were all 'being sustained only by the prospect of rich booty,' writes Esquemeling.

They were about 120 miles west of Portobello, and anchored close to the Isla Largo Remo in a small inlet in Naos Bay, which now forms part of the northern end of the Panama Canal. As the ships rode their anchors Morgan called together his captains and outlined his plan, careful this time that they were not being overheard.

Some of the men protested at the intended target saying that they did not have the numbers to attack the city. Portobello was the third strongest city on the Spanish Main after Havana and Cartagena, and no fleet of ships could penetrate its harbour because of the sixty cannon that were in the three castles overlooking the entrance and the rest of the harbour. It would be suicide. Esquemeling tells us that Morgan's response to the naysayers was, 'If our numbers are small our hearts are great, and the fewer we are the better shares we shall have in the spoils.' Once again, Morgan's gift of oratory, his charisma and dynamic personality, shone through and the rest of the men unanimously agreed to the venture.

Morgan's fleet had carried or towed behind them canoes for moving through shallow inlets and cays where their larger ships could not navigate. While these canoes were being readied for the journey six emaciated Englishmen – who had been prisoners of the Spanish and forced into hard labour – arrived, bringing much needed intelligence.[4]

According to some sources these men had been part of the original garrison at Old Providence before it had been retaken by the Spanish. Indeed, Morgan states this in his report. Their news was that levies were being raised throughout Panama 'against Jamaica, and also by some prisoners who had made their escape from Providence that Prince Maurice and diverse Englishmen were kept in irons in the dungeon of the castle of the town, they thought it their duty to attempt that place.'[5] This was in addition to the levies they had learned of during their siege of Puerto del Príncipe 'that the like levy had been made in all the islands, and considerable forces were expected from Vera Cruz and Campeachy, with materials of war to rendezvous at the Havannah, and from Portobello and Cartagena to rendezvous at St Jago of Cuba, of which he immediately gave notice to Gov Modyford.'[6]

Armed with this information Morgan now had even greater justification for attacking Portobello. Morgan picks up the story:

> So leaving their ships on 26 June, 40 leagues to leeward of Portobello at Bogata, they took to their canoes, twenty-three in number, and rowing along the coast landed at three o'clock in the morning, and made their way into the town.[7]

According to Esquemeling the place where they landed was the village of Estero Longa Lemo and from here they marched until they reached an outpost of Portobello, where they captured a sentry. The man guiding them was one of the six English prisoners; he knew the roads well as he had been working on them and the fortifications of the town. The buccaneers captured the sentry without firing a shot. They quickly bound him and took him to Morgan, 'who questioned the sentry as to the arrangements of the town's defences and the strength of the garrison, and the prisoner told what he knew.'[8] With the bound sentry in front of them, the buccaneers marched for about fifteen minutes to the first castle, which they surrounded. Using the sentry as the go-between, Morgan demanded the garrison surrendered to him but they refused and instead began firing on the buccaneers. It was a lost cause. The castle would soon fall, but the firing had done one thing – it had raised the alarm for the rest of the town.

> And seeing that they could not refresh themselves in quiet, they were enforced to assault the castle, which they took by storm, and found well supplied with ammunition and provisions, only undermanned, being about 130 men, whereof seventy-four killed, among which 'the Castiliano' was one.[9]

This castle was called San Geronimo. Now with the first castle in their possession the buccaneers made a terrifying discovery. In its dungeon were eleven English prisoners in chains who Morgan tells us had been there for two years. Indeed, these prisoners confirmed the story that:

> a great man had been carried thence six months before to Lima of Peru [sic] who was formerly brought from Porto Rico, and also that the Prince of Monte Circa

had been there with orders from the King of Spain to raise 2,200 men against us out of the Province of Panama which Portobello stands in, the certainty whereof was confirmed by all the grandees.[10]

The great man was Prince Maurice.

The detail for the raid on Portobello comes almost exclusively from Esquemeling and it is to him that we turn to once again. However, his bias towards Morgan is evident in his text. We already know that his reference to the first castle, known as San Geronimo, being blown up with the Spaniards inside was untrue because the castle was still intact some years later. That means that we have to take what he has written as being a little suspect. Unfortunately, Morgan did not provide the details in his report.

If we think back to the debacle of the English garrison on Old Providence, and the way in which the Spanish betrayed the prisoners by not acting honourably, the man behind that action was Sanchez, the mayor of Portobello. He was now in the second castle – Fort Triana, or Santiago, depending on the source – with hundreds of soldiers.

This castle was located in the town and overlooks the harbour. Morgan could not bring his ships into the harbour until its guns were silenced. The smaller castle, San Felipe, on the other side of the harbour, also covered the way in and it too needed to be captured. Morgan sent a section of men to take San Felipe while he concentrated most of his forces on Fort Triana.[11]

Having seen the state of the English prisoners they'd just freed from the larger castle, the buccaneers wanted revenge. While it is not evident they knew that Sanchez was in Fort Triana, one has to assume that the English prisoners knew this and had passed this information on to Morgan and his men. This would have given the buccaneers even more reason for taking Fort Triana to settle the old score over Old Providence. Their blood was up. So many of the buccaneers were excellent marksmen and 'sharpshooters because of their earlier life and now they hid on the roofs of the houses round Triana and picked off the Spanish gunners as they reloaded and ran out their guns.'[12]

Esquemeling states that the battle raged all morning, with both sides trying to gain advantage.

Still the invaders could not conquer the fort. Their ships lay in the harbour mouth and no one could enter for the withering fire from the forts on both sides. Finally, as they had lost many men and were gaining no advantage, the buccaneers began throwing in hand grenades and endeavoured to burn down the gate of the fort. But when they came in close for this attack the Spaniards soon made them turn back, for they hurled down at least fifty pots full of gunpowder as well as huge stones, which did much damage among the raiders.

The fight was taking too long and Morgan had already lost good men. He needed something to rouse the men and make one last push. Those he had sent to take San Felipe came to his rescue when he and his buccaneers saw the English flag raised over this fort and its guns became silent. 'They saw the English flag flying from the smaller fort and a troop of their fellows approaching, shouting "Victory!",' writes Esquemeling.

However, Fort Triana was still a problem, for not only was Sanchez in the castle but so were the leading citizens of Portobello, as Esquemeling explains, 'with their gold and silver and jewels and the silver ornaments from the churches'.

Buoyed by the success of the men who had taken San Felipe, Morgan rallied his troops and ordered a dozen huge ladders to be built for scaling the walls of Fort Triana.

The chronology of events in this battle differs from source to source. For example, Stephen Talty, in his book *Empire of Blue Water*, states that San Felipe Castle was not taken by the buccaneers until the following day. Indeed, he says that the flag that was raised was the red flag, which stood for no quarter. 'The men swarmed over the ramparts and cut down the last of the defenders in their section of the castle, then raised the infamous red flag.'[13] So this means the flag that the English saw was not at San Felipe but in another section of Santiago (Fort Triana) because the main body of men were still 'assaulting the front gate of the castle and soon joined up with their compatriots. Seventy-four of the Spanish defenders lay dead, including the castellan.'[14]

Talty's account is based on Esquemeling's, as well as on Spanish reports, so there is likely considerable accuracy in his detail. However, if we go back to the account of the battle as detailed by Pope in his book *Harry Morgan's Way*, which is similar to Esquemeling's, we come to a part in the story that is contentious.

> Morgan had a dozen huge ladders made, broad enough for four men to climb at the same time. He fetched out all the monks and nuns, and the Governor was informed that unless he surrendered the fort these people would be made to set the scaling ladders against its walls.

The governor replied that the buccaneers would not take the fort as long as he was alive. So, according to Esquemeling, the ladders were indeed brought out, 'carried by the monks, priests and women, urged on by the buccaneers, who never thought the governor would fire on his own people – but he spared them as little as he had the raiders.' Their cries for the governor to give up the castle fell on deaf ears and the governor ordered his men to open fire.

> But Captain Morgan was fully deceived in his judgment of this design for the Governor, who acted like a brave soldier in performance of his duty, used his utmost endeavour to destroy whosoever came near the walls. The religious men and women ceased not to cry to him and beg of him, by all the saints of heaven, to deliver the castle, and spare both his and their own lives; but nothing could prevail with his obstinacy and fierceness.

Many of these individuals were killed but the ladders were placed against the walls and the buccaneers swarmed up them, 'having fireballs in their hands, and earthen pots full of powder; all which things, being now at the top of the walls, they kindled and cast in among the Spaniards.'

The interesting point about this part of the story, where Morgan effectively uses the priests and nuns as human shields, is that Morgan later won a libel suit over Esquemeling's publishers, which we will look at in detail later. So this particular incident may or may not have any foundation in truth – yet it remains in most translations.

Esquemeling provides us with the detail of the end of the battle:

> The Spaniards could no longer resist nor defend the castle, which was now entered. Hereupon they all threw down their arms, and craved quarter for their lives; only the governor of the city would crave no mercy, but killed many of the pirates with his own hands and not a few of his own soldiers; because they did not stand to their arms. And though the pirates asked him if he would have quarter; yet he constantly answered, 'By no means, I had rather die as a valiant solider, than be hanged as a coward.' They endeavoured as much as they could to take him prisoner, but he defended himself so obstinately, that they were forced to kill him, notwithstanding all the cries and tears of his own wife and daughter, who begged him, on their knees, to demand quarter, and save his life.

According to Esquemeling, by night of the first day the buccaneers had taken all three castles. Remember that Talty states they had yet to take San Felipe. Indeed, his account states that Morgan sent 200 men to take that fort, which was held by a handful of Spaniards, and after a brief fight the castellan surrendered it to Morgan under generous terms of capitulation.[15]

But the buccaneers, states Talty, reneged on the terms of surrender, which allowed the Spaniards to leave the fort with their muskets and flags flying.

They were stripped of everything but their swords, and the castellan, now weighed down by guilt, asked for a vial of poison, which he was given and he drank it.[16]

With the town now in their hands, Esquemeling states that the buccaneers 'fell to eating and drinking, as usual; that is committing in both all manner of debauchery and excess, so that fifty courageous men might easily have retaken the city, and killed all the pirates.'

Pope suggests that Esquemeling now enters the realm of fantasy because he states that Morgan's men, unable to extort riches from their prisoners, began to torture them, and some died under this treatment. Talty does not mention this in his book either.

Panama City was not much more than 70 miles away and had been alerted to the attack on Portobello by a Spanish horseman who had escaped and managed to get to Panama. Esquemeling states that this rider alerted the viceroy of the Province of Panama, Don Juan Perez de Guzman, who then began to raise an army of 3,000 men and set out to retake Portobello.

> He employed all his care and industry to raise forces to pursue and cast out the pirates thence; but these cared little for his preparations having their ships at hand, and determining to fire the city, and retreat.

Stephan Talty tells us that the person alerted was the president of Panama, Don Agustin de Bracamonte, and it was he who sent drummers through the streets of Panama trying to drum up enough men for the army to take back Portobello. He also states that Bracamonte had 800 men at his disposal, who immediately left for Portobello without the necessary provisions to keep them sustained. The provisions caught up later.[17]

The story that Esquemeling tells at this point is that Morgan had all the loot they'd gathered loaded onto the ships, which had been sailed into the harbour. With all three castles now in his hands, Morgan turned to the prisoners and demanded 100,000 pieces of eight as a ransom for the town, or he would burn it to the ground. To get the money, he demanded the prisoners send two men to the president of Panama. The president was already on the march with his forces when these two men arrived and gave him 'an account of all'.

Morgan was alerted to the oncoming army marching over the mountains and through the jungles towards them by the native Indians, who, as we have seen, were no friends of the Spanish. The Spanish treated the Indians very badly and many of the various buccaneers on expeditions in this part of the Spanish Main had made friends with the disgruntled Indians. Hearing of the approaching army, Morgan decided to lead a force of approximately 100 men into the jungle, down the only passable road (not much more than a track) up to a narrow pass where he knew the oncoming forces would have to go through. Here he set up an ambush and waited.[18]

It wasn't long before the forward sentries he'd posted announced the Spanish forces were massing in the narrow passage. The Spanish had no chance against Morgan's well-armed men, who 'at the first encounter put to flight a good party of those of Panama,' writes Esquemeling.

After this ambush the Spanish had no real force left to take back Portobello. They would have to give in to Morgan's demands. So for the final word on this action we will turn to Morgan himself, who states:

> On the fifth day arrived the President of Panama with about 3,000 men; whom they beat off with considerable damage, insomuch that next day he proffered 100,000 pieces of eight for delivery of the town, castles, and 300 negroes, which being paid, they repaired on board leaving the town and castles in as good condition as they found them.[19]

Part of the loot that Morgan loaded onto his ships was the brass cannon they'd found in the castles. 'In the first castle there were thirty brass guns besides iron, in the second, thirteen, all brass, and in the third, fourteen guns.' This is quite likely the reason why it took so long to load the booty into the ships.

The handing over of the money was not quite as sudden as Morgan claims. According to Stephen Talty there was considerable negotiation between him and the Spaniards (under Bracamonte). The sum that Morgan demanded was 350,000 pesos. Negotiations went back and forth until the sum of 100,000 pesos in cash was finally agreed upon. Esquemeling picks up the story:

> Thus in a few days more the miserable citizens gathered the contributions required, and brought 100,000 pieces of eight to the pirates for a ransom of their cruel captivity: but the President of Panama was much amazed to consider that 400 men could take such a great city, with so many strong castles, especially having no ordnance, wherewith to raise batteries.

With the money agreed and received – gold coins and silver – and the rest of the loot loaded onto the ships, Morgan and his men sailed away from Portobello. Their haul amounted to more than 250,000 pieces of eight plus the money they would receive from the sale of goods such as cloth, linen and silks, as well as the slaves they'd taken. At their prearranged rendezvous point off Cuba, the buccaneers divided up their plunder and set sail for Jamaica.

Morgan had shown the Spanish that he could attack their heart with virtual impunity and how vulnerable the Spanish were.

They further declared to the world that in all this service of Portobello, they lost but eighteen men killed and thirty-two wounded, and kept possession of the place thirty-one days; and for the better vindicating themselves against the usual scandals of that enemy, they aver that having several ladies of great quality and other prisoners they were proffered their liberty to go to the President's camp, but they refused, saying they were now prisoners to a person of quality, who was more tender of their honours than they doubted to find in the President's camp among his rude Panama soldiers, and so voluntarily continued with them till the surrender of the town and castles, when with many thanks and good wishes they repaired to their former houses.[20]

Chapter 9

The Oxford Incident

The riches gained by Morgan and the rest of the buccaneers during their raid on Portobello were mostly squandered the moment they arrived back in Port Royal. While the raid had been daring and dangerous, Morgan's next mission would cement his reputation as the most successful buccaneer of the age. It would prove beyond doubt just how much of a brilliant tactician he was as well as how much the Spanish feared him.

To relate this adventure we return to our regular sources, Esquemeling, Talty, Pope, Breverton and Morgan himself. But before we examine the Maracaibo affair and the near disaster the mission could have been, it is worth putting into context the times and environment of Jamaica, specifically Port Royal.

The riches seized at Portobello were divided up at Cow Island off Hispaniola. In cash they had 250,000 pieces of eight, which was a very large amount at the time. In addition were the materials, gold and silver that would be sold to merchants in Port Royal.

> His ships were low in the water with their freight of gold and silver, silks and satins, furniture and weapons, and the chained slaves in the hold soon to be sold to the planters.[1]

The buccaneers had suffered heavy casualties in this siege, some to action but most to tropical disease, so much so that less than 400 men rendezvoused at Cow Island for distribution of the booty. This meant greater shares for each man. Philip Lindsay tells us that shares were distributed according to the wounds suffered by the men – how serious they were – and according to rank. As commander-in-chief, Morgan would get 5 per cent of the total amount. Modyford, as the king's representative, would also receive a sum. The rest would be apportioned appropriately.

With the loot distributed they sailed into 'the broad harbour, guns firing, flags and pennants flying to anchor off The Point.'[2]

The city of Port Royal was built on the end of a sand spit that acted as a breakwater against the sea. This sandy peninsula (The Point) formed a natural harbour, which, as Lindsay tells us, was about 7 miles long and 4 miles wide. It was a deep water harbour that could take ships of more than 1,000 tonnes. Many people had settled along this sand spit, which boasted warehouses, fortifications and large 'merchant palaces' as well as the 'ramshackle dens of debauchery near the wharves'.

The currency in this city of sin was gin and whoring and any sailor or privateer could get just about anything he could think of provided he had the money. There were plenty of people – harlots, merchants, con artists, card sharks and more – prepared to relieve the buccaneers of their hard-fought plunder.

> A cask of rum, a deck of cards, or a dice-box, an opulent harlot with skilled caresses, and these rascals, devils to the Spaniards, became children to be gulled in expert hands.[3]

In Port Royal what little law existed revolved around money. For example, if a buccaneer spent all his money on gambling, drinking and whoring and found himself unable to pay any debts he may have racked up, he could be sold as a slave to his creditor until the debt was paid or worked off.

The Point was away from the places frequented by the finer gentry and it is unlikely that Morgan took part in the debaucheries of his men. After all, he was a married man, a plantation owner, and he moved in the highest society in Jamaica. He was feted by the planters and wealthy merchants while also spending time with Modyford, for there was much to discuss regarding the raids and the dispatches that needed to be sent back to London. However, Lindsay states that Morgan was a heavy drinker and probably did his drinking 'on plantations or in the luxurious merchant palaces, chiefly away from The Point, arguing how best to invest his profits.'

Of course with such wild behaviour the riches earned by the buccaneers were soon gone and once again many found themselves penniless. 'They were all very liberal, and in a short time came clamouring to their captain to put to sea; for they were reduced to a starving condition.'[4]

It would not be long before Morgan was once again planning a new mission with the approval from Modyford.

But in Port Royal not everyone was involved in the debauchery and deplored the actions of the buccaneers, along with the industries that catered for their desires. John Styles, a wealthy merchant, wrote to the Secretary of State, complaining that:

> The number of tippling houses is now doubly increased, so that 'there is not now resident upon this place ten men to every house that selleth strong liquors.'

> There are more than 100 licensed houses, besides sugar and rum works that sell without licence; and what can that bring but ruin, for many sell their plantations, and either go out for privateers, or drinking themselves into debt, sell their bodies or are sold for prison fees. Since Styles has been a prisoner there have been twenty sold thence; 'so interests decrease, negro and slaves increase,' yet were not this course taken, the prisons would not hold the prisoners.[5]

While complaining about the behaviour of the buccaneers in town and the sinful industries that had built up to cater to their needs there were also allegations of prisoner abuse that Styles claimed to have overheard the buccaneers boasting about in the taverns.

> It is a common thing amongst the privateers, besides burning with matches and such like slight torments, to cut a man in pieces, first some flesh, then a hand, an arm, a leg, sometimes tying a cord about his head, and with a stick twisting it till the eyes start out, which is called 'woolding'. Before taking Puerto Bello, thus some were used, because they refused to discover a way into the town which was not, and many in the town, because they would not discover wealth they knew not of: a woman there was by some set bare upon a baking stone and roasted, because she did not confess of money which she had only in their conceit; this he heard some declare boasting, and one that was sick confess with sorrow: besides the horrid oaths, blasphemies, abuse of scriptures, rapes, whoredoms, and adulteries, and such not forborne in the common highways and not punished, but made a jest of even by authority.[6]

From the research done for this book it appears that the allegations put forward by Styles went largely unheeded. Perhaps it was a question of Morgan being so successful that the authorities, in this case, Modyford, looked the other way. There is no direct evidence that links Morgan with any act of torture. But with hundreds of men under his command and the men scattered throughout the towns and cities he sacked, he could have no way of knowing what any one man or group of men were doing. Yet a commander should always be responsible for his men – shouldn't he!

While the only true English evidence that points towards cruelty and torture is Esquemeling, we know we must be mindful of his bias and embellishments about the misuse of prisoners. It also depends on which translation of Esquemeling's book is used, as we shall see in later chapters. The Spanish reports that Stephen Talty cites regularly in his book do not run to the same flights of fancy as those of Esquemeling, nor do they always support every detail of the expeditions, so we are left without knowing for sure if these events took place.

Other events around this time are described and explained differently depending on the source used. The origin for Morgan's next mission is also a little murky. Morgan still had his commission as an admiral, which put him in charge of Jamaica's forces and second only to Sir Thomas Modyford, the governor. Both men believed that the Spaniards were preparing for an attack on Jamaica – according to intelligence that Morgan had received on the Portobello raid. They also believed that the best way to keep the enemy at bay was to attack his heart, forcing him to hold back his forces in a defensive posture while he wondered where the next attack was coming from. The best targets were along the Spanish Main in either New Spain or Cuba. Of the targets they identified, Cartagena was the most important, and the wealthiest. With a powerful enough force Morgan could sack the city.

Cartagena was the port through which the gold and silver from Peru flowed to Spain and was the largest along the Main. This also made it the best port from which to launch an attack on Jamaica.[7]

While one can assume from the way that Pope describes the relationship between Modyford and Morgan that the men by and large agreed to this expedition, Lindsay is more specific in his terminology:

> therefore he gave Morgan further powers and sent him out again under sealed orders with his ferocious army, and he even committed himself and his government openly to the expedition by sending the 300-ton fifth-rate frigate *Oxford*, thirty-four guns and a crew of 160 men, under the command of Edward Collier who held the King's commission, to join the buccaneers.[8]

Morgan was once again sailing away from Port Royal with ten ships and more than 800 men towards the old rendezvous point, Cow Island, off south-west Hispaniola. It was October 1668, and while Morgan waited off Cow Island the first warship intended purely for the defence of Jamaica arrived from England. The *Oxford* was a frigate that had a crew of 125 men and twenty-six guns. It was twelve years old and no longer in the service of the Royal Navy. It was to be a private man-of-war, owned and operated by the Jamaican government. The problem was, however, that the government could not afford to run her. Indeed, the government of Jamaica did not have the infrastructure, men or resources to run its own navy so the *Oxford* would have ended up being in the service of the people who could run a navy – the buccaneers. Under the command of Edward Collier, Modyford ordered the frigate to be refitted, victualled and sent to meet up with Morgan at Cow Island. 'The *Oxford* frigate is to face Cartagena and will sail about five days hence.'⁹ Collier was an experienced privateer and well known to Morgan. However, according to Pope, Modyford ordered Collier to deal with a French pirate who was known to have joined Morgan's fleet at Cow Island. The French ship *Le Cerf Volant* had attacked a British ship from Virginia and Modyford wanted Collier to get the pirate. The *Oxford* sailed for Cow Island and found the French pirate ship riding its anchor in the island's anchorage with the rest of Morgan's fleet. The French captain and crew were then arrested by Collier and both the *Oxford* and *Le Cerf Volant* returned to Port Royal so the French pirates could stand trial for robbery and piracy. The French captain was sentenced to death but this was later commuted by Modyford.¹⁰

However, *Le Cerf Volant*, armed with fourteen guns, was quickly refitted and renamed the *Satisfaction* and sailed, in consort with the *Oxford*, back to Cow Island. Aboard the *Satisfaction* was Dr Richard Browne, a surgeon who had come to Jamaica aboard the *Oxford*. He regularly communicated with Sir Joseph Williamson, Secretary of the Privy Council, and Lord Arlington, Secretary of State, providing them with detailed reports of everything he saw and experienced during his time in the West Indies. Browne wrote a letter, dated 20 January 1669, to Joseph Williamson about the arrest and return to Port Royal. He described the situation:

His Majesty's ship *Oxford*, commanded by Captain Edward Collier, came to anchor 29 October, at the Isle of Vacour, on the coast of Hispaniola, where were several English and French privateers belonging to Jamaica, and two French men-of-war, one being the *Cour Volant* of Rochelle, Captain La Veven commander, that robbed Isaac Rush, of Virginia, Master of the Commonwealth, of twelve barréls of pork, a barrél of butter, and another of flour. Captain Collier sent his Lieutenant to command La Veven aboard, but he answered that it was not usual for any captain of a man-of-war of France to be commanded out of his ship. The next morning, Captain Collier weighed, and came close to him, intending to board him, when La Veven came aboard; upon his commission being demanded he made several evasions, but subsequently produced one from Monsieur de Beaufort to La Veven, but on his taking Rush's provisions, he went by the name of Captain la Roche of Toulon, and Rush coming into the Isle of Vacour the next day, maintained that he was the same man, whereupon Captain Collier, believing he was no other than a pirate, had him brought aboard his ship, 'in order to his trial' at Jamaica, and commanded all the French, to the number of forty-five, on board the *Oxford* also.¹¹

From this letter it is pretty clear that Browne was an eyewitness and this is corroborated later in the letter when he states that Collier set sail in Veven's ship for Jamaica, where he was put on trial for his crimes. He does not mention anything about the *Oxford* returning with Veven's ship to Jamaica and then sailing back to Cow Island with the *Satisfaction* (the former *Le Cerf Volant)* because by that time the *Oxford* had been destroyed.

The sources used for this book mostly claim that the *Oxford* did return to Port Royal as escort to the French ship, and that her crew waited for the French ship to be condemned as a prize and renamed the *Satisfaction*, and then returned with the latter ship in tow. So we have a discrepancy in the account of this affair and what actually took place varies depending on the text used by the historian. One thing that is clear is that Browne was an eyewitness, if we take his letter at face value. He describes the destruction of the *Oxford* in a personal way, relating what he was doing and how he managed to survive at the time the *Oxford* was destroyed.

Before we look at the destruction of the frigate in greater detail it is worth looking at Esquemeling's account of the French pirate incident.

> The French pirates belonging to this great ship had met at sea an English vessel; and being under great want of victuals, they had taken some provisions out of the English ship, without paying for them, having, perhaps, no ready money aboard; only they gave them bills of exchange for Jamaica and Tortuga, to receive money there. Captain Morgan having notice of this, and perceiving he could not prevail with the French captain to follow him, resolved to lay hold on this occasion, to ruin the French, and seek his revenge. Hereupon he invited, with dissimulation, the French commander, and several of his men, to dine with him on board the great ship that was come to Jamaica, as is said. Being come, he made them all prisoners, pretending the injury afore-said done to the English vessel.

Because we have the letter from Richard Browne we know that Esquemeling's account is at best an exaggeration of the facts or, at worst, a complete fabrication. The great ship that Esquemeling refers to that belonged to the French was likely *Le Cerf Volant*, 'of twenty-four iron guns'. The great ship from Jamaica is very likely the *Oxford* frigate. Esquemeling leaves Captain Collier's role in this affair completely out of his account and transfers Collier's actions to Morgan. He does not name any of the ships, nor the French captain, in the way that Browne did. So in this case it is Browne's report of the incident of *Le Cerf Volant* and the French crew that we will take as being the most accurate. It leads into the destruction of the *Oxford*. Esquemeling's account of the frigate's destruction will be looked at first as he provides some detail, but whether that detail is accurate is left up to the reader to decide.

> Morgan, presently after he had taken these French prisoners, called a council to deliberate what place they should first pitch upon in this expedition. Here it was determined to go to the Isle of Savona, to wait for the flota then expected from Spain, and to take any of the Spanish vessels straggling from the rest. This resolution being taken, they began aboard the great ship to feast one another for joy of their new voyage, and happy council as they hoped: they drank many healths, and discharged many guns, the common sign of mirth among seamen. Most of the men being drunk, by what accident is not known, the ship suddenly was blown up, with 350 Englishmen, besides the French prisoners in the hold; all which there escaped but thirty men, who were in the great cabin, at some distance from the main force of the powder.[12]

Esquemeling does not state who sat where when the powder magazine went up. Also, Esquemeling claims that the buccaneers decided to sail to the Isle of Savona off the eastern part of Hispaniola before they decided what the target should be for this new expedition. Our other sources, including Pope, suggest that at the council of war called upon the *Oxford* it was decided that Cartagena would be the target. Either way, it was after the council of war that the *Oxford* was destroyed. This is what Browne had to say about the event:

> While the captains were at dinner on the quarter-deck, the Oxford blew up, when 200 men were lost, including Captain Aylett, Commander of the *Lilly*, and captains Bigford, Morris, Thornbury, and Whiting, only six men and four boys being saved. The accident is supposed to have been caused by the negligence of the gunner. I was eating my dinner with the rest, when the mainmasts blew out, and fell upon captains Aylett, Bigford and others, and knocked them on the head; I saved myself by getting astride the mizen-mast.[13]

Pope goes further in his detail of this account. He states that Morgan and the rest of the captains went down into the 'great cabin' of the frigate, where they began a hearty meal. Instead of sitting at the head of the table, Morgan sat on one side of it in the middle, with Captain Collier sitting on his right. Captains Bigford, Whiting, Thornbury and Aylett sat opposite Morgan, as did John Morris the younger. His father sat on the same side as Morgan, as did Browne, who sat at the far end of the table. Those who sat on Morgan's side miraculously survived the explosion while those on the opposite side perished.

Indeed, when the ship's magazine erupted and blew the ship to pieces, the effect of the blast threw the men into the air. They hit the water, surrounded by the debris from the disintegrated frigate and floating human body parts. Fortunately, the men on the other ships were quick to react and launched their boats, which rowed amongst the wreckage picking up survivors. They managed to save Browne, Collier, two cabin boys, the elder John Morris and, of course, Admiral Morgan.[14]

Chapter 10

Attack on Maracaibo

Gave him account about a month since of the unhappy blowing up of the *Oxford* frigate and the taking of *M. La Vivon*, of the *Cour Volant*, of eighteen guns, which was condemned as a pirate; she is now called the *Satisfaction*, and victualled for four months, to go as a privateer against the Spaniards in the Bay of Campeachy.

With the destruction of the *Oxford*, Morgan now had to change his plans. The firepower he needed to take Cartagena disappeared when the frigate blew up. It had only been in the service of Jamaica for a few months and now Morgan had to contend with a smaller fleet with fewer men and less firepower than he had with the *Oxford*, so that meant Cartagena was out of the question.

Rallying the fleet, Morgan sent out a call for more privateers to join him on his expedition. The primary means of doing this was by sending the *Satisfaction* back to Jamaica. Morgan hoped the men on that ship would send the word out to the privateers in Port Royal, Tortuga and beyond with a message to meet him at the new rendezvous point at the Isle of Savona a month later.

Morgan and the rest of his fleet left Cow Island and sailed into the teeth of a strong easterly wind that delayed his journey round the False Cape and Punta Beata by three weeks, exhausting their food and water. With his provisions so low and his men weak he had no choice but to land near Santo Domingo, where, Esquemeling states, Morgan ordered some of the men from the ships to go inland to find water and provisions.

But it was not that easy. His men killed many cattle and while they did they were watched all the time by the Spaniards, who had set a trap by 'gathering a great herd of cows, and set two or three men to keep them. The pirates, having spied them, killed a sufficient number, and though the Spaniards could see them at a distance, yet they could not hinder them at present, but as soon as they attempted to carry them away, they set upon them furiously,' writes Esquemeling. This running fight meant that the buccaneers had to flee. But they did so by degrees, taking enough meat with them that could be salted away in casks on board the ships. According to Esquemeling, many Spanish were killed in these attacks.

He tried again to resupply by sending a mission to Hispaniola, but the men on this mission returned empty-handed having been harried by a large contingent of Spanish soldiers.

When the fleet finally arrived at the Isle of Savona they were very weak. Since leaving Cow Island they had been heading windward, their ships battered and beaten by high rolling seas that pitched the ships violently. The men had been constantly working to keep their vessels afloat. Most of the ships in the fleet were small, as Dudley Pope states, they were little more than 'large boats whose crew had to spend most of their time at the pumps or bailing with calabash shells.'[1] The men were exhausted, their clothes constantly soaked and their provisions difficult to keep from spoiling in such small vessels because of the lack of cabins or shelter.

However, once they arrived at the anchorage at Savona, Morgan's heart must have fallen, for there were no other privateers there waiting to join him. 'Having hitherto resolved to cruise on the coasts of Caraca, and to plunder the towns and villages there, finding himself at present with such small forces he changed his resolution by advice of a French captain in his fleet.'

At this juncture it is worth reiterating that the only real eyewitness account we have of Morgan's actions on this part of his expedition comes from Esquemeling.[2] However, to use the vernacular, he is the only game in town. Yet at the heart of his book is the character of Morgan himself: the man we seek, the kind of leader he was and that he was a man of his age.

No one today could do what Morgan did. He stood astride the line between law and order and criminal behaviour. Esquemeling refers to him as a pirate, which infers that he was, like Blackbeard, a common criminal. But Morgan was not a criminal; he was a military man and his actions, as we have seen, were entirely against an enemy of England.

While the detail of the Maracaibo raid comes primarily from Esquemeling, the character of Morgan and his actions should be evaluated in an objective light, taking Esquemeling's bias against Morgan away. So while Esquemeling is the primary source to understand the essence of Morgan it is necessary to look at this account through the eyes of other historians.

The French captain referred to by Esquemeling had been on an expedition to Maracaibo with the brutal French buccaneer Francis L'Ollonais. The city was attacked on that raid by a fleet of eight ships and 650 men, the unknown French captain advised Morgan. As a result of that attack, this French captain knew 'all the entries, passages, forces and means, how to put in execution the same again.'[3]

Map of Lake Maracaibo with Guajira and Paraguana peninsulas and Nederlandse Antillen in the French language.

Having listened to the advice from the French captain, Morgan decided to head for Maracaibo. He put the proposal to the rest of his captains and they all agreed. The plan as outlined by the Frenchman was a good one. The people of Maracaibo had not been attacked since L'Ollonais had raided them and they would be complacent. Indeed, they may even have seen that attack as a unique event, one that couldn't happen again because the defences were better now and no one could get past them. It couldn't happen again, could it?

In his biography of Morgan, Dudley Pope describes the course that Morgan's fleet would have to take and the geography of the area to get to Maracaibo. The goal was to sail for the Dutch Island of Curaçao in the Gulf of Venezuela. This coastline, which runs east and west, and was at the time the coast of the province of Caracas (Venezuela), borders with Columbia at its western end. Here the Gulf of Venezuela 'funnels down at its inshore side to become a narrow channel, like the neck of a flask, and then opens out again into the almost circular Lake of Maracaibo.'[4]

Having agreed the plan the fleet now weighed anchor and set sail for Curaçao. Fifty miles west of Curaçao, and almost exactly in the centre of the entrance to the Gulf of Venezuela, lies the island of Aruba. The journey from Savona to Curaçao was 400 miles and when Morgan sighted the Dutch island, instead of heading for it, he turned the fleet towards Aruba and anchored there for a couple of days. According to Esquemeling, this island had a small garrison to defend it and it was primarily populated with Indians who were under Spanish rule. 'The Inhabitants exercise commerce or trade with the pirates that go or come this way: they buy of the islanders sheep, lambs and kids, which they exchange for linen, thread and like things,' writes Esquemeling.[5] He also states that the island was very dry and barren but was full of dangerous insects, snakes and spiders.

Morgan purchased sheep, lamb and wood for his fleet and then two days after arriving he quietly ordered the anchors to be raised and the fleet slipped out of the anchorage under the cover of night, 'to the intent they might not see what course he steered.'

Morgan headed for the western side of the Gulf, keeping well out of sight of the Spanish forts and watchtowers along the coast. He continued south, towards the channel that led to Maracaibo. At this point finding the channel became a little more difficult, for the coast along this section of the Gulf consisted of low, long sandy beaches where the surf would break more than a mile from shore, so there were few landmarks for a navigator to find his way towards the channel. After some time, they sighted the village of Sinamaica, which the French captain had been able to identify. Morgan decided to anchor his fleet for the night.

Inside the channel are three islands that Pope tells us almost close it off. They are San Carlos, Bajo Seco and Zapara. These islands 'were low and sandy, fringed here and there with mangroves.'[6] The water level in the channel itself is quite low, 12 feet or less, and the channel at the time when Morgan attacked twisted and turned in a series of bends between the three islands. The most difficult to navigate was the channel around Seco as this island was not much more than a sandy cay. The difficulty lay in the shallow bank of quicksand that ran from Seco to Zapara, which also bore the brunt of the sea and was known as the Bar of Maracaibo.

Morgan raised anchor at dawn and the little fleet headed towards San Carlos, the first of the three islands. However, they soon discovered that the Spanish had not been idle since the attack by L'Ollonais. They'd erected a fort on the island, whose guns covered the channel. Because of the low terrain, Morgan's fleet was discovered by the garrison in the fort shortly after they set sail. Stephen Talty tells us that Morgan's flagship was the *Lilly*, a frigate of fourteen guns. But it would be no match for the Spanish guns in the fort. While the location of the fort was excellent, the Spanish had failed to provide the necessary resources to make it a viable defence.

> Inside, there were just nine men, no doubt astonished by the sudden appearance of the long-dreaded privateers in their peaceful cay. But they knew their duty and began furiously loading and firing the eleven guns as Morgan sailed up to the beach and offloaded his men in the teeth of the barrage, while his gunners provided covering fire.[7]

Morgan knew there was no way they could navigate the channel with the Spanish guns raining fire on them. The guns had to be silenced and the fort taken so the attack on the fort was carried out.

However, it was slow going as on the beach where the men landed there was virtually no cover for the buccaneers, who slowly began working their way forward towards the fort. Spanish cannon balls smashed into the sand near the buccaneers as they ran for the only cover they could find, a sandy ridge. According to Esquemeling, 'the dispute continued very hot on both sides.'

In the late afternoon a gale blew up, which whipped sand into the buccaneers' faces, stinging their eyes, clogging their muskets and pistols while the Spanish continued firing. To the Spanish gunners, the buccaneers below were no more than blurred shapes in the flying sand and grit whipped up by the gale. Still they continued to fire. In addition to this the buccaneers had to contend with the muggy and intense tropical heat. Yet, according to Esquemeling, Morgan and his men 'managed the fight with great courage from morning till dark at night.'

Morgan had not stayed in his ship and sent the men out to take the fort under the command of one of his captains. He was leading this attack himself. It is crucial to point this out because had he not been there it is very likely that his men, upwards of 200 in number, would have been killed if not for his bravery and courage.

As darkness fell, Morgan moved quickly and quietly towards the walls of the fort, expecting the crack of musket fire at any moment. But the Spanish guns were silent. Perhaps the gunners had had enough and were tired from the day-long battle. Morgan moved around the walls of the fort looking for a way in and finally he found one. A gate had been left open. He stepped quickly inside and, 'having examined, he found nobody in it, the Spaniards having deserted it not long before.' There was good reason for the Spaniards to desert the place. As his men quickly joined him and they moved deeper into the building they soon found 'a match lighted near a train of powder, to have blown up the pirates and the whole fortress as soon as they were in it,' Esquemeling writes.[8] He states that the match had been rigged to burn for fifteen minutes before igniting the powder and blowing up the fort. With only minutes to spare, Morgan grabbed the lit match and stamped it out, saving the lives of him and all his men. How did he know there was a burning match there and where he could find it? According to Dudley Pope, he recognized the smell of a slow-burning match and was able to pinpoint its location.

Whatever legendary status Admiral Morgan had at this point with the buccaneers, and it was growing all the time, this action would have given it a real boost.

What had happened to the Spanish gunners manning the fort? 'They'd jumped into a boat and headed into town to raise the alarm.'[9]

Of course, this meant that Morgan had lost the edge of surprise but this loss was softened by the huge quantities of powder that they found in the fort. They found sixteen guns, ranging from 12- to 24-pounders, and proceeded to spike (or nail) them so they could not be used by the Spanish to blast the fleet on their way out of the channel. Spiking, or nailing, a gun usually meant hammering a nail into the touch hole to completely block it and then cutting the head of the nail off. This procedure meant that the only way the gun could be cleared and made usable again was by drilling the nail out of the touch hole, which quite often made the touch hole too large or damaged it.

In addition to the powder, Esquemeling tells us they also 'found many muskets and other military provisions.' These provisions included holsters for the pistols, rests for the muskets, spare ramrods and flints. With the guns spiked, sentries posted and muskets and military provisions made ready for carrying aboard the fleet the next day, Morgan and his men slept securely in the shelter of the fort.

> The next day they commanded the ships to enter the bar, among which they divided the powder, muskets and other things found in the fort: then they embarked again to continue their course towards Maracaibo but the waters being very low, they could not pass a certain bank at the entry of the lake.[10]

The bank that Esquemeling refers to is a bank of deadly quicksand, which meant they could not navigate the channel using their fleet. Morgan turned to his old tried and true tactic – canoes. These were quickly lowered into the water and the men clambered into them, loading them with as much as they required for the upcoming operations. Slowly, they 'rowed into a stiff wind and soon found the shore at the foot of the fort named de la Barra.'[11]

As with the previous day, they landed on shore and began approaching the fort cautiously, and as quietly as possible, keeping low as they moved forward. The same scenario from the day before now played out again as they reached the fort, 'which they found as the precedent, without any person in it, for all were fled into the woods, leaving also the town without any people.'[12]

This fort defended the city, which was also silent and empty, its streets bereft of any kind of movement. According to Esquemeling, the first thing Morgan did was send out search parties throughout the town looking for Spanish soldiers or snipers who may still be hiding and waiting to attack. But they found nothing.

Morgan's men then left their boats and began choosing 'what houses they pleased to themselves, the best they could find'. The main church in the town was taken over as Morgan's headquarters. With the town secure Morgan sent out more than a hundred men to look for people, the wealthiest and most influential of the town, to find out where they had hidden their valuables. The following day the men returned with fifty mules and thirty prisoners. 'On these innocent wretches they exercised the most horrible torments, thereby endeavouring to extort a confession, where the rest of the inhabitants, and their riches were concealed.'[13]

The above quote comes from Charles Leslie's book, *A New History of Jamaica*, which was published in 1740, after Esquemeling's book, and much of his account of the exploits of Morgan and his men is based on Esquemeling's. It is his account that tells us these prisoners were tortured, put on the rack, by the buccaneers. Some of the tortures included stretching their limbs with cords and then beating them with sticks while others were placing lit matches under the fingernails of the prisoners, which were then allowed to burn.

'Others had slender cords or matches twisted about their heads, till their eyes burst out.' Those who had nothing to say or had no fortune to hand over died. 'These tortures and racks continued for three whole weeks, in which time they sent out daily parties to seek for more people to torment and rob, they never returning without booty and new riches.'[14]

However, as this book is about the character of Morgan, this barbarous activity needs to be taken seriously. Was he aware of it? Did he order it to take place? Did he participate in this cruelty? Were his captains, the men under his command, involved in organizing this torture or was it set up and carried out at a much lower level of command?

In this passage, as in other passages where Esquemeling accuses the buccaneers of torture and cruelty, he does not explicitly mention Morgan as taking part. Whether or not Morgan was aware of it, or ordered it, or rather just let it happen and ensured he had no direct part in it is something we will never really know for sure.

Dudley Pope points out that the rack and other instruments of torture were not things that the buccaneers brought with them. They were already there in the town, just as they would have been in any other town across the Spanish Main. They were there for the Spanish administration and religious leaders to use on their own people, to keep the population in check.[15]

It is likely that Morgan took a house in Maracaibo for himself while supervising operations in the town. He would have spent a large amount of time in the church, which Esquemeling said was set up as a headquarters or 'common *corps du guard*'. Therefore there is a possibility that Morgan may not have heard the screams of the prisoners being tortured as the rack could have been in another building in another part of the town. In his earlier raids we have seen him treat his prisoners with respect and honour, especially the ladies, so people being tortured may not have been Morgan's decision.

After three weeks, Morgan had about a hundred of the most influential and wealthiest families of the town along with their valuables and goods. Anything else of value that the buccaneers could find had been stripped out of the town and loaded onto their ships, which by this time had managed to navigate the bar and had anchored off Maracaibo. Every day, canoes loaded with booty and provisions went out to the ships. Cattle were killed, salted and loaded on board.

But Morgan was restless. He decided that he'd taken all that he could from the people and town of Maracaibo and set his sights on sailing south into the Lake of Maracaibo to 'look for purchase'. The French captain who had sailed with L'Ollonais knew Gibraltar at the far end of the lake and was sure that he could guide Morgan and the fleet to that town, which was wealthy and ripe for the picking.

Listening to the Frenchman's advice, Morgan and his captains decided on a course of action. They would set sail for Gibraltar. Morgan ordered the fleet to be ready to sail. Soon they weighed anchor and left Maracaibo. This was the point at which things began to go wrong.

Chapter 11

The Gibraltar Excursion

Having exhausted the riches that lay in Maracaibo Morgan had set his sights on Gibraltar at the southern tip of Lake of Maracaibo. From questioning all his prisoners he'd found a dozen or so who were known in Gibraltar. These people would be his messengers and his hostages.

He knew from the accounts that were coming in from interrogating[1] prisoners and from the Indians living in the villages near Maracaibo that the Spanish were concentrating their troops in Gibraltar. Whatever wealth lay in that town he was going to have to fight for it.

Five miles from the town, Morgan ordered the fleet to anchor. A canoe was slowly hoisted down onto the water and the prisoners climbed one by one down into the vessel, with buccaneers manning the oars. One of the buccaneers had a white flag and as they rowed away from the fleet and headed towards the town, they raised this white flag as a sign of truce.

At the town, the prisoners were set free but they had been given specific instructions 'to require the inhabitants to surrender, otherwise Captain Morgan would certainly put them all to the sword, without any quarter.'

This time, the Spaniards were defiant and as Morgan brought the fleet close to the town within the range of the guns at the fort they were 'saluted with a furious Fire from the Cannon of the Place; But this noways [*sic*] damped their Spirits, these Showers of death only animated them with the greater Fury.'[2]

Morgan sailed his little fleet out of range of the guns and ordered the fleet to lower their anchors. Now he could see the town and he studied it for some time. On one side was a wooded area that had accessible beaches for canoes. He could easily land his men on those beaches and then they would march through the woods to the town. He'd done it before and knew it wouldn't be difficult. They waited overnight and began the assault in the morning.

They marched towards the town, not by the common way, but crossing through the woods, which way the Spaniards scarce thought they would have come; for the beginning of their march they made as if they intended to come the next and open way to the town, hereby to deceive the Spaniards; but these remembering full well what Lolonais [*sic*] had done but two years before, thought it not safe to expect a second brunt, and hereupon all fled out of the town as fast as they could carrying all their goods and riches.[3]

When they entered the town, Morgan and his buccaneers found the place empty. As with Maracaibo, the buccaneers set up houses for themselves and Morgan set up a temporary headquarters. He sent out search parties to look for the inhabitants of the town hiding in the woods. But this initial attempt at locating the wealthy and their riches failed, unlike in Maracaibo.

Morgan changed his strategy, realizing that at some point the people in hiding were going to have to come back to their plantations and country houses for provisions for 'they could not live on what the woods afforded,' writes Esquemeling. Morgan divided his men into many smaller search parties and sent them out in all directions to the plantations and country houses, where they would wait for the Spaniards to return for supplies.

This strategy soon paid off as the buccaneers brought to Morgan's headquarters more than 250 prisoners. Day and night, Morgan and his captains questioned these people, asking them the same thing over and over: where had they hidden their wealth, who else was hiding in the woods and where was their treasure?

However, how these prisoners were treated is a key question. Let's not forget that Esquemeling's account is crucial to understanding the events that took place on this expedition. But how accurate are his accounts is also in question.

For example, he states that when the buccaneers arrived in Gibraltar and found the city empty he claims that they found one man 'who was born a fool'. The buccaneers demanded information from this man, a mentally disabled individual who was incapable of answering their questions. Over and over they asked him where the inhabitants of the town had gone to and where they'd hidden their wealth. The poor man could not answer them. The buccaneers tortured him. 'They presently put him to the rack, and tortured him with cords; which torments forced him to cry out: "Do not torture me anymore but come with me, and I will show you my goods and my riches."'

According to Esquemeling the man then led the buccaneers to a dilapidated cottage where he gave them the few items he had, which were of no value, and three pieces of eight. This man told them he was the brother of the governor of Maracaibo and for some reason, known only to Esquemeling, they tortured him again. At that point the story moves on and the fate of this poor fool is never explained.

Esquemeling then provides another account of the inhumane actions of the buccaneers when he states that they 'brought back an honest peasant with two daughters of his, whom they intended to torture as they used others, if they showed not the places where the inhabitants were hid.' This peasant knew where some of the town's inhabitants were hiding and told the buccaneers so. He took them to these places but the Spaniards had moved on, 'farther off into the thickest of the woods, where they built themselves huts, to preserve from the weather those few goods they had.'

Esquemeling tells us that the buccaneers believed the man had deceived them so they promptly hung him from a tree. What happened to his daughters is anyone's guess.

Interestingly, Pope does not mention either of these two incidents in his biography of Morgan. Nor does he mention the next two incidents that Esquemeling attributed to the buccaneers.

According to Esquemeling, one of the search parties sent to the country houses found a slave (Indian) and offered him 'mountains of gold and his liberty, by transporting him to Jamaica, if he would show them where the inhabitants of Gibraltar lay hid.' This individual took the buccaneers to the place where the Spanish were hiding from the buccaneers, who took them all as prisoners. They commanded this slave 'to kill some before the eyes of the rest; that by this perpetrated crime, he might never be able to leave their wicked company.' According to the account, this slave carried out the orders from the buccaneers with a certain amount of gusto and 'committed many murders and insolences upon the Spaniards.' The rest were brought back as prisoners and became part of the overall 250 prisoners collected and questioned by Morgan.

The final event that Esquemeling recounts is perhaps the most bizarre. He states that among these prisoners was a Portuguese man who was reported by one of the slaves to be very rich. This, Esquemeling tells us, was a false accusation. The man tried to tell the buccaneers that he only had 100 pieces of eight to his name, which had been stolen two days earlier by his servant. Naturally, the buccaneers didn't believe him and they committed a wide variety of tortures on him to get him to talk.

Esquemeling then devotes an entire paragraph to the various tortures the buccaneers committed on this man before he finally broke down and paid them 1,000 pieces of eight. 'These he raised, and having paid them, got his liberty; though so horribly maimed, that it is scarce to be believed he could survive many weeks.'[4]

At no time in these accounts does Esquemeling even mention that Morgan had anything to do with torture. He only ever refers to the people who carried out these atrocities as 'the pirates', so the question of truth becomes even more critical in an account of the life of Henry Morgan.

Perhaps the best source to use to see if these accounts have any truth in them is Stephen Talty's book, *Empire of Blue Water*. He suggests that the accounts outlined by Esquemeling should be taken 'with a grain of salt'. Indeed, it is his belief that 'there is little in the record outside of Esquemeling's account to suggest that Morgan was a monster capable of such things.'[5]

He continues by saying that Esquemeling probably made up these accounts of cruelties at the behest of his publisher.

> The innocent fool chattering away to the pirates about his famous relatives, ensuring his own death, and the Portuguese miser who endured a Golgotha just to save 500 pesos – they are beautiful touches.[6]

However, there is no doubt that there were cruelties on these buccaneering expeditions, as Talty points out. Everyone who signed on understood the rules of engagement. People who resisted the buccaneers essentially opened themselves up to all kinds of barbaric treatment at their hands. There was no Geneva Convention about the treatment of prisoners; indeed, there was no policy at all. How prisoners were treated depended on whether or not they resisted, whether or not they paid and especially whether or not they annoyed the buccaneers by calling their bluff. 'There was no policy, that is, except that every last piece of eight should be wrung from every last prisoner.'[7]

Morgan's questioning of his prisoners revealed some interesting information. A slave told him that he could lead Morgan and his men to 'a river of the lake, where he should find a ship and four boats, richly laden with goods of the inhabitants of Maracaibo.' The slave also knew that the governor of Gibraltar was hiding on a small island in the middle of the river, 'with the greatest part of the women of the town'.[8]

Following up on this information, Morgan decided to split his forces and sent 200 men in the canoes to go after the ship and small boats while he would lead 250 men to find the governor and bring him back as a hostage. The governor had built a small fort on the island, 'as well as he could, for his defence; but hearing that Captain Morgan came in person with great forces to seek him, he retired to the top of a mountain not far off, to which there was no ascent but by a very narrow passage.'[9]

Morgan and his men were determined to get to the governor but foul weather made traversing the passage almost impossible. Each man would have to move through the passage in single file and would be at the mercy of anyone above with enough ammunition to pick them off at his leisure. Indeed, Esquemeling states that 'the governor was well provided with all sorts of ammunition: beside, there was fallen a huge rain, whereby all the pirates' baggage and powder was wet.'

On this mission, Morgan lost some of his men and some of the mules carrying 'plate and goods which were taken from the fugitive inhabitants' were swept away. He had no choice but to return almost empty-handed.

The men who Morgan had sent after the boats fared little better. Once again, the Spaniards heard the buccaneers were on the march looking for them and managed to unload the wealth and goods they had on the boats and hid it before they disappeared into the woods. However, they did not unload everything. 'They left both in the ship and the boats great parcels of goods ... which the pirates seized and brought thereof a considerable booty unto Gibraltar.'[10]

The buccaneers had been in Gibraltar for five weeks and now it was time to leave. Morgan knew that over the time they'd been away from Maracaibo the Spaniards would have been able to fortify the channel leading into the lake, which would make his escape difficult indeed.

But he had one more action to perform while still in Gibraltar. He decided to ransom the town and 'ordered some prisoners to go forth into the woods and fields, and collect a ransom for the town, otherwise they would certainly burn it down to the ground.'[11]

The prisoners returned with news that the governor had forbidden them to pay anything for the town. Ignoring this direction from the governor the prisoners asked Morgan for more time, saying they could probably raise around 5,000 pieces of eight and some of the townspeople would act as hostages while the money was collected and paid to Morgan when he reached Maracaibo.

Conscious of the time he'd been away and the need to get back up to Maracaibo, out of the lake and into the open sea before the Spaniards were able to stop him, Morgan agreed to their proposition and immediately began making preparations to leave. He then set all the prisoners free while under the new agreement the Spanish 'delivered him four person[s] agreed on for hostages of what money more he was to receive.' Morgan also held onto the slaves, afraid that if he handed them over to the people of the town they would be burned alive for having helped the buccaneers.

At last, they weighed anchor, and set sail in all haste for Maracaibo; here they arrived in four days, and found all things as they had left them; yet here they received news from a poor distressed old man, whom they found sick in the town, that three Spanish men-of-war were arrived at the entry of the lake, waiting the return of the pirates; moreover, that the castle at the entry thereof was again put into good posture of defence, well provided with guns and men, and all sorts of ammunition.[12]

Morgan quickly called his captains together and ordered the one with the fastest vessel to set sail to investigate this alarming news. The following day this captain returned, telling Morgan that the news the old man had related was true. There were three men-of-war at the entrance to the lake; one of thirty-six large guns and twelve small guns; another of twenty-six guns and twelve smaller guns; and the third of sixteen large and eight small guns.

That was it. It was over. How could Morgan possibly get out of this situation? His fleet was outgunned in every respect. 'Considering the difficulty of passing safe with his little fleet amidst those great ships and the fort; or he must perish.' They could see no way of escaping by sea or by land.

Morgan and his men were trapped.

Chapter 12

Trapped

Captain Morgan resumed new courage, and resolving to show himself still undaunted, he boldly sent a Spaniard to the admiral of those three ships, demanding of him a considerable ransom for not putting the city of Maracaibo to the flames.[1]

While the above statement written by Esquemeling reveals Morgan's state of mind when he discovered that his escape out of the lake into open sea was blocked by the three Spanish warships, he was negotiating from a position of weakness.

The Spanish admiral, Don Alonso Del Campo Y Espinosa, held all the cards. He had far more firepower than had Morgan's entire fleet and in addition to the three warships he also had the guns in the fort on San Carlos. Morgan and his men had taken that fort and nailed or spiked all the guns there. Don Alonso's men had re-drilled the guns, re-mounted and primed them so they were now ready to fire. Also, the Spanish had added more guns to the fort so that they now, including the ships and the fort, had a total of 126 fully functional cannon with which to blast Morgan's fleet out of the water.

The fleet of Spanish warships had been ordered to the Spanish Main by the Catholic king of Spain in revenge for the taking of Puerto Bello and all 'damages and hostilities committed here by the English'. Despite the many protestations the Spanish ambassador had made to the British court the hostilities in the West Indies continued. The response from the government in England and the king had always been that no commissions or letters of marque had been given to any privateer to commit hostile acts on the subjects of Spain. Yet they persisted. Having had enough, the Spanish king ordered a fleet of six warships be equipped and commanded by Admiral Don Augustine de Bustos. Don Alonso was his vice admiral.

The biggest ship of the fleet had forty-eight large guns and eight smaller guns and was the NS *de la Soleda*, while the second largest ship, *La Conception*, of forty-four guns, was under the command of Don Alonso. The fleet set sail from Spain for Cartagena but when it arrived, the larger of the two ships named above 'received orders to return to Spain, being judged too big for cruising these coasts.'[2]

With the two largest ships gone and Don Augustine with them, that left Don Alonso in charge of the *Magdalen*, thirty-six large and twelve small guns and a compliment of 250 men; the *Santa Louisa*, twenty-six large and twelve smaller guns and a crew of 200; the *La Marquesa*, sixteen great guns and eight small cannon and 150 men; and the NS *del Carmen*, with eighteen large cannon, eight smaller guns and 100 men.

Don Alonso left Cartagena and sailed for Campeachy to catch the English but on the way they encountered rough weather and the NS *del Carmen* was lost. Upon arrival at Santo Domingo, the Spanish received news that the buccaneers had passed that way and were heading for Caracas. Don Alonso, determined to hunt this fleet down, immediately set sail for Caracas. 'Here we found them not, but met with a boat, which certified us they were in the lake of Maracaibo.'[3]

Don Alonso immediately set sail for the Lake of Maracaibo and discovered that Morgan was in Gibraltar. He set about creating a trap for the buccaneers, knowing full well they would have to sail through the channel and past the castle to get to the open sea.

Don Alonso held the upper hand. He had greater firepower and more men than the buccaneers, as well as the tactical advantage. Morgan and his fleet would have to sail through the channel. There was no other way they could leave.

The Spaniard that Morgan had sent to Don Alonso, with his threat of razing Maracaibo to the ground if the Spaniards did not let them pass, returned two days later with Don Alonso's reply:

> I let you understand by these lines that I am come to this place, according to my obligation, near that castle which you took out of the hands of a parcel of cowards; where I have put things into a very good posture of defence, and mounted again the artillery which you had nailed and dismounted.[4]

The reply from Don Alonso had been written in Spanish and so needed to be translated, which it was. Once that was done, Morgan could be in no doubt about this opponent's intentions. 'My intent is, to dispute with you your passage out of the lake, and follow and pursue you everywhere, to the end you may see the performance of my duty.' The letter then described the terms for Morgan's safe passage out of the lake and back to Jamaica. For their safe passage the buccaneers would have to surrender everything they had taken, which included slaves and all the other prisoners. At this time Morgan still had the four hostages from Gibraltar, who would only be freed when the people of Gibraltar paid their ransom.

Then came the threat. If Morgan didn't surrender all the booty, slaves and prisoners, Don Alonso would 'command boats to come from Caracas, wherein I will put my troops, and coming to Maracaibo, will put you every man to the sword.' Adding to this threat, Don Alonso wrote, 'I have with me very good soldiers, who desire nothing more ardently than to revenge on you, and your people, all the cruelties, and base infamous actions, you have committed upon the Spanish nation in America.'[5]

Don Alonso's reply had been written on board his flagship, the largest of the three warships, the *Magdalen*, and was dated 24 April 1669.

Perhaps a testament to Morgan's leadership ability is his intuition and understanding of the men he led. Rather than simply gathering his captains together for a council of war, Morgan had all the men gather in the hot square in the centre of Maracaibo, where, according to Esquemeling, he asked them for advice. The letter from Don Alonso had been translated into English and French and Morgan read this letter out to his men.

After he read the letter, he put a question to them. Would they rather surrender everything they'd obtained for their freedom or would they rather fight their way out?

The answer was unanimous: 'They had rather fight to the last drop of blood, than surrender so easily the booty they had got with so much danger of their lives,' Esquemeling tells us.

While they had all decided to fight, how were they going to do it? According to Esquemeling, one of the buccaneers in the crowd suggested they could defeat the *Magdalen* by using a fireship manned with only twelve men. The vessel proposed for this fireship was the one that had been taken in the river of Gibraltar. To fool the Spanish they needed to fill the decks with logs of wood, standing upright and wearing hats and caps, which from the flagship would look like men on the deck. Portholes were to be cut and logs stuck out from them to make the ship look like it had more guns than it actually had. Finishing off the deception, the buccaneers hung English colours at the stern, 'to persuade the enemy she is one of our best men-of-war going to fight them.'[6]

The buccaneers agreed to the plan and Morgan ordered the preparations for the fireship to start immediately. In the meantime, he would try once again to negotiate with Don Alonso. It would be far better to leave the lake without losing any ships from his fleet or men. He sent two people under a flag of truce to Don Alonso. Morgan knew that he had something to offer. He still had all the slaves taken from Gibraltar, plus the Spanish hostages taken in lieu of the outstanding ransom that still needed to be paid and, finally, there was the town of Maracaibo that he still held. Don Alonso's reply to Morgan's original demands had mentioned none of these. So Morgan proposed that for safe passage for his men and his ships he would leave Maracaibo untouched, release the slaves and the four prisoners from Gibraltar without paying any ransom. This was the proposal the two men gave to Don Alonso.

The Spanish admiral rejected the proposals out of hand and sent back a message to Morgan that said, 'If they [the buccaneers] surrendered not themselves voluntarily into his hands, within two days, under the conditions which he had offered them by his letter, he would immediately come and force them to do it.'[7]

So now Morgan would have to fight. The preparations were well under way. According to Esquemeling, all the slaves and prisoners were tied up and placed under guard, while the rest of the buccaneers scoured the town gathering up as much 'pitch, tar and brimstone they could find'.

'Likewise, they made several inventions of powder and brimstone, with great quantities of palm leaves very well anointed,' Esquemeling wrote. Under each of the logs disguised as cannon they laid large amounts of powder and cut holes in the ship to ensure that once ignited the powder would have a maximum blast range.

> Thus they broke open also new portholes where, instead of guns, they placed little drums of which the negroes make use. Finally the decks were handsomely beset with many pieces of wood dressed up in the shape of men with hats, as monteros,[8] and likewise armed with swords muskets and bandoleers.[9]

Morgan ordered that the prisoners should be put into one of the bigger boats while the women, 'plate, jewels, and other rich things' were put into the largest boat. Other vessels were loaded with bulkier goods and, as Esquemeling tells us, 'each of these boats, had twelve men aboard, very well armed.' Morgan then called his men together and roused them to fight to the last drop of blood and give the Spanish no quarter.

Fully prepared, on the evening of 29 April 1669 Morgan and the buccaneers were ready to sail. The fireship would go first and head directly towards the largest of the three Spanish ships, the *Magdalen*, and the rest of the buccaneer fleet would split up and attack the other two Spanish ships, with Morgan leading the attack on the second largest ship, the thirty-eight-gun *Santa Louisa*.

On 30 April the buccaneers set sail covering 20 miles before they came within sight of the Spanish men-of-war anchored across the channel. By this time the light was fading and rather than attack at night, Morgan ordered his fleet to drop their anchors. The attack would take place in the early morning.

As the day dawned the Spanish watched as the English fleet came sailing towards them with the fireship in the lead. Of course at this point there was no hint of flame, no sign of any smoke to give away the ruse. The fireship headed directly for the *Magdalen*. According to Pope this was a classic move where a ship would steer directly for the enemy ship and, at the last moment, turn to fire its broadside at the other vessel.[10]

Indeed, the *Magdalen* did fire some shots at the approaching ship but her Spanish gun crews were waiting for the fireship to turn so they could destroy the smaller vessel with a broadside. From the yards and rigging the fireship had many grapples hanging loosely on ropes so they would catch the *Magdalen's* rigging and force the two ships to come together so the fire could have maximum effect.

As the fireship approached within a few yards of the *Magdalen* the Spanish realized they'd been duped. Smoke poured out from the hatches as explosions throughout the fireship suddenly erupted. The few buccaneers on board ran aft and dived into the water, climbing into their boat that had been towed behind the fireship. Burning tar and pitch and pieces of blazing wood flew into the air from the explosions landing on the Spanish ship, the flames spreading like wildfire. Using whatever they could find the Spanish frantically tried to push the burning fireship away but it was no use. The powder under each of the logs that had been used to represent guns ignited, sending the burning logs onto the decks of the *Magdalen*. No matter what the Spanish did they were doomed as quite suddenly the flames on the fireship reached the magazine and the resulting explosion tore the ship apart, sending flaming wreckage all over the *Magdalen*. 'The flame seizing her timber and tackling soon consumed all the stern, the fore part sinking into the sea, where she perished.'[11]

The captain of the second Spanish ship, *Santa Louisa*, realizing that the flagship was lost and there was a high probability of another fireship coming for his vessel, cut his cable and sailed the ship directly for the beach and for San Carlos Castle, 'where the Spaniards themselves sunk her, choosing to lose their ship rather than fall into the hands of the pirates.' This ship, according to Esquemeling, was also set on fire so that the buccaneers could not salvage anything from her. However, the third ship, *La Marquesa*, had no chance to escape as the buccaneers boarded her and took her crew prisoner.

Morgan now ordered his men to take the boats and look for survivors. When the flames had enveloped the *Magdalen* many of her crew had jumped into the water to avoid the fire and they now clung to whatever wreckage they could. They would not accept any help from the English. 'They would not ask or take any quarter, choosing rather to lose their lives than receive them from their hands,' wrote Esquemeling.[12] Don Alonso had managed to escape the flames and make his way to the castle.

One of the prisoners that Morgan found was a pilot who was not Spanish and was happy to answer any questions Morgan put to him. It was this man who related the story of how the Spanish men-of-war came to be anchored in the channel waiting for Morgan under Don Alonso's command. The pilot told Morgan how, when Don Alonso had received Morgan's refusal to surrender, he 'gave a very good supper to all his people; he ordered them not to take or give any quarter.' This Morgan now knew accounted for so many of the Spanish floating in the water refusing to be saved, choosing to drown instead.

With such a resounding victory many of the buccaneers ran ashore intending to take the castle but were repulsed by heavy and accurate fire from the Spanish gunners. 'This they found very well provided with men, great cannon and ammunition – they having no other arms than muskets and a few fireballs in their hands.'[13]

For the rest of the day the buccaneers fired at the castle with their muskets. Under the cover of darkness they stealthily moved up to the walls to throw in their fireballs, but the Spanish fire was just too great for them to succeed. Having lost many men in the process they eventually gave up and returned to their ships.

Morgan transferred his flag over to the *La Marquesa*, a much larger and faster ship than the fourteen-gun vessel he'd been using after the destruction of the *Oxford*. He turned again to the pilot, who also told him that there had been considerable gold plate and other riches on the *Magdalen* when it went down. Morgan ordered one of his ships to anchor as close to it as possible and begin salvage operations. The ship Morgan dispatched set about recovering as much of the ship's treasure as possible while doing its best to keep out of range of the guns from San Carlos Castle.

So while the salvage operations were going on, and those Spanish who would be pulled from the water were taken prisoner, Morgan still had a bigger problem. How was he going to sail his fleet intact past the guns of the castle into open sea with all of the booty they'd taken?

He might have won a great victory but it would be a hollow one if he and his men remained trapped and unable to get home.

Chapter 13

Breakout

On the face of it, one could say that Morgan held all the cards. Two of the three Spanish men-of-war under the command of Don Alonso had been sunk. The third, *La Marquesa*, had been captured by the buccaneers and Morgan had transferred his flag to that ship. But the problem was the castle, San Carlos. It was in the hands of the Spanish and was bristling with guns, all pointing towards the channel, so any ship that Morgan tried to get through would be blasted to bits. The castle had the higher ground and more firepower than Morgan's combined fleet. Even the attacks by the buccaneers on the castle had proved to be fruitless as the Spanish resistance had been too strong for the buccaneers and many men had been lost in the process. Yet Morgan knew that something had to be done. He could not sail his fleet up the channel to open sea without coming under fire from San Carlos.

To make matters worse, Don Alonso had escaped the inferno of the *Magdalen* and managed to get to the castle, which was now under his direct command. This meant that the garrison there, reinforced days earlier by Don Alonso, would not easily give in. Morgan ordered his best snipers to position themselves in such a way so that any Spanish soldier who appeared on the battlements of the castle would be shot. The men had dug themselves in on the beach so they would have some protection from any cannon fire from the castle. The buccaneers now watched and waited. In the castle, the Spanish did the same. The firing had stopped. Both sides were at an impasse.

Morgan knew that he could not fight his way out so he had to do something that he was unaccustomed too – bargaining. Maracaibo was still empty and under his control. Morgan sailed the rest of the fleet back to Maracaibo, according to Esquemeling, 'where he refitted the great ship he had taken and chose it for himself.'

He then sent a messenger to Don Alonso, 'demanding of him a ransom of fire for Maracaibo; which being denied, he threatened entirely to consume and destroy it.' Don Alonso refused the ransom, but the rest of the Spanish, 'considering the ill-luck they had all along with those pirates and not knowing how to get rid of them, concluded to pay the said ransom.'[1]

Despite Don Alonso's refusal to negotiate, the people of Maracaibo began bargaining with Morgan, asking him what he wanted in return for leaving the town alone. They finally decided on 20,000 pieces of eight and 500 head of cattle, for which Morgan would release his prisoners and not set fire to the town.

> The cattle were brought the next day, with one part of the money; and, while the pirates were busied in salting the flesh, they made up the whole 20,000 pieces of eight as was agreed.[2]

With the beef aboard and the ransom paid, Morgan said goodbye to Maracaibo for the last time and headed back towards the channel. However, he had not released the hostages as he'd promised. Don Alonso's intractability had left Morgan with little choice but to use the hostages as his only remaining bargaining tool. Esquemeling writes that Morgan 'wished the prisoners to agree with the governor [Don Alonso] to permit a safe passage to his fleet, which, if he should not allow, he would certainly hang them all up in his ships.'

Morgan sent a group of prisoners to Don Alonso with his request, ensuring that many more remained in his custody. The prisoners pleaded with the Spanish governor, but to no avail. Esquemeling states in his book that Don Alonso replied: 'If you had been as loyal to your king in hindering the entry of these pirates, as I shall do their going out, you had never caused these troubles, neither to yourselves nor to our whole nation, which hath suffered so much through your pusillanimity.'[3]

By this time, Morgan had anchored his fleet near the ship that he'd assigned to conduct salvage operations on the wreck of the *Magdalen*. In the midst of the bleak situation Morgan received some good news. The buccaneers had managed to salvage 15,000 pieces of eight from the wreck.

Yet the problem still remained. Even if Don Alonso had agreed to let the fleet pass without firing on it there was nothing to stop the Spaniard issuing orders to fire on the buccaneers once they were in range. In the past the Spanish had gone against their word and there was no reason to trust them now, but it was the only option open to Morgan.

The prisoners Morgan sent to Don Alonso returned with his answer. It was no. He would not allow safe passage for the fleet. The hostages would have to die.

> The Spaniards returned with much consternation, and no hopes of obtaining their request, telling Captain Morgan, what answer they had received; his

answer was, 'If Don Alonso will not let me pass, I will find means how to do it without him.'[4]

At this point, according to Esquemeling, Morgan decided to divide the booty equally into each ship of his fleet so that no one vessel would have the lion's share of their takings, 'fearing he might not have an opportunity to do it in another place, if any tempest should rise and separate the ships, as also being jealous that any of the commanders might run away with the best part of the spoil.'

According to the laws of the Brethren, each of the buccaneers came forward and declared on oath how much they had. The accounts from each of the men and ships were added up and found 'to the value of 250,000 pieces of eight in money and jewels, besides the huge quantity of merchandise and slaves: all which purchase was divided into every ship or boat, according to its share.'[5]

Time was running out for Morgan. It was certainly on Don Alonso's side. It would only be a matter of days before Spanish reinforcements arrived from Panama and other Spanish cities on the Main. Morgan would end up facing a force of thousands if he remained bottled up, so he had to come up with a plan, and do it fast.

This book is about the character of Morgan, what makes him unique and why he should always have more than a passing footnote in history. He was a brilliant strategist and tactician. He was able to adapt to his environment and willing to take risks in order to achieve his objectives.

On the other hand, Don Alonso was a nobleman and 'could not imagine that he could be out-thought by scum like the Brethren.'[6] In addition, he represented the King of Spain and as such the complete arrogance that nothing could defeat him – certainly not a band of pirates. Another of his main concerns, according to Pope, was how he would be seen in Madrid, especially if he failed. This was his overriding motivation. Indeed, every note he wrote was copied and sent to his masters in Madrid.

> Don Alonso's real audience for the note, which was no doubt copied in triplicate, was back in Madrid, awaiting word of Morgan's demise. He was building a legal case for the disaster that was unfolding.[7]

While he had called Morgan's bluff, one has to wonder just how well his masters in Madrid would have taken the burning of Maracaibo and the execution of the hostages – all Spanish – because he refused to let Morgan pass.

While Morgan was capable of adapting quickly, Don Alonso was rigid, traditional, bound by duty to his king and, more importantly, bound by his arrogance and belief of his superior birthright. He was far more comfortable in his ship firing a broadside at his enemy than he was besieged in a castle.[8]

Morgan drained every bit of information he could from the pilot, treating the man with great respect and very well in the process, so much so that the pilot joined Morgan as a buccaneer. Part of the information Morgan received told him about the character of the man he was facing. While Morgan was a brilliant and subtle tactician, Don Alonzo was the reverse.

Morgan realized that the Spanish guns in the fort were almost entirely facing seaward so as to blast the fleet as they sailed through the channel to the open sea. After studying Don Alonso's tactics, Morgan came up with an ingenious plan. He realized that if the Spanish admiral suddenly saw a large force of buccaneers landing on the island this would signal their intention to attack the fort from the landward side, where his defences were weakest.

The buccaneer fleet was anchored just out of range of the castle's guns, and close to the ships the shoreline was covered in mangrove trees that grew right at the waterline, some more than a dozen feet high. The foliage was thick and a perfect place for men to hide while they prepared a land assault against the fort.

As the day wore on, the Spanish, watching the buccaneers from the ramparts, saw boats filled with men, armed to the teeth with muskets, swords, pikes and so on, leave the buccaneer ships and head towards the shore, where they disappeared behind the mangrove trees. The boats would then row back to the ships with what looked like only two or three men rowing them back. Throughout the day, boat after boat, filled with armed men, rowed to the shore and returned with just the rowers. From Don Alonso's perspective the conclusion was obvious: the buccaneers were landing men in readiness for a full-scale land attack, which would most likely take place under the cover of darkness.

Convinced this was the case, Don Alonso ordered the guns pointing towards the sea to be shifted to the landward side of the castle so that their arc of fire would sweep the area that the buccaneers would have to travel to make their attack. Men pushed and pulled, sweating in the tropical heat, as each gun was slowly hauled across the castle to the landward side.

Night fell quickly and the Spanish waited for what they believed would be the sudden crash of muskets and cries of charging men signalling the attack. Instead, they heard only the familiar sounds of the tropical night. No muskets, no cries … nothing. They waited. Don Alonso must have wondered what the buccaneers were waiting for.

Finally, they heard what they had been waiting for – cannon fire. But this was from the seaward side and there were seven shots altogether. Racing to the seaward side of the fort, Don Alonso's heart sank. Morgan had tricked him. In the darkness the fleet had passed the fort on the tide and once out of range raised their sails. The seven shots had been a mocking salute by Morgan.

Realizing what had happened, Don Alonso ordered the guns to be moved back to the seaward side and this was done quickly. The Spanish gunners began laying down a furious barrage, but it was no use. The buccaneer fleet, now anchored in the seaward side of the channel, were out of reach.

How had Morgan tricked the Spanish? Esquemeling explains how the wily Welshman outwitted Don Alonso for the second time:

> They rowed towards the shore, as if they designed to land: here they hid themselves under branches of trees that hang over the coast awhile, laying themselves down in the boats; then the canoes returned to the ships, with the appearance of only two or three men rowing them back, the rest being unseen at the bottom of the canoes: thus much only could be perceived from the castle.[9]

With that part of the subterfuge done, Morgan waited until night for the ebb tide that flowed north from the Lake of Maracaibo into the Gulf of Venezuela. Quietly, he ordered the fleet to raise their anchors and slowly the ships drifted on the tide into the gulf, *La Marquesa*, Morgan's flagship, leading the fleet. As each ship passed the fort, they raised their sails and fired a single salute, hence the seven shots of cannon.

Anchored in the gulf, out of reach of the Spanish guns, one can only imagine the relief felt by the buccaneers, who must have all laughed heartily at beating the Spanish yet again. Perhaps Don Alonso and his men could hear this laughter in the darkness. The furious barrage of gunfire that the Spanish fired into the darkness of the night did no damage to the buccaneers.

The following day, Morgan let the hostages from Maracaibo go as they had paid their ransom. Under a flag of truce they were loaded into canoes and rowed ashore, where they were received by Don Alonso, who gave them a boat so they could all return to their homes. However, aboard *La Marquesa* were prisoners from Gibraltar who had still not paid their ransom.

From the events in these pages it appears as if the Spanish were inept and incapable of fighting the Brethren and defeating them. However, Stephen Talty, in *Empire of Blue Water*, tells us that this is not the case:

> The Spanish did regularly defeat pirates in battle throughout the history of their New World possessions, and the historical records are littered with tales

of buccaneers who ended their days on the enemy's beaches or in his prisons. Just not Morgan.[10]

It is this statement that brings this story into context and makes Morgan's exploits so remarkable. Indeed, few commanders in history have been able to do what he did. That's why he was a legend amongst the Brethren, because he was the exception rather than the norm.

Free and successful, Morgan and his largely intact fleet left the Gulf and sailed as rich men for Port Royal.

Chapter 14

Revenge

The Name of Morgan was now famous at home, and terrible abroad. He himself promised greater things than he had yet attempted; and nothing was thought impossible for such Courage to perform.[1]

M organ's daring Maracaibo raid had once again humiliated the Spanish and they were understandably furious. Port Royal gave the returning heroes a huge welcome when Morgan and his fleet sailed into the harbour at Port Royal on 17 May 1669. When the buccaneers swarmed ashore with their newly won wealth the merchants, innkeepers and prostitutes did their best to relieve them of it while the city celebrated. While they caroused Morgan met with the governor, Sir Thomas Modyford, in Spanish Town to brief him on his exploits.

Modyford, however, was not best pleased. Morgan was supposed to have sacked Cartagena as it was from this place that the Spanish could possibly have mounted an invasion on Jamaica; Maracaibo and Gibraltar were too far away to constitute a threat to the island. Modyford also knew that once King Charles II and his government heard about the raids, they too would be furious and there would be some form of repercussion. Peace still existed between Spain and England and so the government in London wanted to distance itself from the actions taking place in the West Indies.

Prior to the return of the buccaneers a ship had arrived in Port Royal from London. The *Isabella* carried a letter from Charles Modyford, Thomas Modyford's son, stating that the government in London denounced the Portobello raid. The Spanish government demanded full satisfaction from this raid but they had not yet heard of Morgan's latest exploits. However, they soon would.

In London, the king and his government did not want to disgrace Modyford by providing Spain with an abject apology as Modyford was part of the machine of government and so, by implication, the whole of the English government was to blame. Instead the government dithered while it decided on what course of action to take. In the meantime, the inactivity of the English government served to increase the anger in Madrid to the point that the Spanish government commanded their governors in the West Indies to attack British ships and settlements in the region. Once these orders had been received commissions were issued by the governors of the Spanish Main, Cuba, Hispaniola and New Spain to any Spanish ship to turn privateer and attack the English, particularly those sailing out of Port Royal. The minutes of the Council of Jamaica, dated 29 June 1670, made plain the relationship existing between the English and the Spanish in the West Indies at that time:

> From the Queen Regent of Spain, dated 20 April 1669, her Governors in the Indies are commanded to make open war against His Majesty's subjects, and that the Spanish Governors have granted commissions and are levying forces against the English.[2]

A letter written by Modyford's brother, Sir James, emphasizes the situation, stating that the Spanish 'have denounced war against us in Cartagena, and given out commissions.' He goes on to say that the information coming from Spanish traders was that they 'have daily in expectation twelve sail of frigates from Europe who have commissions (as all ships shall have that come into the Indies) to take all English they can light on.' Sir James ended his letter with an ominous warning: 'For the Duke of Albemarle's death, that only befriended us, this war, our making a blind peace, no frigates, nor orders coming, gives us cruel apprehensions and makes many remiss.'[3]

In London, the Duke of Albemarle, George Monck, had been the most sympathetic ear in the king's circle. He was the leader of the anti-Spanish faction and believed in empire. For him and his supporters, Jamaica was part of the empire and so should have all of the protection and prosperity of any other colony. For him, the buccaneers of Jamaica represented a hard and heavy stick with which 'to prod and dislodge the Spanish. And so Monck argued their case with vehemence.'[4]

Almost at the other end of the scale was Lord Arlington, Secretary of State. He wanted closer, peaceful relations with Spain and the actions of the buccaneers were putting this objective into real jeopardy. According to Stephen Talty, Arlington had spent many years in Spain; he identified with their causes and understood them perhaps more than any other man in the English government. He believed that a treaty with Spain that recognized the English colonies in the region would be the best way to end the hostilities. Yet while the English emissary in Madrid, William Godolphin, worked tirelessly to negotiate such a treaty the Spanish continued to demand reparations. They wanted Modyford removed from office and something done about Morgan.

Arlington's response to the increasing Spanish anger was that the actions of the buccaneers were in response to Spanish hostilities in the region.

In addition, London was still reeling from the Great Fire of 1666 and the subsequent plague that swept through the city and the rest of the country. On the military front victories were few and far between. Twice the Dutch had humiliated the navy so the news of Morgan's exploits struck a chord with the common people. He was, as Talty states, a 'Protestant Avenger', and a hero.[5]

Modyford was no fool. He had to do something to appease London, especially with letters coming in from his son relating the king's increasing anger with Modyford and the buccaneers. On 14 June 1669, the town crier marched through the streets of Port Royal with a drummer proclaiming that Modyford had withdrawn all the commissions for the buccaneers, including Morgan's.[6] Officially, their exploits were over and now Modyford could point to this as a result. He knew that the Maracaibo affair had not yet reached London. He also knew that he was going to need a defence and set about writing a lengthy letter to Lord Arlington outlining his reasons for granting commissions to the buccaneers against the Spanish. He testified to the 'aversion he had for the privateers', and recalled 'his affectionate letters to the Spanish governors', since his arrival in Jamaica. He mentioned his harsh treatment 'by imprisoning them, executing some and restoring their prizes to the great hazard of the peace.'[7]

However, once Modyford realized he may have made a powerful enemy of the buccaneers:

> who not only knew all their ports, bays, and creeks, but every path in the island, and had many correspondents on shore, and that some of them were gone to the French at Tortuga and Hispaniola, and the rest preparing to go, and could better attempt this place than we could defend it, Modyford found the fatal error he was running into, and having notice of the Dutch war by Lord Arlington's despatch of 12 November 1664, he changed his behaviour so effectually that he persuaded all in or near this harbour to undertake against the Dutch at Curaçao, giving them suitable commissions.

The narrative Modyford sent to Arlington was a potted history of everything he had done concerning the buccaneers from his arrival in Jamaica up to the recent raids on Maracaibo and Gibraltar:

> He advised the Duke of Albemarle of the state of this place in relation to the privateers by letters of 6 March 1665; in answer to which he had orders of 30 May 1665 to grant or not commissions against the Spaniards, as to him

should seem most advantageous for His Majesty's service, and letters from Lord Arlington, that from the Lord General he should receive His Majesty's directions touching the privateers, and also letters from the Lord Chancellor to the same purpose, and from Sir James Modyford, and also His Grace's own letter in Feb 1667, confirming all the former, and that after the peace with Spain, as by the abstracts annexed may appear. The privateers meantime were driven to leeward, and the admiral fell in with the island of Providence and without any commission took it; to which Modyford sent a governor, which was not only approved of at home, but another governor under the broad seal of England authorized and sent. Yet notwithstanding this full power he would not proceed to grant commissions until the council of this island unanimously affirmed it was for the good of the island and gave their reasons hereto annexed and thereupon in March 1666, there being also war with France, he granted commissions, which was approved by His Grace, his end being only to keep them from joining with the French, but they had only commissions for taking ships, and none for landing. He always reproved them for so acting, especially in the business of Puerto Bello and Maracay; to which they made their defence by writing, which he sent home, but never received any answer to. Meantime, by reason of their numbers and not knowing the sense at home, he thought it prudential to forbear punishing them; and, receiving an intimation of His Majesty's sense in his son's letters, and also advice of the intentions of the Spaniards to attempt them, the galleons being daily expected in the Indies, and the New Spain fleet already there, in order to detain the privateers on the island, he repealed all their powers.[8]

Modyford continued his narrative by saying that the king's fifteenth shares of the raids he would keep:

to be employed in fortification, which may be about £600 and His Royal Highness's tenths he always sent home to Sir William Coventry and Mr Wren for His Royal Highness's account. To myself [the buccaneers], gave only £20 for their commission, which never exceeded £300.

With a bold flourish, Modyford ended his narrative demanding that any 'bold maligners and rash talkers against his actions' come forth and challenge the validity of his statements.

In Jamaica the rest of the year was quiet but filled with the tension of waiting for something to happen. When would the Spanish strike? How would they strike? The island of Jamaica was an English colony surrounded by Spanish colonies and the Spanish refused to accept that England owned the island.

In the autumn of 1669, William Godolphin, representing Charles II, was in Madrid trying to negotiate a treaty that would get the Spanish to recognize Jamaica as English.

For there to be any possibility that a treaty could be negotiated, all privateering would have to stop; there should be no revenge for past injustices (they would need to be forgotten); Spain would have to recognize British-held territory; and trading between the two nations would be allowed to flourish. This was no easy matter, for Godolphin needed to ensure the Spanish signed a treaty with such conditions.

In the meantime, Morgan spent the rest of the year with his wife, Elizabeth, and began extending his plantations by searching for land that no one owned and then applying for it. He found more than 800 acres in Clarendon Parish that had the Minho River as one of its boundaries. According to Pope, the land near the village of Chapleton is still called Morgan's Valley. Already a landowner, Morgan was extending what he had, being interested in clearing the land and planting crops – mostly sugar – as with his other plantations. One of the captains who had been with Morgan on many of his expeditions, Captain Edward Collier, acquired 1,000 acres also in Clarendon Parish.

As the year ended and the New Year of 1670 arrived, Morgan could look to his extended family and be proud. His wife's father, old Colonel Edward Morgan, had left his estate to his two sons, and they had made it a going concern. All the Morgans had rallied around to help. Elizabeth and Henry remained childless. However, Elizabeth's younger sister, Anna Petronilla, who had married Major Robert Byndloss, had one son and was again pregnant, while the old colonel's third daughter, Johanna Wilhelmina, married Colonel Henry Archbold. The families were all landowners and planters. They, along with the other plantation owners, held the greatest power and influence in the little colony, although the Morgan family's power would soon begin to fade. All the landowners believed that Morgan was the only person in Jamaica capable of defending the island. He was a hero and everyone looked up to him.

In London the balance of power was shifting. The Duke of Albemarle, George Monck, died early in 1670 of dropsy, thus depriving the anti-Spanish faction in the Privy Council of a leader. The subsequent vacuum paved the way for the pro-Spanish group, headed by Lord Arlington, to cast their power in the Privy Council, helped, of course, by the king's Catholic sympathies.

What this meant in Jamaica was that the buccaneers were more out of favour than ever before and were to be controlled. However, the buccaneers would soon be needed again.

Modyford was trying to hold together a truce with the Spanish in the West Indies and in January 1670, as a gesture of goodwill, he decided to free some Spanish prisoners. He also decided that a friendly letter to the governor of Cuba would be an excellent way of showing his good faith as well as the good faith of the English in Jamaica. Carefully, he chose a ship, registered in Jamaica, under the command of Bernard Claeson Speirdyck, a Dutchman known throughout Port Royal as Captain Bernard. The ship was the *Mary and Jane*.

In addition to the prisoners and the letter, the ship also carried cargo that the Spanish wanted and needed. Setting sail, he landed the prisoners and cargo in Manzanillo and then set sail back towards Jamaica. However, everything went badly wrong when he spied what appeared to be a ship flying English colours. Sending a boat over to enquire, the ship suddenly turned and headed straight for the *Mary and Jane*, firing a broadside into her. This ship turned out to be a Spanish privateer, the *San Pedro y la Fama*, under the command of Captain Emanuel Rivera Pardal.

> Five or six days afterwards a Spanish Armadilla was fitted from Cartagena, with eighty-six men, Captain Manuel de Rivera, a Portuguese, saying he had letters of reprisal from the King of Spain for five years through the whole West Indies, for satisfaction of the Jamaicans taking Puerto Bello. On 27 February, Capt Barnard spied a sail with an English ancient, and sent two men to see who it might be; the men were detained and the frigate fired a broadside, they answering one another with the like salutes about three hours. Next day, after a sharp dispute of about four hours, the Captain being killed and the ship on fire in the forecastle and astern, they yielded. The English lost only one man and one boy besides the Captain, the enemy by their own report having lost thirty-six, and several with their legs shot off. Eight or ten days after the Spaniards gave them their own longboat and provision to carry them to Jamaica, carrying four men with them prisoners.[9]

This action described in a deposition by Cornelius Carstens, the purser of the *Mary and Jane*, was included in a letter Modyford sent to Arlington dated 20 April 1670. That letter also included two other depositions that illustrated the level of hostility the Spanish had against the English in Jamaica:

> Depositions of Capt John Coxend and Peter Bursett. About ten weeks ago deponents were aboard of Capt Thomas Rogers, commander of a privateer of Jamaica, in the Bay of Campeachy, who sixteen days before, having been assaulted by a Spanish man-of-war from Cartagena, did in his own defence board and take it, where said Rogers took, amongst other prisoners, an Englishman by name Edward Browne, who had revolted from his allegiance and lived with the

Spaniards of Cartagena. Said Browne being examined by deponents declared that there was war proclaimed in Cartagena by beat of drum against Jamaica.[10]

Another deposition taken roughly the same time reinforces this point:

Deposition of Nicholas Hicks, gent. Being in the island of Corisa in November last, he happened into the company of one Prince, an Englishman, then pilot or master of a Spanish ship from Puerto Bello, who told deponent that the Spaniard had made proclamation in Puerto Bello that they would give no quarter to any Englishman, merchant or man-of-war, and he was sure they would never have peace with the Englishmen.[11]

Even this was not absolute proof of the Spanish intentions. For Modyford to act he needed something in writing from a Spanish governor that would provide him with the foundation for which he could retaliate.

On 5 May Modyford again wrote to Arlington, enclosed another deposition, this time from William Lane, the boatswain on the *Amity*, a ship out of Bristol under the command of William Cands that had been bound for Nevis from Madeira. Lane's deposition stated:

about nine weeks past, 35 leagues to Wind ward of Antigua, a Spanish frigate boarded the *Amity* and took her. The Captain's name was Don Francisco, who sent his prize to Carthagena, and put the English ashore at Corasa, showing that Governor his commission, which was from old Spain against the English and French, and not to give quarter to any Jamaicans, or French that belong to Tortuga.[12]

Modyford hoped that the presence of yet another deposition indicating the Spanish actions would prompt Lord Arlington to write back and give him permission to retaliate, but for the rest of the month of May there was no response from London.

Finally, Modyford received the proof he needed that Spain was granting commissions against Jamaica signed by local governors when two small Jamaican merchant ships, sailing off the Yucatán Peninsula, were attacked by the *San Nicolas de Tolentino*, a Spanish ship intending to take the two Jamaican ships as prizes. However, the tables were reversed and the *San Nicolas* was taken and brought back to Port Royal. Amongst her papers was a copy of a commission where Don Pedro Bayona y Villa Nueva, governor of Santiago de Cuba, had been given permission by the Queen Regent of Spain to use all necessary force permitted in the articles of war by attacking ships, land and other possessions held by the English.[13]

> Whereas by copy of a commission sent by Wm Beck, Governor of Curaçao, to Gov Sir Thos Modyford, from the Queen Regent of Spain, dated 20 April 1669, her governors in the Indies are commanded to make open war against His Majesty's subjects, and that the Spanish governors have granted commissions and are levying forces against the English.[14]

Then, in June, the Spanish pushed the war up a notch when news arrived in Port Royal that men from two Spanish ships had landed on the north coast.

> The Spaniards have landed to leeward, burnt many houses, taken prisoners, and marched off. They last appeared off Wealthy Wood, but finding armed men on the shore, stood off to sea.[15]

By the time a hastily assembled militia appeared on the scene the ships had left. A few days later, the population of Port Royal sighted three Spanish ships off the coast, heading westward. They came in close as if to land an invasion force and continue burning plantations and houses but soon sailed away when the militia arrived. However, the following day the Spanish did land and more houses were burned and more prisoners taken.

On 29 June, Modyford called an extraordinary meeting of the Council of Jamaica, held at King's House in Spanish Town, to discuss the situation. It didn't take them long to make a unanimous decision. This decision, reflected in the minutes of the council, evoked the latest instructions Modyford had from the king, which stated he was to take the necessary action, with advice of the council, to meet an emergency 'as fully and effectually as if you were instructed by us'.[16]

That decision was to give Morgan back his commission.

> In accordance with the last article of His Majesty's instructions to Gov Modyford 'in this great and urgent necessity', it is ordered that a commission be granted to Admiral Henry Morgan to be commander-in-chief of all ships of war belonging to this harbour, and to attack, seize and destroy the enemy's vessels with powers herein set forth.[17]

Around this time a proclamation arrived from the Spanish challenging Morgan personally. It came from Captain Rivera Pardal, who was the leader of the Spanish ships that had landed on the northern coast, setting fire to many houses and taking prisoners.

I, Captain Manuel Rivero Pardal, to the chief of the squadron of privateers in Jamaica. I am he who this year have done that which follows. I went on shore at Caimanos, and burnt twenty houses, and fought with Captain Ary, and took from him a catch laden with provisions and a canoa. And I am he who took Capt Baines, and did carry the prize to Carthagena, and now am arrived to this coast, and have burnt it. And I come to seek General Morgan, with two ships of twenty guns, and having seen this, I crave he would come out upon the coast and seek me, that he might see the valour of the Spaniards. And because I had no time I did not come to the mouth of Port Royal to speak by word of mouth in the name of my king, whom God preserve.[18]

Once again, the safety of Jamaica had been thrust onto Morgan's shoulders. Although by the end of June he had not yet received the commission from Modyford, Morgan was already busy setting up and recruiting his force. It would not be difficult. For many buccaneers, the death of Captain Barnard at the hands of Rivera festered and his public challenge to Morgan was seen by most as an insult to the Brethren.

On the second day of July, Lieutenant Colonel Robert Byndloss mobilized the Port Royal Volunteers. That same day Morgan received his commission from Modyford. It began by retelling the directive from the Queen Regent of Spain to her governors in the Indies to 'make open war against the subjects of His Majesty', and that already the Captain General of Paraguay and governor of St Jago of Cuba had:

executed the same, and in most barbarous manner landed his men on the north side of Jamaica, firing all the houses and killing and taking all the inhabitants prisoners they could meet with; and the rest of the governors are diligently gathering forces to be sent to St Jago, their rendezvous and magazine, for invasion and conquest of this island.

Modyford continued, saying that by the virtue of the king and from the advice of the Council of Jamaica Morgan was appointed as commander-in-chief:

of all the ships fitted or to be fitted for defence of this island, and of the officers, soldiers, and seamen upon the same, and commands him to get said vessels into one fleet, well manned, armed and victualled, and by the first opportunity to put to sea for defence of this island, and to use his best endeavour to surprise, take, sink, disperse or destroy the enemy's vessels, and, in case he finds it feasible, to land and attack St Jago or any other place where he shall be informed are stores for this war or a rendezvous for their forces, and to use his best endeavours to seize the stores and take, kill, or disperse the forces.[19]

Modyford ended the commission by saying that Morgan was to follow orders from the king, the Duke of York or himself. Copies of this commission were sent to the Duke of York. Along with the instructions in the commission, Modyford wrote another set of instructions for Morgan, far more detailed, specifically on the conduct of his expedition. He wrote that Morgan should ensure the sailors and soldiers were on the 'old pleasing account of no purchase, no pay, and therefore that all which is got shall be divided amongst them, according to the accustomed rules.' He continued by saying that for those Spaniards who submitted to the authority of the English government they were to be given 'mercy and enjoyment of estates and liberty of conscience'. However, if the Spanish did not yield, Modyford instructed Morgan 'with all expedition to destroy and burn and leave it a wilderness.' In the treatment of Spanish prisoners Morgan was to:

> inquire what usage our prisoners have had, and what quarter has been given to ours, and give the same, or rather, as our custom is, to exceed them in civility and humanity, endeavouring to make all people sensible of his moderation and good nature and his inaptitude and loathness to spill the blood of man.[20]

England and France were at peace so Morgan knew he could once again rely on the French buccaneers at Tortuga, and so he set a rendezvous for 24 October at that island. One of the largest of the Jamaican ships was the *Satisfaction*, which had been out of Port Royal for a year and a half. Onboard this ship was surgeon Richard Browne, who was thoroughly bored with his eighteen-month long voyage. The ship finally did return to Port Royal in the early part of August before Morgan had set sail for Tortuga. He made Browne the surgeon general of the expedition.

> Found that two Spanish men-of-war had been on these coasts, burnt several houses, taken some prisoners and provisions, and had left a challenge both in Spanish and English; on which account the Governor and Council have made war with them, and Admiral Morgan is preparing a fleet with 1,500 men for some notable design on land, and Browne goes with him as Surgeon General.[21]

But Modyford was walking a tightrope. He'd heard nothing from Lord Arlington and had no idea how Godolphin was getting on with negotiations in Madrid. His son Charles was able to send him bits and pieces from London about the political scene there. Since the death of the Duke of Albemarle Modyford knew that he now had no friend in the Privy Council and that he needed to find if not a friend then a sympathetic ear. He also knew that there was an inner circle in the Privy Council of five men who were the closest to the king and therefore had the most influence with His Majesty. Arlington was one of these men, as Albemarle had been, but with the duke gone, now Modyford needed an ally.

He chose to write to Lord Ashley, justifying everything he had done, the reasons for pursuing the war against the Spanish at a time when London was trying to negotiate peace. In his letter dated 6 July 1670, Modyford told Lord Ashley that the Spanish had been preparing for the war since April 1669. He wrote that the buccaneers would never 'be planters, he has employed to keep the war in their own country, and judge you, my Lord, in this exigent, what course could be more frugal, more prudential, more hopeful – the men volunteers, the ships, arms, ammunition their own, their victuals and pay the enemy's, and such enemies as they have always beaten.'[22]

Modyford went on to state that the Spanish had already attacked Jamaica, putting many houses to 'fire and sword', taking prisoners and challenging the English to come out and fight. He ended his letter by asking Ashley to 'mediate with His Majesty as that according to his instruction this proceeding may have its due ratification.' With the letter Modyford included as many documents as he could that would prove his course of action was just: the council minutes of 29 June, the depositions from the purser of the *Mary and Jane* and other crews, the challenge from Captain Rivera, the commission to Morgan as well as a copy of the 29 April commission by the Queen Regent of Spain telling her governors in the West Indies to make war with Jamaica. In turn, Modyford wanted approval from the king.

Yet by early August nothing had arrived from London. On the 14th, Morgan led the fleet of buccaneers out of Port Royal and they sailed to the western end of the island, anchoring at Bluefields Bay, where they continued to prepare for the expedition ahead.

Finally, on 18 August, a ship arrived bringing a letter from Arlington, which was dated 12 June. It made for sober reading:

> Ever since Sir Wm Godolphin's going last into Spain, they have daily expected
> he would be able to bring that court to some articles that might make them live
> like good neighbours in the West Indies, they affording us a safe retreat in their

ports, and wood, water, and refreshments for money, forbearing to ask freedom
of trade, which neither we in our Leeward plantations nor they in any parts of
America, according to their ancient constitutions, can admit of: this they would
hardly agree to, such have been their resentments for what the privateers have
done.[23]

Of the buccaneers, Arlington charged Modyford with ensuring that 'in
whatsoever state the privateers are at the receipt of this letter, he keep them so
till we have a final answer from Spain.'[24] From the letter Modyford knew that
Arlington clearly either had no idea of the gravity of the situation in Jamaica
or really cared about the colony at all.

The letter put Modyford in an even more difficult situation. Arlington
had said in his letter he'd received Modyford's letter dated 20 March and so
would have been aware of the death of Captain Barnard and the capture of
his ship. Yet Arlington dismissed these acts. Modyford was now charged with
keeping the privateers where they were, which was at sea, and 'forbear all
hostilities at land.'

Modyford decided to follow the orders as best he could and so sent word for
Morgan to return to Port Royal from Bluefields Bay. When Morgan arrived
he hurried to meet the governor. Modyford told Morgan of:

His Majesty's pleasure, strictly charging him to observe the same, and behave
with all moderation possible in carrying on this war. He replied that he would
observe these orders as far as possible, but necessity would compel him to land
in the Spaniards' country for wood, water and provisions, or desert the service,
and that unless he were assured of the enemy's embodying or laying up stores
in their towns, for the destruction of this island, he would not attempt any of
them.[25]

Morgan returned to the fleet anchored at Bluefields Bay and prepared to set
sail for the rendezvous point. Back in Jamaica, Modyford sent a long letter,
dated 20 August, to Arlington, telling him he had obeyed His Majesty's
wishes.

Little did either men know that storm clouds were gathering for them both.

Chapter 15

Back at Sea

A small frigate of nine guns, Captain John Morris, commander, sent by Sir Thos Modyford to Admiral Morgan, captured the frigate of Captain Emanuel Rivera of fourteen guns and good store of ammunition, granadoes and stink pots. Rivera was shot through the neck and immediately died. This is that same vapouring captain that so much annoyed Jamaica in burning houses and robbing the people and sent that insolent challenge to Admiral Morgan. The frigate is now added to our fleet.[1]

In order for Morgan to build his fleet he sent out a call-up notice or, as Esquemeling states, he wrote 'letters to all the expert pirates' at Tortuga as well as to the hunters and planters of Hispaniola inviting them to join him.

Having done that, and satisfied Modyford that he would follow the orders from London, Morgan and his fleet set sail from Bluefields Bay and headed for the rendezvous at Tortuga. However, on the way, he diverted the fleet northwards to the coast of Cuba, looking for any sign of a Spanish fleet. There was no sign of the enemy. Leaving Captain John Morris commanding the *Dolphin* to cruise the South Cays and Manzanillo area, Morgan ordered the fleet to sail eastwards to Santiago. Again, there was no sign of enemy ships. After this brief reconnaissance the fleet began cruising down the coast of Cuba, letting the Spaniards know that there was a British fleet out there just waiting for the Spaniards to come out and fight. No one did.

Late August and early September were in the middle of the hurricane season in the West Indies and as Morgan's fleet sailed towards Tortuga they were hit by a tropical storm that howled through the rigging of their ships. The men hurried in the driving rain and gale force winds to haul down the sails. The ships big and small corkscrewed on the rough seas, whipped up by the winds. Waves smashed across the decks and the men were quickly soaked, especially those in the small vessels that had little shelter on their decks. The gales scattered the ships but fortunately none were lost and by 2 September, they'd all reached Tortuga safely.

The storm also affected John Morris commanding the *Dolphin*, who, seeking shelter against the gales, sailed into a cove on the eastern shore of Cuba. Accounts differ from one source to another as to whether he found a ship already there or whether the ship sailed into the cove after he did, but the ship he came across was a Spanish man-of-war. Even more coincidental is that it was commanded by Manuel Rivero Pardal, 'the vapouring Admiral of St Jago, who had been sent there double manned, and with eighty musketeers on land.'[2] This frigate was the *San Pedro y la Fama* and had 'fourteen guns and good store of ammunition, granadoes and stink pots.'[3]

According to Stephan Talty, Rivero was delighted at the sight of the *Dolphin* as his frigate had fourteen guns to the *Dolphin's* ten. It should have been a pushover but Rivero did not know he was facing hardened and experienced buccaneers[4] who knew their weapons and how to use them effectively. A battle quickly ensued and the *Dolphin* fired the first shots. 'At the first volley the Spaniards left their guns, and the captain, running to bring them back, was killed by a shot in the throat, after which the men leapt overboard.'[5]

Most of the men from the *Fama* dived into the water as the buccaneers approached and, as Talty states, shot the Spanish as they desperately tried to swim away. Only five prisoners were taken by Morris, who when he boarded the Spanish frigate discovered three commissions authorizing the Spanish to attack the English at Jamaica. These commissions were sent via Morgan to Modyford, who sent them on to Lord Arlington, 'whereby His Lordship will find him [Pardal] a person of great value amongst them, and empowered to carry the royal standard in the maintop; also the original canvas challenge, which was nailed to a tree near the west point of this island, whereby a guess may be made of the man's vanity.'[6]

The captured *Fama* was taken by Morris to join Morgan's fleet, now anchored in the channel between Tortuga and Hispaniola.

As more and more privateers arrived and joined the fleet, Morgan soon realized he had a major problem to deal with – provisions for all the men. Esquemeling wrote about the numbers of men that joined the expedition:

> These people upon this notice flocked to the place assigned, in huge numbers, with ships, canoes, and boats, being desirous to follow him. Many, who had not the convenience of coming by sea, traversed the woods of Hispaniola, and with no small difficulties arrived there by land.

Morgan called a council of all the captains in his fleet to put in motion the plan to build up the massive amount of food they would need for everyone. Skilled marksmen were sent out in parties to hunt in the woods of Hispaniola, 'where they killed a huge number of beasts and salted them,' Esquemeling writes. Crucially, they needed maize, to grind into flour to make bread, along with other foodstuffs, so a large group of 400 men, in five ships under the command of Vice Admiral Collier, were sent to the Spanish Main to gather up as much maize as they could. There was another reason why Morgan sent out this little raiding party. He wanted information on what the Spanish were doing – as much information as he could get. In the meantime those men left behind on the ships and smaller vessels sweated in the baking heat repairing sails, rigging, masts and anything else on their ships damaged by the early September gales. But on 7 October another storm struck, this one worse than the one before.

> On the 7th inst so violent a storm assaulted the fleet that all the vessels except the Admiral's were driven onshore, but all except three are fetched off again; he has more men than shipping, which has encouraged some merchantmen to go up to him.[7]

So with the ships damaged from the 7 October storm the men of the fleet continued to repair their vessels and make them ready for the long expedition ahead.

What does not come through in the sources and even in Esquemeling's work, but is implied, is that this expedition, unlike Maracaibo, was not entirely about booty or loot. This was in response to the declared war by the Spanish on the English in the West Indies and it might account for the unusually high numbers of men who arrived at Tortuga in any way they could to serve with Morgan.

As far as Collier is concerned his little fleet of five ships had sailed towards the largest and best grain ports 'usually best stored with maize of all the parts thereabouts' of the Spanish Main, Rio de la Hacha. This was westward, beyond the Gulf of Venezuela.

When Collier's fleet arrived at the mouth of the Rio de la Hacha they were in sight of land but the wind suddenly died and they were becalmed. They'd travelled 450 miles only to be becalmed within sight of their target. 'The Spanish inhabitants along the coast, who had perceived them to be enemies, had sufficient time to prepare themselves, at least to hide the best of their goods,' wrote Esquemeling. Indeed, the people of the port had been through this before and knew what the presence of the fleet meant. When the port had been a prosperous fishery it had been attacked by corsairs so the people of the town knew what to expect. Finally, when the wind did get up, Collier was able to land his men 2 miles from the town.[8]

Taking the town should have been easy for Collier and his men as it had only one fort with four guns but on this occasion there was a large galleon present, the *La Gallardina*, which added an extra forty Spaniards to the fort. Despite this, Collier demanded their surrender but these Spanish, aware of who they were dealing with, replied that they would only lay down their arms by force. This ship had been the consort to Rivera's ships that had attacked Jamaica, set houses on fire and taken prisoners. 'The men probably suspected that burning houses and leaving posted threats had not endeared them to Morgan's men.'[9] So for the next twenty-four hours the Spanish fired their cannon at Collier's men, but realizing they were achieving nothing, they finally gave up. The buccaneers stormed the fort and the ship and then moved into the town. Collier had two of the Spanish soldiers executed, according to Talty. Indeed, the buccaneers found some of the soldiers hiding under mattresses as they entered the fort.

During the time when Collier's fleet had been becalmed the people of the town had been able to hide all their goods as well as a large portions of maize, the main reason Collier had come to this little backwater. The *La Gallardina*, however, was a different story because it was 'lade with maize, and now almost ready to depart', Esquemeling states. This was perfect for the buccaneers as they now had a ship ready to go filled with maize.

The town was now in the hands of Collier and his men. Most of the townspeople had fled into the nearby woods and teams of buccaneers were sent out to find them, seize their valuables and take prisoners. It's at this point that Esquemeling tells us the buccaneers tortured the Spanish prisoners. 'Some were forced, by intolerable tortures, to confess; but others, who would not, were used more barbarously.'[10] This cruelty is corroborated by Talty in his book when he states that the buccaneers freely roamed the countryside looking for booty, taking prisoners and torturing them.[11]

The buccaneers found some 'plate and movables' in the way of booty yet despite their efforts they missed a sizeable sum of 200,000 pesos that the Spanish had hidden in the fort itself.[12]

> Yet, not content with what they had got, they dispatched some prisoners into the woods to seek for the rest of the inhabitants, and to demand a ransom for not burning the town. They answered they had no money nor plate; but if they would be satisfied with a quantity of maize, they would give as much as they could.[13]

As obtaining maize was the main reason why Collier had come to this little port he accepted the Spanish proposal. Within three days, 4,000 bushels of maize had been loaded onto Collier's ships by the Spanish, 'desirous to rid themselves of that inhuman sort of people.' Finally, after spending fifteen days in the town, the fleet set sail for Hispaniola, 'to give account to their leader, Captain Morgan, of all they had performed.'

In all, Collier and his fleet had been away for five weeks. What had been going through Morgan's mind at the time no one can say, although Esquemeling takes a crack at it. He believes that Morgan may have thought that Collier's fleet had been captured by the Spanish or he feared that they may have taken a great galleon, made a fortune for themselves and decided not to rejoin the fleet. Whatever anxieties, they were dispelled when instead of a fleet of five ships arriving, seven arrived. *La Gallardina* was one of those ships, along with a merchantman that Collier had taken along the way. There is an interesting dichotomy between Pope and Talty in the telling of this incident. For example, Talty states that *La Gallardina* was already at Rio de la Hacha when Collier arrived. Pope states that the same ship was captured by Collier on the way back from Rio de la Hacha and that only when Collier began questioning its captain did he discover that it had been the consort to Rivera's ship.[14] Either way, this ship was a godsend for Morgan. It was a ten-gun, 80-ton privateer and gave Morgan another fighting ship.

More important, however, was the information that the crew of *La Gallardina* had for Morgan, who had the captain of *La Gallardina* sign a written statement. The ship had just sailed from Cartagena, where the Spanish were up in arms against the excesses of the English. The information was that 'the president of Panama, Don Juan Perez de Guzman, had issued commissions against the English to several ships, which had since taken English prizes.' Indeed, a fleet had been fitted out in Spain for the express purpose of attacking Jamaica.

> In September came advice from Old Spain, wherein the Governor was commanded to prosecute the war against this island, and much blamed for having done nothing all this time. The like letters were despatched to all the other governors, by which His Lordship may have some aim at the violence of their intentions and the little force they have to execute them.[15]

Morgan now had a mixture of English and French ships in his fleet. Seven French ships had joined him, the largest of which was the *St Catherine*, with a crew of 110 and fourteen guns. Next was the *St Pierre*, with ten guns and upwards of ninety men, and even the tiny *Le Cerf*, managing to mount only two guns but was packed with forty men, was part of the French contingent. On the beach, more French buccaneers slept, waiting and hoping to be taken on. Morgan knew that all the ships were full so he handed *La Gallardina* over to the French under the command of Captain Gascoine.[16]

Morgan divided the maize amongst the men of the fleet and around 23 November set sail for Cape Tiburon. This is a stretch of coastline at the southwest tip of Hispaniola. This rugged peninsula is home to many sheltered bays, which provided excellent anchorages for ships heading towards Jamaica, the Spanish Main, Cuba and so on. Morgan anchored his fleet in the sheltered side of Cape Tiburon.

> No sooner were they arrived, but they met some other ships newly come in join them from Jamaica; so that now their fleet consisted of thirty-seven ships, wherein were 2,000 fighting men, beside mariners and boys. The admiral hereof was mounted with twenty-two great guns, and six small ones of brass, the rest carried some twenty; some sixteen, some eighteen, and the smallest vessel at least four; besides which, they had great quantities of ammunition and fireballs, with other inventions of powder.[17]

Finally, the whole fleet was assembled and Morgan duly dispatched a vessel with a letter for Modyford telling him of the fact. However, the size of the fleet was too large for one man to handle so Morgan decided to split the fleet into two squadrons. One would be commanded by Vice Admiral Edward Collier and the other would be commanded by Morgan. Morgan's flagship, the *Satisfaction*, was the largest ship in the fleet and one of only two that had been purpose-built for war. The other was the *La Gallardina*. Despite Esquemeling's statement above about the smallest vessels having at least four guns, we know from Pope that some had no guns at all. For example, one of the smallest ships, the *Prosperous*, of only 10 tons, was commanded by Patrick Dunbar and held sixteen men, yet it had no guns. The *Free Gift*, of only 15 tons and commanded by Roger Kelly, had only two guns, yet it carried forty buccaneers. There was the 12-ton sloop *Betty*, commanded by William Curzon, with twenty-five men. Then there was the *Thomas*, commanded by Humphrey Thurston, and the *Port Royal*, under the command of James Delliat. The experienced captains, such as John Morris, Lawrence Prince and Joseph Bradley, were there with their ships. Richard Norman, commanding the ten-gun *Lilly*, and Thomas Rogers, commanding the twelve-gun *Gift*, were part of the fleet and both men had been with Morgan at Maracaibo.[18]

With all these ships and men Morgan decided to redo the Brethren agreement. First he ensured that every captain received a commission 'to act all manner of hostilities against the Spanish nation, and take of them what ships they could, either abroad at sea, or in the harbours, as if they were the open and declared enemies of the King of England.'[19]

The new articles that Morgan drew up were more generous for everyone but especially so for the wounded. First, the king got his usual fifteenth share, while the Duke of York received an eighth share. Morgan gave himself 1 per cent, while each captain received 'the shares of eight men for the expenses [*sic*] of his ship, besides his own. To the surgeon, beside his pay, 200 pieces of eight for his chest of medicaments.' Morgan allotted the carpenters an additional 100 pieces of eight over their salaries. As far as the wounded were concerned, anyone who lost both legs would received 1,500 pieces of eight as compensation or fifteen slaves; the loss of both hands was 1,800 pieces of eight or eighteen slaves; one leg or one hand was six slaves or 600 pieces of eight and one eye was 100 pieces of eight or one slave. Anyone who showed bravery in battle, 'either by entering first any castle, or taking down the Spanish colours, and setting up the English, they allotted fifty pieces of eight for a reward.'[20]

Finally, Morgan called a council of war to decide what target they should attack. Because of the different languages the discussion would take time. Morgan ordered that a committee should be set up to provide recommendations for the next target and report back to a full council. This was duly done and three cities were chosen: St Jago, Cartagena or Panama. St Jago in Cuba was dismissed because of the poor weather along the coast and the chances that most of the fleet would be lost in the gale winds. Cartagena was too heavily defended, so that left Panama, the heart of the Spanish Main.

Morgan put it to the full council of war and it was unanimously agreed. Panama was the target. However, they had no information about the city and before they attempted it their goal would be to capture Spanish prisoners or find reliable guides who knew the place. The best place to find that was the island of Old Providence and the council of war determined that recapturing that island was their first priority. He sent a letter dated 6 December to Modyford, 'advising that he was 1,800 strong, whereof 200 or 300 French and thirty-six ships, and was under sail to make further discoveries of the enemy, having by prisoners been informed that about Carthagena, Puerto Bello and Panama, soldiers were listing against the galleons came, to be transported against this island.'[21]

The fleet set sail for Old Providence on 8 December 1670.

Chapter 16

To Old Providence and Beyond

The account of the taking of Old Providence by Morgan and his men comes largely from Esquemeling. In his own report, Morgan is very brief about the whole affair. But as this book is about trying to discover the character of Morgan it is worth going into as much detail as we can in order to study what made him the gifted leader he was.

The buccaneers took six days to cross the 575 miles to Old Providence. We must remember that in Morgan's day there were no electronic navigational aids that the ships of today enjoy. The charts that Morgan had were ones that the buccaneers had drawn themselves on their voyages or existing ones that they added to.

It's worth taking a brief moment to look at how the buccaneers did navigate, for we have described in this book some very lengthy journeys of hundreds of miles. These were not easy journeys as they would be today. Dudley Pope describes in some detail how the navigators of Morgan's time would plot their course and be able to find their destination. The key for any navigator at that time was knowing the latitude of their destination. He could find his north or south latitude by taking a reading of the position of the sun at any given time then 'measuring the angle with a backstaff, the forerunner of the modern sextant.' However, to get the east-west longitude the navigator would then need to make an accurate measurement 'of the distance he had sailed from a known position'. Fortunately, the latitude of Old Providence was known by the buccaneers, so getting to it was relatively easy for them.[1]

Old Providence is recognizable from a distance for its three peaks and it was on the sixth day out of Cape Tiburon that the buccaneers sighted the island. Although the Spanish had added four cannon for covering the anchorage there was no sign of them as Morgan's fleet approached. Even within range, the cannon remained silent. Morgan sent a boat to the mouth of the river to see if there were any other vessels that might 'give intelligence of his arrival to the inhabitants and prevent his designs.' There were no vessels to provide a warning.

Esquemeling tells us that the following day Morgan's fleet anchored in a bay called Aguade Grande, where the Spanish had built the battery that housed the four cannon. As they were unmanned Morgan was able to land upwards of a thousand men 'in divers[e] squadrons' by sending the boats back and forth as quickly as they could go in case the Spanish were hiding and should suddenly appear and open fire. Once the men had been landed they began 'marching through the woods, though they had no other guides than a few of his own men, who had been there before, under Mansvelt.'[2]

Arriving at the governor's residence they found that the Spanish had built another battery, which Esquemeling states was called the Platform, but this too was deserted. The Spanish garrison had in fact moved to the smaller adjoining island, Santa Catalina (St Catherines), 'which is so near the great one, that a short bridge only may conjoin them.'[3]

The Spanish had fortified this island, putting up forts and batteries all the way around it and making it virtually impregnable. Once they saw the buccaneers approaching they 'fired on them so furiously that they could advance nothing that day, but were content to retreat, and take up their rest in the open fields, which was not strange to these people, being sufficiently used to such kind of repose.'

But the men were hungry, having not eaten since they'd landed on the island. To make matters worse, that night as they lay in the open fields with little shelter, 'it rained so hard that they had much ado to bear it, the greatest part of them having no other clothes than a pair of seaman's trousers or breeches, and a shirt without shoes or stockings,' wrote Esquemeling. To provide some warmth the Dutch author tells us that the men tore down 'a few thatched houses' and set fires to help keep themselves dry and warm.[4]

The following morning, having still not eaten anything, the men marched on under rain that fell 'as if the skies were melted into waters'. While the heavens opened and rain fell in sheets on the unfortunate buccaneers, the Spanish continued to fire at them from the forts. At this point in the narrative, Esquemeling tells us that the men were 'reduced to great affliction and danger, through the hardness of the weather'. Their spirits were so low that the men began talking of returning to the ships, where they could dry out and have something to eat.

With morale rapidly ebbing away we see Morgan displaying his great leadership, his strength of character keeping his men inspired despite their dreadful circumstances. He decided enough was enough and ordered that a canoe be made ready and sent across to the governor of the island under the flag of truce. According to Esquemeling, Morgan sent a message to the governor stating that:

if within a few hours he [the Governor] delivered not himself and all his men unto his [Morgan's] hands, he did by that messenger swear unto him, and all those that were in his company, he would most certainly put them all to the sword, without granting quarter to any.[5]

Of course this was a huge bluff on Morgan's part. His own men were hungry, tired and wet. They were lightly armed with muskets and the rain had meant that while their powder may have remained dry, the slow match that was needed to fire the matchlocks and pistols needed to be dried out. The buccaneers hung strips of this slow match from anything they could find – branches, twigs … anything – so they could dry in the sun. They faced an enemy who had nine forts, forty-nine cannon, loads of ammunition and stores, 1,220 muskets and more. The Spanish could hold out for days while the buccaneers could not. The Spanish had the shelter and the stores the buccaneers did not. The largest of the forts, St Jerome, had twenty cannon, a 20-foot deep ditch surrounding it and was built of stone. For the buccaneers to try to take it with what they had would be folly.

In short, the Spanish could hold out and keep up the fight while the buccaneers could not. Morgan was relying on his reputation and the fear that the Spanish had of him and his buccaneers. Deep in his heart Morgan must have known that the governor could have put up such resistance that would have made taking the island by force impractical.

By the time the two-hour deadline had passed, the rain had stopped and the governor's reply arrived in 'two canoes with white colours, and two person to treat with Captain Morgan', reported Esquemeling.

For whatever reason, the governor decided he would surrender the island to Morgan. Whether it was because of the fierce reputation of Morgan and his buccaneers and the fear they struck in the hearts of the Spanish or the governor's desire to ensure the safety of the island's women and children, we shall never know. It was more likely a combination of factors. However, to achieve this surrender Morgan would have to adhere to certain conditions. 'He desired Captain Morgan would be pleased to use a certain stratagem of war, for the better saving of his own credit, and the reputation of his officers both abroad and at home.'[6]

During the two hours that Morgan had given the governor, the man must have worked out the details of these conditions, for they were complex indeed. First Morgan was to lead some of his troops to the bridge that joined 'the lesser island to the great one', where he would attack St Jerome fort. While he was doing that, his fleet would anchor near the next largest fort, Santa Teresa, land troops and attack it while also landing troops near the St Mathew batteries. These troops were then to take the governor prisoner as he attempted to get to St Jerome:

using the formality, as if they forced him to deliver the castle; and that he would lead the English into it, under colour of being his own troops. That on both sides there should be continual firing, but without bullets, or at least into the air, so that no side might be hurt. Thus having obtained two such considerable forts; the chiefest of the isle, he need not take care for the rest, which must fall of course into his hands.[7]

Morgan agreed to these rather strange circumstances and, as Esquemeling states, insisted that the conditions and details of the governor's proposal be kept to the letter. So this 'false battle' began that evening with Morgan and his troops storming St Jerome, 'with incessant firing from both the castles, against the ships, but without bullets, as was agreed.' Morgan and his men quickly took both forts, 'forcing the Spanish, in appearance, to fly to the church.'

The following day the buccaneers began to quell their hunger as they set about putting the forts and the island to rights. They slaughtered and roasted cattle, poultry and 'all sorts of victuals they could find, for some days; scarce thinking of anything else than to kill, roast and eat.'

They also set about making fires, presumably to dry out their clothes and powder by tearing down the houses and using the timber for firewood. Having done this, the buccaneers then gathered all the prisoners they'd taken on the island and discovered there were 459 in all. Of those, 190 were soldiers of the garrison, there were forty married couples and forty-three children, and thirty-four slaves with eight children, who Esquemeling tells us belonged to the King of Spain. In addition there were eight bandits on the island (Esquemeling calls them banditti), plus thirty-nine 'negroes belonging to private persons; with twenty-seven female blacks and thirty-four children.'[8]

They disarmed the Spanish prisoners and then began a stocktake of the island's forts and castles. For example, in St Jerome, the fort closest to the bridge, they discovered 'eight great guns, of 12, 6 and 8 pounds carriage; with six pipes of muskets, every pipe containing ten muskets,' writes Esquemeling. On top of that they discovered another sixty muskets and enough powder and ammunition for all the ordnance in the fort.

The fort of St Mathew had three 8-pounder guns, according to Esquemeling, while the largest of the forts, Santa Teresa, had 'twenty great guns, of 18, 12, 8 and 6 pounds; with ten pipes of muskets, like those before, and ninety muskets remaining, besides other ammunition.' This was the fort with the deep ditch dug round it and the thick stone walls. It had only one entry point, which was a door in the middle of the castle, and was impregnable on the seaward side. Inside the fort were four cannon mounted on a high platform that covered the port so it could shoot at any ships attempting to anchor there. On the landward side was a narrow path 3 or 4 feet wide that led up to the entrance to the fort. St Augustine was the forth fort and had only three cannon – 8- and 6-pounders, while the fifth fort, La Plattaforma de la Conception, mounted only two 8-pounders. The sixth fort, San Salvador, also had only two cannon. Like these two, the seventh fort, Plattaforma de los Artilleros, also had only two cannon while the eighth, the Santa Cruz, had three cannon. St Joseph's fort, the ninth, mounted 'six guns of 12 and 8 pounds, besides two pipes of muskets and sufficient ammunition'.

The buccaneers also discovered more than 30,000 pounds of powder and ammunition, which they took on board their ships, and then set about tearing down all the forts except St Jerome, where they kept the prisoners under guard. They also 'stopped and nailed' all the guns so that they would be useless to the Spanish.

While the buccaneers were busy carrying out their work on the forts Morgan and his captains[9] were working out what to do next. Since the objective was Panama they needed a foothold on the Isthmus of Panama. The best place for that was Chagres, which lay at the mouth of the Chagres River. By using the river they could cross the isthmus in canoes and small boats to Venta Cruz, where they could then march on Panama itself.

But, as with all his other expeditions, Morgan needed intelligence. He needed to know as much as possible about the land, the geography, the defences – everything that he could possibly know about the place – before he set sail. Esquemeling tells us that there were some bandits or *banditti* in the employ of the Spanish and it was to these men that Morgan turned to act as guides 'and show him the securest ways to Panama, which if they performed, he promised them equal shares in the plunder of that expedition, and their liberty when they arrived in Jamaica.'[10] The three men agreed to Morgan's proposals so he ordered that four ships be made ready to sail for Chagres and that these ships would carry 400 men.

Captain Bradley's *Mayflower* led the little fleet away from Old Providence on 18 December. Their destination was Chagres and at the mouth of that river was one of the key obstacles that they would have to overcome – San Lorenzo fort and the many batteries within it.

Morgan's prayers must have gone with them.

Chapter 17

The Battle at San Lorenzo

Had it not been an Accident, which determined them to surrender, it would probably have repelled all their Assaults.[1]

W as it good tactics or good strategy for Morgan to send a small force to Chagres before the main fleet arrived? Such a strategy would certainly give him the intelligence he needed of the area and if the men he sent could secure a foothold and take the castle then the move downriver to Panama itself would be much easier, knowing that their escape route was covered. Could Morgan have been thinking of Maracaibo, where his fleet had been trapped, and he didn't want that to happen again?

Perhaps the real question here is, why didn't Morgan go with this fleet with the idea of bringing the rest of the men and ships to Chagres Castle once it was taken? Would not his charisma and ability to lead have been paramount for the men in the task of taking Chagres?

We could ask many questions about why Morgan chose to send a small force to Chagres without actually going and leading that force himself. The work taking place on Old Providence and the smaller island of Santa Catalina was not as important as ensuring a safe passage for the fleet to Panama. But perhaps there were other reasons for Morgan wanting to stay on Old Providence.

If we remember back to when Colonel Mansfield originally took Old Providence and left a small garrison there, which was subsequently captured by the Spanish, there was some doubt as to whether or not Morgan was on that expedition. If he had been, then perhaps his remaining on the island while sending a small fleet to Chagres was to ensure that every last piece of Spanish presence was removed or torn down in retribution for the way the English prisoners had been treated by the Spanish in Portobello. Perhaps he wanted to ensure that this time the English presence would remain on this island.

Whatever his reasons, Morgan remained behind while Bradley's little fleet set sail for Chagres.

However, across the world in Europe the times were changing and these changes would have a deep effect on both Morgan and Modyford as well as on buccaneering itself. Sir William Godolphin, who had for some considerable time been negotiating a peace treaty between Spain and Britain, finally signed the treaty in Madrid on 11 July 1670. Key to this treaty was the recognition by Spain of the territories and lands in the Americas and the West Indies already occupied by Britain. For Jamaica it meant that Spain had given up her claim to the island. It was now British. It also meant that both countries would cease hostilities and that the task of dealing with the buccaneers and stopping their raids into Spanish territories now lay firmly on British shoulders.

It would not be until 18 November that the treaty was ratified in London and once this was done it would take another eight months for the treaty to be published throughout the colonies. So it was a little more than a year from the day it was signed in Madrid that it arrived in Jamaica.

With the new treaty signed Lord Arlington now decided it was time to get rid of Modyford and put someone in place that would not be so friendly towards the buccaneers. After all, the situation had changed and there was now no threat to Jamaica.

Thomas Lynch had been the Chief Justice in Jamaica five years previously and since Modyford dismissed him he'd travelled to London and stayed there, even though he had a large plantation on the island. For Arlington, Lynch was ideal – he came from a good family in Kent, was the grandson of a bishop and was still a youngish man at thirty–eight. Like Morgan, he'd originally gone to Jamaica with Venables.

In September 1670, Lynch was told he would be the next lieutenant governor of Jamaica. He could not be appointed governor while Modyford remained in office. On 3 December, Lynch was knighted by the king and a few days later married the daughter of Sir Edward Herbert. The woman in question, Vere, was also the sister of the Earl of Torrington, so not only had Lynch come from a respectable family, he had married into another respectable family. Shortly afterwards he received two important documents, one was his commission and the other contained the orders to strip Modyford of his commission as governor of Jamaica.

Of course, Morgan knew nothing of this. Modyford had an inkling of the changes in London through the private letters he'd received from his son, Charles. Even though he knew that the treaty had been signed he had no official letter from London. Undaunted, he set about writing to Arlington, building his case, telling him that he:

had despatched to the Admiral, before the first of these expresses arrived, a copy of the articles of peace with Spain, intimating that though he had them from private hands and no orders to call him in, yet thought fit to let him see them, and to advise him to mind His Lordship's letter of 10 June, and to do nothing that might prevent the accomplishment of His Majesty's peaceable intentions; but the vessel returned with Modyford's letters, having missed him at his old rendezvous, however, has returned her to the main with strict instructions to find the Admiral out.[2]

While Modyford was doing his best to ensure he justified his actions to Lord Arlington, Morgan was hundreds of miles away on Old Providence planning the next phase of the Panama expedition. He'd just dispatched Bradley in three ships with 400 men to take and secure the mouth of the Chagres River. That meant, of course, taking San Lorenzo Castle.

According to Dudley Pope, there were two routes the buccaneers could take for crossing the isthmus to get to Panama. The first was the route down the Chagres River to Venta de Cruze and then onto Panama by foot, horse or mule. The second was by using a narrow track or path from the city of Portobello to Venta de Cruz. It is here that the Chagres River and the land route meet. Now the land route could only be used in the dry season but the Spanish used that route for transporting their gold and silver by horse or mule as they did not want to risk losing valuable cargo such as this in the river in a capsize or being swept away by currents. Since Morgan's last attack on Portobello he knew that the Spanish would have greatly increased the defences around the town, so using the land route was not a practical option.[3] That left the Chagres River route and the attack and capture of San Lorenzo Castle.

We have a description of the entrance to the Chagres River and of San Lorenzo Castle, mainly from Esquemeling, but also from our other sources. The castle itself had been built on the north side of the mouth of the river. The castle, or fort, was not a single structure but more of a sprawling affair built on different levels as distinct but connected structures on the first of three peninsulas that jutted out into the river. 'The castle is built on a high mountain at the entry of the river, surrounded by strong palisades, or wooden walls, filled with earth, which secures them as well as the best wall of stone or brick,' wrote Esquemeling.

He goes on to state that on the northern side of the mouth of the river, the castle is 'surrounded by the river, which here is very broad'. At the foot of the mountain a fort had been built to house eight large guns 'commanding the entry of the river'. Lower down, closer to the water's edge, were two batteries of six guns each, which were for defending the mouth of the river. 'At one side of the castle are two great storehouses of all sorts of warlike ammunition and merchandize, brought thither from the island country. Near these houses is a high pair of stairs hewn out of the rock, to mount to the top of the castle.' These stairs were the only way up to the castle. At the top of the mountain where the castle sat, a ditch divided the peak into two parts and Esquemeling tells us it was some 30 feet deep. The only way to get into the castle was by using the drawbridge that the Spanish had built over the ditch.[4] In addition, on the westward side was a small port, which was capable of anchoring small vessels only, 'besides, before the castle, at the entry of the river, is a great rock, scarce to be described but at low tide.'[5]

Why go into such detail in describing this place? Morgan doesn't in his official report but Esquemeling does. The idea here is to show just how much work the Spanish had done to fortify their territory and how seriously they took the threat of Morgan and the buccaneers. But, more importantly, it is to show the magnitude of Morgan's task and what the cost would be for him to take and secure this castle.

When Bradley arrived in the *Mayflower* just off the entrance to the river, the Spanish began firing their cannon at the three ships. Bradley soon realized that he was completely outgunned. While the Spanish guns bellowed, Bradley surveyed the fort and the cliffs through his telescope. There was no way he could attack from the sea. The cliff was steep, the rock sheer and slippery, not to mention the guns – especially the battery closest to the water; they would destroy the small boats he would have to use to make a seaward landing.

Ruling out the sea, he decided to attack by land and sailed further up the coast until 'they came to anchor in a small port, about a league from the castle,' wrote Esquemeling. The following morning, Bradley led his 400 buccaneers from the shore on a march through thick jungle. The men hacked their way through the 'mire and dirt' and the vicious undergrowth of the humid jungle. This exhausting march lasted until two o'clock in the afternoon, when they suddenly found themselves in a clearing very close to the fort, despite the fact that their guides 'had served them very exactly.' The Spanish sentries on the fort immediately opened fire on the buccaneers 'that they lost many of their men by its shot, they being in an open place without cover.'[6]

From his study of the fort Bradley had seen that the walls were made with wood and earth, which would be difficult to breach under normal circumstances. However, if the wooden planks of the walls were set on fire they would eventually collapse as they burnt; the earth would also collapse and that would create breaches through which the buccaneers could rush in and take the castle. That was Bradley's plan and it was the reason why the buccaneers had brought so many fireballs or fire pots with them. These weapons were made of either cast iron or pottery, filled with combustible materials and set alight by cloth being stuffed into the opening and lit just before they were thrown at the target.

However, Bradley had lost part of his force in the first melee when they'd arrived out in the open in front of the fort. He had men dead and wounded, and the first attack in daylight using the fireballs had failed. 'They advanced towards the castle with their swords in one hand, and fireballs in the other. The Spanish defended themselves very briskly, ceasing not to fire at them continually,' wrote Esquemeling of the first attack. 'The pirates making some trial to climb the walls, were forced to retreat, resting themselves till night.'

The night attack was a different story. While the snipers of the buccaneers concentrated on the Spanish soldiers the rest hurled fireballs at the walls and the gate. A fire started somewhere inside the castle, though how it started is unclear.

> One of the pirates being wounded with an arrow in his back, which pierced his body through, he pulled it out boldly at the side of his breast, and winding a little cotton about it, he put it into his musket, and shot it back to the castle; but the cotton being kindled by the powder, fired two or three houses in the castle, being thatched with palm-leaves, which the Spaniards perceived not so soon as was necessary; for this fire meeting with a parcel of powder, blew it up, thereby causing great ruin, and no less consternation to the Spaniards, who were not able to put a stop to it, not having seen it time enough.[7]

Whether or not this story is true is debatable. It could be another of Esquemeling's embellishments. The fact that one of the buccaneers was able to pull an arrow that had gone through his body out from the side of his chest seems a little over the top, especially when this same man had the foresight to wrap cotton around the shaft of the arrow and then fire it with his musket back into the castle. The pain and shock of having the arrow go through him and be stuck in him could have made it difficult for him to think clearly. But then, these men were hardy, much hardier than we are in the twenty-first century, so perhaps it was true – or partly true.

But the significance of this fire is that it was the beginning of the end for the Spanish because they soon found themselves surrounded by flames. Wherever they could, the buccaneers set fire to the planks, while the Spanish inside the castle tried desperately to put the fire out, 'which caused great confusion because of their want of water,' wrote Esquemeling, who continued to set the scene. 'The fire thus seen at once in several parts about the castle, gave them great advantage against the Spaniards, many breaches being made by the fire among the pales, great heaps of earth falling into the ditch.'

By midnight the fire was out of control and most of the walls had collapsed. The Spanish continued to resist but the buccaneers would 'creep on the ground, as near as they could, and shoot amidst the flames against the Spaniards on the other side, and thus killed many of them from the walls.'[8]

For Bradley this was a waiting game. By morning there were massive breaches in the walls, and where they had collapsed the earth had fallen into the ditch, creating earthen bridges for the pirates to cross. The governor of the castle, Don Pedro de Lisardo, had ordered his guns to be moved to cover these large gaps but it was to no avail. By this point the buccaneer snipers were picking off the gunners as they moved the cannon and tried to fire. Pedro de Lisardo took twenty-five men and defended one of the gaps but was killed along with most of his men. With that the buccaneers stormed in and took the castle. Most of the Spanish had been killed.

> Understanding that the Castle of Chagraw blocked the way, it was determined to attack it, which was done by Lieutenant Colonel Joseph Bradley with 470 men, who after fighting in the trenches from three o'clock till eight the next morning, stormed the place. The enemy refused quarter, which cost them 360 men, while ours lost thirty killed and seventy-six wounded, whereof the brave Bradley was one, who died ten days after. Leaving 300 men to guard the castle and ships under Major Richard Norman, they started on 9 January 1671, with 1,400 men in seven ships and thirty-six boats up the river.[9]

When the Spanish surrendered to the buccaneers they found that only thirty of the entire Spanish garrison of 314 troops remained alive, and of these, twenty were wounded. All thirty were taken prisoner by the buccaneers. Interestingly, not one officer had survived.

However, upon demanding of the prisoners that they tell them everything they knew, the buccaneers soon realized they'd lost the element of surprise. Eight or nine of the Spanish soldiers in the lower gun emplacements had deserted and headed straight for Panama with news of the buccaneer invasion. Worse was to come. A deserter from the buccaneers during the operation at Rio de la Hache had made his way to Panama with news that the English and French buccaneers under Morgan were assembling a fleet to attack Panama.

The governor of Panama, Don Juan Perez de Guzman, might have been a sick man with erysipelas (an acute bacterial skin infection), but his mind was clear enough to understand what the news meant. He sent an additional 164 men to reinforce the garrison of 150 men at San Lorenzo. In addition, he'd sent another 200 men to reinforce the garrison at Portobello should the buccaneers land there. All these men, according to Esquemeling, had been given 'much provision and ammunition'. The buccaneers also discovered from the Spanish captives that the governor had ordered ambushes be placed at key points along the Chagres River and 'that he waited for them in the open fields of Panama with 3,600 men.' This would have included artillery, cavalry and infantry so an extremely formidable force up against the relatively lightly armed buccaneers.

While the cost of the battle had been horrendous for the Spanish it had also been bad for the buccaneers. They'd lost a quarter of the men they landed with and Captain Bradley was mortally wounded. Those buccaneers who were fit to work began moving downriver to Chagres town, rounding up slaves and others they could find to get them to work on rebuilding San Lorenzo Castle. With Bradley so ill, Captain Richard Norman took over as commander. He must have wondered why on earth Morgan was taking so long to arrive.

Back at Old Providence Morgan had not been idle. He was doing all he could to ensure that the island, and especially Santa Catalina, the smaller island, was made ready to be 'the perpetual possession of the pirates', according to Esquemeling. He also 'embarked all the provisions that could be found, with much maize, or Indian wheat, and *cazave*, whereof also is made bread in those parts.' So while he made the entire fleet ready to depart, he ordered that all the houses and forts on Santa Catalina be burnt, with the exception of St Teresa, 'which he judged to be the strongest and securest wherein to fortify himself at his return from Panama.'[10]

By New Year's Day 1671, the *Mayflower* and her two consorts had sailed into the river and anchored so they were protected by the guns of the fort, battery and castle. To get to this anchorage they had to gingerly sail around the 'great rock' that Esquemeling wrote about, which could not be seen except at low tide and Dudley Pope refers to as Laja Reef.

Work had been under way on rebuilding the walls since 29 December, shovelling back the earth between the wooden walls in order to get the castle back into working order. The following day, when the lookouts on the walls of San Lorenzo finally spotted the sails of Morgan's fleet, a great feeling of relief swept through the buccaneers. They watched as Morgan's flagship, the *Satisfaction*, led a fleet of more than thirty ships towards the mouth of the river. It had taken the fleet eight days to sail from Old Providence to the mouth of the Chagres River on the Isthmus of Panama.

From the walls of the castle the buccaneers could clearly see the reef under the surface of the water, but Morgan and the men onboard the *Satisfaction* couldn't have seen it as they were heading straight for it. With a sudden jolt and grinding crash the ship hit the reef, as did the *Port Royal* and two other ships coming in behind it. Immediately, the buccaneers of the stricken ships managed to board their boats and take off most of the provisions and powder before the ships were broken up on the rocks. The provisions Morgan had carefully overseen at Old Providence had been saved. Morgan had decided to leave 150 men garrisoned in San Lorenzo to protect the fleet, where another 150 men were left.[11] This was his escape route once they'd achieved what they had set out to do.

'Captain Morgan was brought into the castle with great acclamations of all the pirates, both of those within, and those newly come,' writes Esquemeling. Indeed, he states that in the river were some Spanish ships that were probably coastal vessels, each with two large iron guns and four smaller brass cannon. These vessels were largely used to carry goods up and down the river and along the coast to Portobello and Nicaragua. Along with these ships, the buccaneers also captured four smaller vessels and all the canoes they could find.

As the rest of the fleet skirted around Laja Reef and anchored under the guns of the battery and the fort, Morgan inspected the work being done on San Lorenzo. He needed this castle to be strong and fortified enough to withstand an attack by the Spanish and so ordered that all the prisoners, including those he'd brought with him from Old Providence, be put to work on the rebuilding.

Now his attention turned to Panama. He would take 1,200 men and lead them to Panama carrying 'little provisions with him, hoping to provide himself sufficiently among the Spaniards, whom he knew to lie in ambuscades by the way.'[12]

However, before he left he had one last task to do – bury an old friend. Charles Bradley had died.

1. Morgan at Porto Bello. (Originally published in Howard Pyle's 'Buccaneers and Marooners of the Spanish Main', *Harper's Magazine*, August–September 1887)

2. Puerto del Príncipe (now Camagüey) being sacked in 1668 by Morgan. (From the Project Gutenberg eBook of *On the Spanish Main*, by John Masefield)

3. Henry Morgan recruiting for the attack. (Originally published in Howard Pyle's 'Buccaneers and Marooners of the Spanish Main', *Harper's Magazine*, August–September 1887)

4. Henry Morgan destroys the Spanish fleet at Lake Maracaibo, Venezuela.

5. Map showing Chagres Castle. (From Project Gutenberg e-text 19396 from the Project Gutenberg eBook of *On the Spanish Main*, by John Masefield)

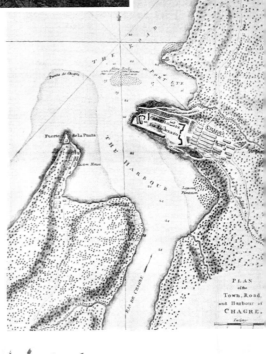

6. Submerged palms and battery casemates of Old Port Royal. (Date 1907, *Popular Science Monthly*)

7. A drawing of Port Royal before the earthquake that destroyed it. (Date 1892, *Popular Science Monthly*)

8. A closer view of the submerged remains of Port Royal. (Date 1907, *Popular Science Monthly*)

9. San Lorenzo Fort as it is today. (Image by Editorpana, Wikimedia Creative Commons Attribute Share Alike Licence)

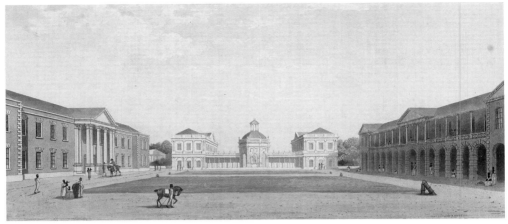

10. King's Square, St Jago de la Vega (Spanish Town), 1820–24. (From *A Picturesque Tour of the Island of Jamaica*, by James Hakewell, Hurst & Robinson, London, 1825)

11. The Golden Vale, Portland Jamaica, circa 1820–24. (From *A Picturesque Tour of the Island of Jamaica*, by James Hakewell, Hurst & Robinson, London, 1825)

12. Harbour Street Kingston Jamaica, circa 1820–24. (From *A Picturesque Tour of the Island of Jamaica*, by James Hakewell, Hurst & Robinson, London, 1825)

13. Bryan Castle, Great House, Trelawny, Jamaica, circa 1820–24. (From *A Picturesque Tour of the Island of Jamaica*, by James Hakewell, Hurst & Robinson, London, 1825)

14. The Bog Walk, circa 1820–24. (From *A Picturesque Tour of the Island of Jamaica*, by James Hakewell, Hurst & Robinson, London, 1825)

15. The Bridge over the White River, St Mary's, Jamaica, circa 1820–24. (From *A Picturesque Tour of the Island of Jamaica*, by James Hakewell, Hurst & Robinson, London, 1825)

16. Kingston and Port Royal from Windsor Farm, Jamaica, circa 1820–24. (From *A Picturesque Tour of the Island of Jamaica*, by James Hakewell, Hurst & Robinson, London, 1825)

17. Spring Garden Estate, St George's, Jamaica, circa 1820–24. (From *A Picturesque Tour of the Island of Jamaica*, by James Hakewell, Hurst & Robinson, London, 1825)

18. Bridge over the Rio Cobre, Spanish Town, Jamaica, circa 1820–24. (From *A Picturesque Tour of the Island of Jamaica*, by James Hakewell, Hurst & Robinson, London, 1825)

19. *The Capture of Puerto Bello.* This painting is based on an engraving from a panoramic painting by Samuel Scott. In the summer of 1739, during a debate in the House of Commons relating to the deteriorating situation with Spain in the West Indies, Captain Edward Vernon claimed he could take the Spanish town of Puerto Bello, Panama, on the north side of the Isthmus of Darien with six ships of the line. He was taken at his word, promoted to vice admiral and given six ships to redeem his pledge. The war became known as the War of Jenkins' Ear. (Oil on canvas, by George Chambers Snr, dated 1838. National Maritime Museum)

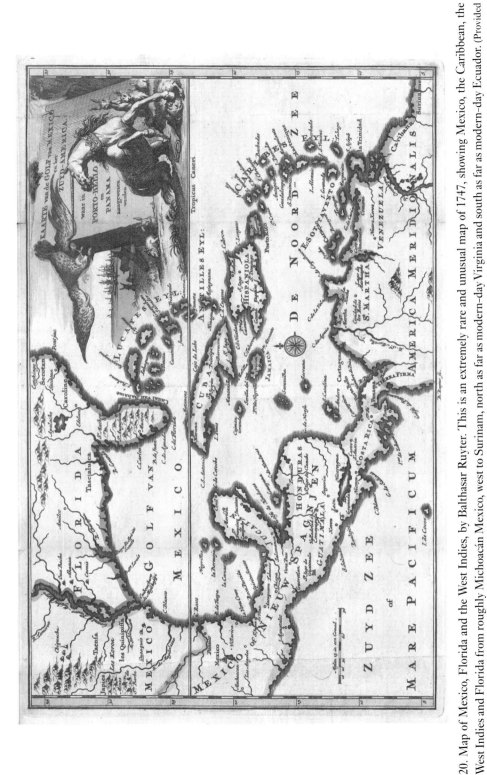

20. Map of Mexico, Florida and the West Indies, by Balthasar Ruyter. This is an extremely rare and unusual map of 1747, showing Mexico, the Caribbean, the West Indies and Florida from roughly Michoacán Mexico, west to Surinam, north as far as modern–day Virginia and south as far as modern–day Ecuador. (Provided to Wikimedia Commons by Geographicus Rare Antique Maps, a specialist dealer in rare maps and other cartography of the fifteenth, sixteenth, seventeenth, eighteenth and nineteenth centuries, as part of a co-operation project. It is in the public domain in the United States and other countries)

Chapter 18

The Road to Panama

The Hardships this Party underwent were surprising, they not only struggled with common Difficulties, but likewise encountered Famine and every kind of Misery. They were reduced to feed upon the Leaves of Trees, and to take unheard-of Methods to preserve their Lives.[1]

It's at this point in the narrative that perhaps Morgan's judgement comes into question. At Chagres Morgan left 300 men split between the castle and the fleet now anchored at the foot of the gun batteries, under the command of Major Richard Norman. 'They started on 9 January 1671, with 1,400 men in seven ships and thirty-six boats up the river,' Morgan wrote in his official report. Interestingly, Pope follows along with Esquemeling's number of 1,200 men.[2]

Morgan decided not to take any provisions, having left them with the fleet anchored under the protection of San Lorenzo Castle. His decision was based on the hope that they would find food along the way. He knew the Spanish had set up ambushes for him and so he assumed that these ambushes would have food. There were also plantations that they could raid for provisions, so there should have been no problem with victualling his men. The main reason for this decision was that the men would have to travel light. Morgan knew the rainy season was over and the river was at a low level. If there was too much weight in the boats they would not be able to haul them over the rough terrain to skirt difficult stretches of river that they couldn't negotiate. It would mean going aground at the low points in the river, which would slow them down even more.

Although Morgan believed that food and water could be obtained during their journey to Panama, he knew it would be much harder to obtain dry powder and dry match, so every man would have to carry not just the dry powder and match, but also ammunition, a cutlass and a pike. Each man would also need a blanket to keep away the insects and a jacket to keep out the rain. None of these things could be found along the way. Morgan made his decision and began the journey.

While much of the Chagres River has been assimilated into the Panama Canal, in Morgan's time it twisted and turned to such a degree that it was almost three times longer than the distance directly between Chagres and Venta de Cruz. Branches of the river would fork off in different directions, sometimes almost as wide as the river itself, making it difficult for the buccaneers to know the right way to go. If it hadn't been for their guides the expedition would have been lost.

On day one of the journey, Esquemeling tells us they travelled 6 leagues and arrived at a place called De Los Bracos, where Morgan sent the men ashore 'to sleep and stretch their limbs, being almost crippled with lying too much crowded in the boats.' After resting Morgan ordered the men to go to the plantations in the area to look for food as well as for the enemy. He needed to know as much as he could about the enemy's strength. But the buccaneers found no food and no enemy. The Spanish had fled and taken everything with them. As hunger pains began to stab, that night the men slept restlessly.

On the following morning they again began rowing downriver. The buccaneers had two kinds of vessels for this expedition. There were the larger river vessels with single masts, sails and oars, which were designed for carrying cargo, and large canoes or boats, which had to be rowed.[3]

As the day wore on, the going became more difficult. The river became shallower and was littered with tree trunks and branches that had washed down from the hills during the rainy season. The buccaneers pulled out the trunks that blocked their way and hacked at the branches that were causing the river to bottle up or were overhanging to such a degree that they made visibility almost impossible. Progress was also hampered by sudden torrential rain squalls, which soaked the buccaneers completely in a matter of minutes and then departed as quickly as they'd arrived, leaving a scorching sun blazing in their wake.

By evening they arrived at the village of Cruz de Juan Gallego, where, Esquemeling tells us, they 'were compelled to leave their boats and canoes, the river being very dry for want of rain, and many trees having fallen into it.'[4]

Turning to the guides, Morgan wanted to know if the way ahead was going to be as difficult as the journey to reach this village had been. The guides told him that in '2 leagues' the jungle thinned along the riverbanks, making the overland journey easier. Morgan decided they would spend the night in the village, which was also empty of provisions and enemy. Realizing he would need the boats for his return journey, he ordered that 160 men remain behind to guard them in case the Spanish should decide to attack and cut off his escape route.

To these, Captain Morgan gave order, under great penalties, that no man, on any pretext whatever, should dare to leave the boats, and go ashore; fearing lest they should be surprised by an ambuscade of Spaniards in the neighbouring woods, which appeared so thick as to seem almost impenetrable.[5]

On the morning of the third day, the buccaneers, minus the 160 men left behind with the boats, began to hack their way through the jungle, continuing their journey towards Panama. The boats they'd left behind were the larger vessels, which were unable to go any further. The canoes were now carried overland by the men who were not hacking away at the jungle. In the intense, humid heat it was hard going, especially as hunger pains continued to gnaw at their stomachs.

The way became so difficult that Morgan 'thought it more convenient to transport some of the men in canoes (though with great labour) to a place further up the river to a place called Cedro Bueno,' wrote Esquemeling. The canoes went back into the water and the slow process of moving up the difficult river began again. Not all the men were transported at once and the canoes had to come back for the rest so that 'about night they got altogether in the said place.' At Cedro Bueno the buccaneers hoped to find Spaniards and Indians with food but instead they found nothing. There were no Indians, no Spanish and, most of all, no food.[6]

Day four and the buccaneers were still hungry. At this point, tired of lifting the canoes and carrying them through the stifling jungle to skirt shallows in the river and to then put them in again time after time, the buccaneers wanted to cut their way through the jungle and leave the canoes behind. Realizing that morale was low Morgan agreed but instead split the force, with most of the buccaneers being led overland by one of the guides while the rest, led by another guide who, according to Esquemeling, 'always went before them, to discover, on both sides the river, the ambuscades. These had also spies, who were very dexterous to give notice of all accidents, or of the arrival of the pirates, six hours, at least, before they came.'[7]

What of the Spanish during this? Don Juan had chosen Francisco Gonzalez Salado to create a defence between Chagres and Venta de Cruz to try to bottle up the buccaneers in the jungle rather than fight them on the plains before Panama. To do this, four ambushes (stockades, according to Stephen Talty) had been built and Salado had chosen 400 men to man them. The idea was to pick off the buccaneers as they rowed up the river to the point where so many would be lost that the invasion would fail and the buccaneers would be forced into a retreating battle. But these stockades did not have artillery; the men were armed as lightly as the buccaneers.

In addition to this were the Indian guerrillas, some of whom had been languishing in Panama's jails. Three Indian captains offered Don Juan a proposal. Let them out of prison, give them men and arms to attack the buccaneers and, if they succeeded in stopping the invasion, the charges would be dropped. If not, they would die. It was a simple proposition and one that appealed to Don Juan. He had nothing to lose and accepted the proposal. The three Indian leaders set off into the jungle with 150 men to attack the buccaneers.[8]

According to Stephen Talty in his book *Empire of Blue Water*, the Spanish had been manning the first ambush and had moved into the woods just before the buccaneers arrived at De Los Bracos on the first day. Indeed, he states that Spanish sharpshooters, hiding in the woods, had the buccaneers in range of their muskets. Yet they did not open fire.

We can speculate on why they didn't start firing. For the most part, Salado had been expecting a force of around 400 buccaneers, the same number that had attacked San Lorenzo. Remember that some Spanish soldiers had deserted their gun positions at the fort and headed for Panama with the news of the arrival of the buccaneers. But this was Bradley's force and was around 400 men. The Spanish, who arrived breathlessly in Panama with news of the invasion force, would only know that there were around 400 men. As a result the Spanish and Indians that manned the ambushes would have been overwhelmed by a force nearly four times larger than what they expected. Once the buccaneers opened fire they would have had their range and position and the ambushers would not have survived.

But there was also another reason, as Talty points out. These buccaneers were not here to take land and occupy it. They were essentially intent on robbing the Spanish and then departing. They were not going to enslave the population; they were not going to force people to live a certain way. They would simply arrive, rob and pillage, and then leave. The settlers – Indians, Spanish soldiers and their families – were not fighting for their freedom so 'if you could hide from the buccaneers, you could live another day, and every soldier and militia member knew that.'[9]

Back in Panama, Don Juan was disgusted that his forces did not put up a fight. This meant that the closer the buccaneers came, the more likely he would have to send out forces to meet them on the plains in front of the city.

Meanwhile, the buccaneers marched on and around noon on the fourth day the guide of the canoes spotted an ambush near 'a post called Torna Cavallos'. They stormed ashore to find the ambush so recently deserted and all provisions taken except 'a few leathern bags, all empty, and a few crumbs of bread scattered on the ground where they [the Spanish] had eaten. Being angry at this they [the buccaneers] pulled down a few little huts which the Spaniards had made, and fell to eating the leathern bags, to ally the ferment of their stomachs, which was now so sharp as to gnaw their very bowels.'

So hungry were the men that Esquemeling tells us they made a banquet of these leather bags. To make them edible they sliced them into strips, which they beat between two stones and then rubbed, 'often dipping it in water, to make it supple and tender. Lastly they scraped off the hair, and broiled it. Being thus cooked, they cut it into small morsels, and ate it, helping it down with frequent gulps of water, which, by good fortune, they had at hand.'[10]

Having had their feast, they continued on their march and by evening arrived at Torna Munni, where the Spanish had made another ambush. Like every village, settlement and post they'd come across so far the enemy was nowhere to be seen and there was no food, 'the Spaniards having been so provident, as not to leave anywhere the least crumb of sustenance.'

On day five they arrived at Barbacoa but it too was, like all the other places, deserted and free of any provisions left by the retreating Spanish. Not far from the settlement were plantations, which the buccaneers searched, but 'could not find any person, animal, or other thing, to relieve their extreme hunger. Finally, having ranged about, and searched a long time, they found a grot, which seemed to be but lately hewn out of a rock, where were two sacks of meal, wheat and like things, with two great jars of wine and certain fruits called plantanoes.' Knowing his men were badly off and desperate for food, Morgan ordered it to be shared out to those that were most desperate, the ones that now needed to be carried in canoes because they were too weak to walk.[11]

With those small provisions having been consumed the sixth day saw the men eating 'leaves of trees and green herbs or grass such as they could pick, for such was the miserable condition they were in,' writes Esquemeling. Around noon they arrived at a plantation and found a barn filled with maize. Breaking down the doors the men fell onto the grain, eating it dry 'as much as they could devour; then they distributed a great quantity, giving every man a good allowance.' They continued on, now sustained with maize, until they reached the tiny settlement of Santa Cruz, where they made camp for the night. Here, Morgan began to hear just how unhappy some of his men were. 'Great murmurings were made at Captain Morgan, and his conduct; some being desirous to return home, while others would rather die there than go back a step from that undertaking: others who had greater courage, laughed and joked at their discourses.'[12]

Nevertheless, their sleep was fitful and the following morning, the men checked and cleaned their weapons, discharging them to ensure that the powder and the match were dry and all the muskets and pistols were working.

The seventh day and the buccaneers reached Venta de Cruz. In the distance they could see smoke rising from the town, which they assumed came from the chimneys. This meant people, and the smoke meant people cooking. Esquemeling tells us this gave the buccaneers 'great joy and the hopes of finding people and plenty of good cheer. Thus they went on as fast as they could, encouraging one another.'

Over difficult ground the buccaneers made record time and arrived, sweating and panting from the stifling heat in the town, expecting to find people and food. Instead they found the place deserted, no Spanish, no militia, no Indians, no sign of any food. 'Nothing but fire, for the Spaniards, before their departure, had everyone set fire to his own house, except the king's storehouses and stables.'[13]

However, in the stables they found a large sack, full of bread, and sixteen jars of Peruvian wine, which they immediately began to consume. Very quickly the men began to fall ill, which Morgan realized was very likely due to their 'want of sustenance and the manifold sorts of trash they had eaten'. Instead of saying this to his men, Morgan told them the wine was likely poisoned and had what remained thrown away. He decided to wait for the sickness to pass and so they made camp in Venta de Cruz until the following morning.

Morgan and his men were still only half way. The rest of the journey – another 26 miles – would have to be on land as the Chagres River now wound its way north–east, away from Panama. The canoes had to stay at Venta de Cruz.

How different would this journey have been if Morgan had allowed his army to carry provisions? If he'd ordered that a canoe filled with provisions be taken on the expedition would he have arrived in Venta de Cruz any earlier? Would the men have been in better health and have had the strength to cut through the jungle faster than they did?

There is a fair degree of speculation around this subject but Morgan could not have known that the Spanish would desert each ambush and take every morsel of food with them. He could not have known they would burn their villages and ambushes to ensure the buccaneers could get no provisions at all. This was Don Juan's strategy – to deny the enemy any form of sustenance so that by the time his forces met the buccaneers, they would be too weak to fight.

Up until this point, Morgan and his army had yet to face the Spanish or the Indians. Now that the rest of the journey to Panama was to be over land, the situation was about to change.

Chapter 19

The Flames of Panama

The enemy had basely quitted the first entrenchment and set all on fire, as they did all the rest, without striking a stroke. Was forced there to leave his ships and boats with 200 men to guard them, under command of Captain Robert Delander, and betook themselves to the wild woods. Routed the enemy by the forlorn commanded by Captain Thomas Rogers 2 miles from Venta Cruse, where they arrived on 15th. It is a very fine village where they land and embark all goods for Panama, but they found it as the rest all on fire and the enemy fled.[1]

Venta de Cruz burned overnight while the buccaneers made their camp there, away from the flames, to rest and recuperate from the wine and food they'd consumed the day before.

By morning, Morgan had them up and ready to continue the march. This leg of the journey would be easier. From Venta de Cruz to Panama was a track well-used by mule trains loaded with goods moving back and forth between the towns. From Venta de Cruz the cargo carried by the mules would be transported up the Chagres River to the other side of the isthmus at Chagres for onward transportation. At Venta de Cruz Morgan sent the canoes back upriver to the boats, except for one, which Esquemeling tells us 'he hid, that it might serve to carry intelligence.'

In Panama, Don Juan was getting both anxious and rapidly infuriated. Incoming reports showed that the men he had sent to ambush the buccaneers had fled rather than followed his expectations to stand and fight. He was disgusted with their behaviour and hoped that on the trek from Venta de Cruz, which was now entirely overland, the ambushes that he'd ordered to be set up would do the job. He did not want to fight the buccaneers on the vast savannah plains before Panama.

The city itself had seen better days. About 7,000 people lived in Panama, which had a shallow anchorage being rapidly choked with silt with each incoming tide. Oddly enough, 6 miles to the west, and on the site of present-day Panama, was a town that had a much better, deeper harbour – Perico.

Panama had been laid out with precision in a grid-like pattern. Yet only a few of the houses or civic buildings had been built of stone; the rest were built of wood and timber. Those buildings made of stone included a few private houses owned by the richest people (mostly merchants of the city), the courthouse, the city council's headquarters and the cathedral.[2]

For fifty years, Pope tells us, the city had stagnated but it was still a very rich place. It was the gateway for gold, silver and jewels coming in from the East and although its harbour was no good for any vessel of more than 60 tons, the city had its own version of nobility that revolved around its governor. The houses of the richer merchants that were not built of stone had been built of wood, but in an ornate and lavish style that befitted their owner's wealth. The churches were rich, filled with gold and silver ornaments and religious paraphernalia. Commercially, the largest ships coming up from the south would anchor at Perico and unload their gold and silver into smaller sloops, which would then take this precious cargo up to Panama.

For decades the population of Panama, especially the rich merchants and wealthy nobility of the city, had been safe from any attack, secure in the knowledge that the jungle – filled with poisonous animals, insects and tropical diseases, and so thick that it was almost impossible to get through – had kept them all safe. So when the news arrived that Morgan had attacked Portobello and then Maracaibo, a wave of shock went through the complacent populace. It was reported that the buccaneers were at the mouth of the Chagres River and had taken San Lorenzo. Further reports revealed that a large body of buccaneers was marching on Panama and all the ambushes that had been set up to stop them had failed because those manning them had fled into the jungle. Then came the news that Venta de Cruz had been captured by the buccaneers and put to the flame by the retreating Spaniards. Imagine the fear that tore through the town when they heard that Morgan was only days away. Don Juan reported that once people had heard of the fall of Chagres Castle and San Lorenzo, many spent their days attending mass in the churches and cathedral, where they offered their jewels and rings for deliverance from the English buccaneers.[3]

But that was not Don Juan's only problem. Morgan and his army encountered little resistance from the Spanish. Don Juan had sent men to man the ambuscades to try to stop the advancing English, but he explains in a letter – written after the battle and intercepted on its way to Spain – that they did no such thing:

Having been a day in Guibal and my Men pretty well refreshed, I received a letter from a Negro Captain, called Frado, in which he assured me that the Enemy marched against us with a thousand strong; which News so much discouraged my Men, that they ceased not to importune and press me to return to the Town, protesting they could defend themselves in it to the last. But it being impossible then to fortify it, it having many entrances and the Houses all built of Wood; so soon as the Enemy would once make a breach, we would quickly be exposed to their fury, and forced miserably to think for ourselves; which for reasons I consented not to them. Next morning at break of day, I found myself with not above one third of my Men, the rest having deserted me so that I was forced to return back to the City to chide them to Fight there at Panama, there being no other remedy.[4]

On the morning of the eighth day, Morgan began the march again, sending a party of 200 men ahead to scout out the Spanish and look for ambushes. The countryside they now marched through was a combination of woods, plains and gorges with high mountain peaks, which would bring them onto the wide savannah that lay before the city of Panama.

The well-trodden mule path they were using was narrow, as one of the buccaneers wrote:

The sixteenth we marched on forwards, the Enemy, galling us from their Ambuscades, and by small Parties and we still beating them for a League together; although they had all the advantage of us that could be, by reason of the Ways being so narrow that we could seldom march above four abreast, and was for the most part too deep and hollow.[5]

After about ten hours the buccaneers arrived at a narrow gorge and proceeded to pass through it when, suddenly, 'three or four thousand arrows were shot at them, they not perceiving whence they came, or who shot at them, though they presumed it was from a high rocky mountain.'[6] The buccaneers dived for cover, quickly loaded their muskets and waited for another barrage of arrows. They searched the rocky ledges on both sides of the gorge for any sign of movement but all was quiet. Morgan, impatient to get going, ordered the march to continue when no additional barrage of arrows was forthcoming.

A few hours later, the buccaneers entered a wooded area and saw a group of Indians running away 'to take the advantage of another post, thence to observe their march,' wrote Esquemeling. However, one group of Indians remained behind to stand and fight, which Esquemeling says they did with great courage until their captain was mortally wounded. Even while wounded he tried to attack the buccaneers with his javelin but was shot and killed before he could do any damage.

Their movement along the trail was now easier as the wood gave way to what Esquemeling describes as 'a large champaign, open and full of fine meadows'.

In the distance they could see some Indians on top of a mountain overlooking a pass that the buccaneers needed to move through to continue their march. 'They sent fifty men, the nimblest they had, to try to catch any of them, and force them to discover their companions; but all in vain; for they escaped by their nimbleness and presently showed themselves in another place.'[7]

> About Noon we got safely to this Savannah or open Fields, with the loss of but three men killed outright, and six or seven wounded; and of the Enemy, twenty killed, and one Captain, besides many wounded. About 3 Miles further we took up our Quarters, to refresh our Men, and thank God for the successful service of that day.[8]

The following day, the 17th, Morgan and his army arrived at 'that desired and long wished-for sight, the South Sea, and not far distant from us a goodly parcel of Cattle and Horses feeding. Whereupon our Admiral commanded a general halt to be made; and gave our Men leave to Kill Horses and Beeves enough to feast us all.'[9]

Throughout the morning, the men slaughtered the animals they needed while others gathered as much wood as they could and made fires for roasting the meat. 'Cutting the flesh into convenient pieces, or gobbets, they threw them into the fire, and half carbonaded or roasted, they devoured them, with incredible haste and appetite; such was their hunger, as they more resembled cannibals than Europeans.'[10]

Finally, with their hunger satiated, Morgan ordered the march to continue and around five in the afternoon 'came within sight of the Enemy, where he was drawn up in Battalia, with 2,100 Foot, and 600 Horse; but finding the day far spent, the Admiral thought it not fit to engage, but took up quarters within a mile of them, where we lay very quiet; not being so much alarmed.'[11]

Indeed, Esquemeling states that the men, having come within sight of the enemy and able to see the highest steeple in Panama from their position, showed 'signs of extreme joy, casting up their hats into the air, leaping and shouting, just as if they had already obtained the victory, and accomplished their designs.'[12]

They sounded trumpets and beat every drum they had to celebrate their arrival on the plain that stretched towards Panama and the South Sea, which they could see from their viewpoint. After this outburst the men settled down to a quiet night in their camp, waiting impatiently for the next day so they could attack the Spanish and enter the town of Panama. What thoughts were going through the minds of the buccaneers at this time, no one will ever know.

But we can likely speculate that some of them would have been thinking of the riches they would find in Panama.

As they slept the Spanish fired their largest cannon from gun positions in the city, but the shot fell short of the buccaneers' camp and the guns soon fell silent. Later, fifty Spanish cavalry rode out of the city, beating drums and sounding their trumpets, and stopped short, out of musket range. The Spanish soon returned to the city but kept back 'seven or eight horsemen, who hovered thereabouts to watch their motions.'[13]

This commotion and the remaining Spanish do not seem to have bothered the buccaneers at all. Indeed, Esquemeling tells us that rather than fearing any blockades that the Spanish might erect around them, 'as soon as they had placed sentinels about their camp, opened their satchels, and, without any napkins or plates, fell to eating, very heartily, the pieces of bulls' and horses' flesh which they had reserved since noon. This done, they laid themselves down to sleep on the grass, with great repose and satisfaction, expecting only, with impatience, the dawning of the next day.'[14]

At the same time, Don Juan's camp was 3 miles from Panama on the plain at Guibal. 'In this conjuncture,' he wrote, 'having had the misfortune to have been lately Blooded three times for an Erysipelas, I had in my right Leg, I was forced to rise out of my Bed, and march to Guibal with the rest of the People, which I had raised [in] Panama; where I laid until I understood the exact course of the English enemies' march.'

But fortune was not on Don Juan's side. On the night of the 17th, he received a report from a Negro captain that upwards of 2,000 buccaneers were marching on Panama and suddenly his officers began to beg him to march back to the city, which, they declared, they would defend to every last drop of blood. But so far most of the men Don Juan had around him, many who had made protestations of defending Panama to the death, had fled without firing a shot at the enemy so he knew he could not trust his officers. His mind was made up; the Spanish forces would stay where they were, the English would be stopped at Guibal. He went to bed, his leg throbbing, tired from the difficulties and challenges he'd faced during the day.

However, in the morning everything had changed, for Don Juan discovered that almost two-thirds of his men had deserted, which left him no choice but to march back to Panama.

In the meantime, Morgan had roused his men early fearing a surprise attack from the Spanish camp that was now deserted. When no attack came the buccaneers had breakfast, which consisted of the beef they still had from the day before and some fresh meat from cattle they slaughtered that morning.

As they feasted on large steaks, Don Juan was in Panama desperate to raise an army.

> I arrived on Saturday night at Panama and Sunday morning went to the great Church, where having received the Holy Communion before our Blessed Lady of Immaculate Conception, with great Devotion, I went to the principal guard and to all that were present I expressed myself to this effect. 'That all those who were True Catholics, Defenders of the Faith and Devotos [*sic*] of our Lady of Pure and Immaculate Conception, should follow my person being that same day at four a Clock [*sic*] in the afternoon resolved to march out to seek the enemy and with this caution that he that should refused to do it, should be held for infamous and a coward, basely slighting so precise an obligation.
>
> All proffered me their assistance except those that had slunk from me at Guibal; And when I had drawn them up in order, I carried the chief of them to the great Church, where in the presence of our Lady of Pure and Immaculate Conception, I made an Oath to die in her Defence; And I gave her a diamond Ring of the Value of 40,000 pieces of Eight in token of Compliance with my word and heartily invoked her aide And all present made the same Oath with much fervour.
>
> The Images of the Pure and Immaculate Conception ever since the day of the Fight at Chagres Castle, had been carried in general Procession attended by the Religious, and Fraternity of the cathedral of St Francis, that of the Nuns of our Lady of the Rosario those of San Domingo and those of the Mercedes together with all the Saints and Patrons of the Religious. And always the most Holy Sacrament in all Churches uncovered and exposed to public view. Masses were continually said for my happy success. I parted with all my Jewels and Relics collected in my Pilgrimage, presenting them to the aforesaid Images, Saints and Patrons.[15]

It was now Sunday morning of 19 January and as the buccaneers feasted on their stakes Don Juan was in the market place exhorting as many men as he could to come out and face the enemy. He wrote that after gathering his force he marched for about a mile out of Panama, 'having with me three Field pieces covered with leather and charged. And from that place I ordered another Party with two other Guns, of the Men which came from the River, being above 300, to advance towards the Enemy, which neither did any good.'

That he had a low opinion of his men can be seen in his account when he talks about the composition of his army. It was made up of:

> two sorts, Various Military Men, and faint-hearted Cowards, many of them having all their Estates, or pay due to them, left the Castle of Chagres and

Puerto Belo and a great part of these Men were Negroes, Mulattos and Indians
to the number of about 1,200, besides about 300 more belonging to the Asiento.
Our Fire Arms were few and bad, in comparison of those the Enemy brought;
For ours were Carbines, arquebuses and Fowling pieces, but few Muskets for
they had likewise been left in Puerto Belo and Chagres.[16]

At the buccaneers' camp, having finished breakfast Morgan formed up his men
and inspected them. He gave them a rousing speech to boost their confidence
in the undertaking at hand and then ordered that the march continue on to
Panama. First they headed for the Spanish camp, which was deserted, and
then they set off for Panama itself.

In his report to Modyford, Morgan described the breakdown of his army.
He had carefully thought out his battle plan and formed his men into a tertia
with 'the vanguard led by Lieutenant Colonel Lawrence Prince and Major
John Morris, in number 300, the main body 600, the right wing led by himself,
the left by Colonel Edward Collier, and the rear guard of 300 commanded by
Colonel Bledry Morgan.'[17] Bledry Morgan had joined Morgan in Providence
after bringing a message from Modyford to him. He was no relation to Henry
Morgan, according to Pope.

Don Juan had reason to be a little more jovial than he had been earlier,
for when he weighed up his forces against those of the buccaneers he could
see the superiority. He had two squadrons of cavalry, he had artillery and, in
addition to the infantry, he had two great herds of cattle driven by fifty keepers
– one on his right, the other on his left. Both herds were to be driven into
the buccaneers to completely disorientate them. Also on his right flank he'd
placed one squadron of his cavalry, while on the left was another, commanded
by Don Fransisco de Haro, a man who we will soon see played a pivotal role
in the battle.

Don Juan had also chosen a good place to make his stand. There was a
ravine to his right and beyond that a hill that would act as a guard, and this
would force the buccaneers to come at him from the centre and the left flank.
The right wing of his army he had placed under the command of Don Juan
Portando Bergueno, while the left wing he'd put Don Alonso de Alcandete in
command and he himself would command the centre, behind the guns. So
despite the desertions that had taken place over the preceding days he was
quietly confident that this time all would be well. After all, they were fighting
for the city, for their homes, so they should not desert as the others had done.

Morgan had started his march and was well on his way towards Panama. By
early afternoon they crested a low hill and saw the Spanish waiting for them,
drawn up before the city. Morgan spotted the hill, which for him would have

been on his left, and the ravine beyond it. Morgan realized that Don Juan was expecting the hill and ravine to protect his right flank but instead, Morgan could see the ravine was also a barrier for Don Juan to send reinforcements to Don Bergueno. This meant that the Spanish right flank was the weakest point. Morgan barked out his orders:

> That our officers should wheel our Body of the left, and endeavour to gain a Hill which was hard by, and which if once gained, we should then force the enemy to engage, to their great disadvantage; because he could not be able to bring out of his great Body, and more Men to fight at a time, than we should out of our small and that we should likewise have the advantage, both of the Wind and the Sun.[18]

So they began to march again, heading towards the Spanish right flank.

Don Juan had given orders that no one was to move without his express command. His plan for attacking the buccaneers was 'that coming within shot, the three first Ranks should Fire on their Knees, and after this charge they should give place to the rest to come up and Fire, and that although they should chance to see any fall Dead or Wounded, they should not quit their stations but to the last extremity observe these orders.'[19]

The buccaneer vanguard under Prince was rapidly approaching the Spanish right flank and came under cannon fire as they did. Collier's wing was on the march to take the hill. As they approached, Francisco de Haro suddenly ordered his squadron of cavalry to charge directly towards the buccaneer vanguard, 'so furiously that he could not be stopped till he lost his life; upon which the Horse wheeled off and the Foot advanced, but met with such a warm welcome and were pursued so close that the enemies' retreat came to plain running.'[20]

Upon seeing Haro and the rest of his cavalry tearing towards them, Prince ordered the men to 'double our Ranks to the Right, and close the Files to the Right and left inward, to the close Order; But their jittery Commander could not stop his career till he dropped, losing his life in the Front Rank of our Vanguard.'[21]

The square that Prince had his men form enabled them to protect themselves from the advancing cavalry as well as concentrate their firepower. The first volley of shot not only cut down Haro himself but more than half of his squadron. The rest just wheeled away in complete disorder and, as Morgan states, simply ran away.[22]

The Spanish Infantry on the right wing now came marching in, expecting to find the buccaneers in complete disarray from the cavalry attack. Instead they found the buccaneers waiting for them.

Their Foot advanced to try their Fortunes, but they proved as unsuccessful as their fellows; for we being ready, with our main Body to receive them, with our first Volley gave them such a warm welcome, and pursued our work in hand, with that vigour and briskness, that our friends the Spaniards thought it safest to retreat.[23]

The hill that Morgan had sent Collier to capture had been taken without much of a fight from the Spanish. From this vantage point Collier could see that Morgan was now engaging the Spanish left wing and he could see the vanguard was engaging the Spanish right wing infantry, so he ordered his men to swing around and head down the hill in support of Prince's vanguard, 'which the Foot seeing, and that they, could not possibly prevail, they discharged the shot they had in their muskets, and throwing them down, fled away, every one as he could.'[24] The buccaneers pursued them as most headed for the city, while others headed for anywhere that they could hide and these men were, when discovered by the buccaneers, 'instantly killed without any quarter', according to Esquemeling.

Don Juan now ordered that the herds of cattle be driven into the buccaneers:

just before which, they practised such a stratagem as hath seldom been heard. For while the Foot had engaged us in the Front and the Flanks they had contrived to force in, two great Droves of Oxen, of above a thousand in each, into the Right and Left Angles of our Rear, with intention to break and disorder us: Which design might probably have taken effect, had not our prudent Admiral, with great pretence of mind, spoiled their project, giving order to a small Party to fire at the Drivers, and not at the Cattle, which put the rest into so great a fear, that the Oxen were soon forced back withal. So that this stratagem being, thus defeated, they were in so great consternation, that happy was he that could get first into the City.[25]

Morgan's strategy of shooting the keepers so frightened the animals that instead of running as they should have done, many of them turned back and trampled the retreating Spanish.

The battle was over. It had lasted only a few hours and most of the Spanish were either dead, wounded or had fled towards the city or into the countryside. Whether or not they were killed outright by the pursuing buccaneers is something that appears only in Esquemeling's text. It is well to remember here that he did not like Morgan and that he probably embellished his account of the battle in order to please his publisher.

Don Juan had been let down again. In every part of the defence of Panama the president had been let down by the men he'd gathered to defend the city. In his account of the battle he states again how the men deserted:

> I was at this time in the Right Wing of the Vanguard, watching the Enemies' motion, which was hasty, by the Foot of a Hill, in a narrow place about three musket shot of the left wing of our army. When on a sudden I heard a loud clamour, crying: 'Fall on, Fall on! For they fly!' At which Don Alonso de Alcandete was not able to keep them in their Ranks nor stop them from running away, though he cut them with his Sword, but they all fell into disorder. And I well knowing the Fatality of this gave command that they should drive up the Herds of Cattle, and charge with the Horse.
>
> So putting myself at the Head of the Squadron on the Right Wing saying 'Come along Boys! There is no other remedy now but to conquer or die! Follow me!' I went directly to the enemy, and hardly did our Men see some fall dead and others wounded, but they turned their backs and fled, leaving me there with only one Negro and one servant that followed me.
>
> Yet I went forward, to comply with my word to the Virgin, which was to Die in her Defence, receiving a shot in a staff which I carried in my Hand upright close to my cheek. At which moment came up to me a priest of the Great Church called Juan de Dios (who was wont to say Mass in my House) beseeching me to retire and save myself, whom I twice sharply reprehended, but the third time he persisted, telling me that it was mere desperation to Die 'O that manner, and not like a Christian. With that I retired, it being a miracle of the Virgin to bring me off safe among so many thousand Bullets.[26]

In the end he too had to retreat and head back into the city, with the buccaneers hot on his heels. How he must have felt at this point is only speculation but it is highly likely that he was angry and disgusted with the conduct of the men who had promised they would fight and then had run away at the first sound of gunfire. Once in the city Don Juan tried again to rouse people to mount a defence.

> I endeavoured with all my industry to persuade the Soldiers to engage the Enemy but it was impossible so that nothing hindering them, they entered the City, to which the Slave and Owners of the Houses had put Fire, and being all of Boards and Timber, it was most of it quickly burnt, except the Audiencia, the Governor's House, the convent of the Mercedes San Joseph, the suburbs of Malambo and Pier de Vidas, at which they say, the Enemy fretted very much for being disappointed of their Plunder and because they had brought with them

an English man, whom they called The Prince, with intent there to Crown him King of the Terra Firma.[27]

Unlike Don Juan, Morgan could enter the city with a certain amount of triumph. However, he still met with resistance, as he described in his report to Modyford:

> In the city they had 200 fresh men, two forts, all the streets barricaded, and great guns in every street, which in all amounted to thirty-two brass guns, but instead of fighting commanded it to be fired, and blew up the chief fort, which was done in such haste that forty of their own soldiers were blown up. In the market place some resistance was made, but at three o'clock they had quiet possession of the city, although on fire, with no more loss in this day's work than five killed and ten wounded, and of the enemy about 400. They endeavoured to put out the fire, but in vain, for all was consumed by twelve at night, but two churches and 300 houses in the suburbs.[28]

At this point we start to see there is a question about who really started the fire. Morgan states in his report that the Viceroy (Don Juan) ordered it while Don Juan states quite clearly that the slaves and owners set their own houses on fire. Esquemeling's account is entirely different. He claims that around noon that day, 'Morgan caused fire privately to be set to several great edifices of the city, nobody knowing who were the authors thereof, much less on what motives Captain Morgan did it, which are unknown to this day.'[29]

There would have been great confusion taking place at this time. The Spanish were fighting a rearguard action against the advancing buccaneers; the people of the city were very likely in a panic. There would have been loud gunfire from muskets and cannon. However, the action that Esquemeling describes is unlikely because it goes against the previous actions of Morgan that we have seen in his earlier expeditions. In both Maracaibo and Puerto Bello, he threatened to set fire to the whole town but only if a ransom was not paid for not setting fire to it. In this case, keeping Panama as it was would have been one of the only bargaining chips he had left if he'd needed it. It was not in Morgan's character to be this reckless or this vindictive for no apparent reason.

Indeed, both Don Juan and Morgan state that the fire was started by the Spanish, as does the following account from another man who was there, Captain Bartholomew Sharp:

And now were we forced to put all Hands to work for the quenching the Fire of our Enemies' Houses, which they themselves had kindled to disappoint us of the Plunder; but all our labour was in vain, for by twelve a clock [*sic*] at Night, all the whole City was burnt, except a part of the Suburbs, which with our great industry, we made a shift to save, being two Churches, and about 300 Houses.[30]

The likelihood is that Esquemeling's accusation against Morgan was false, either made up by him because of his dislike for Morgan or demanded by his publishers to create controversy and discredit Morgan.

Another reason why the idea of Morgan starting the fire himself is preposterous is simply because the houses would have contained many valuables, even though the inhabitants would have spirited most of them away. There would have been ornaments, silver cutlery, furnishings – many of silk – and much more that the buccaneers could have taken and sold. To have started the fire himself meant no loot, and that just doesn't make sense.[31]

The buccaneers worked through the night to try to stop the fire from spreading. They used gunpowder to blow up buildings and create breaks in the path of the flames to stop them from spreading, but the wind fanned the sparks and sent them floating across the breaks to the buildings where they would eventually ignite the dry wood.

Thus was consumed the famous and ancient city of Panama, which is the greatest mart for silver and gold in the whole world, for it receives all the goods that come from Spain in the King's great fleet, and delivers all the gold and silver that comes from the mines of Peru and Potozi.[32]

With the city in ruins, the following morning the buccaneers began the slow search through the charred rubble for any valuables that might have been left behind and survived the fire. It was a very slow process. While some parties of buccaneers shifted the wreckage, others spread out across the land and sea. They captured prisoners and forced them to show them where their valuables were or pay ransom for their freedom. Some barques had been captured by the buccaneers in the harbour, which they used, as Don Juan stated in his report:

The English having thus got possession of the Relics of our Town, found a Bark in the Harbour although I had given order there should be none, yet had they not complied with my command, and when they would have set it on Fire, the Enemy came fast and put it out, and with it did us much damage, for they took three more with it, and made great havoc of all they found in the lands around, taking and bring from thence many Prisoners.[33]

The command of this ship Morgan handed over to Captain Searle, who quickly began to make it ready for sea. Once at sea he explored the islands that stretched almost diagonally down the coast. It was Searle who took the three barques to search the coast of Panama for small anchorages or hidden harbours where ships from the city could have hidden until it was safe to return. They searched the islands of Perico, Taboga, Toboguilla and Otoque for people from the city and anything that would point to wealth. Landing at Taboga Island, Pope tells us that they found a large quantity of wine and began drinking it, which was how they managed to miss a large ship that came into the island's harbour looking for fresh water. Searle managed to capture the small party from this ship and soon discovered that it was the *La Santísima Trinidad*, a ship that was filled with silver, jewels and gold from the churches in Panama, the government of Panama and the citizens who had shipped it out of the city for safekeeping, and now here it was right under Searle's nose. Unfortunately, his men were too drunk to do anything about it and the ship left quickly.[34]

The next day, having realized what they'd done, Searle ordered one of the barques to chase the ship, a galleon, but as Esquemeling states, it was in vain, 'the Spaniards who were on board having had intelligence of their own danger one or two days before, while the pirates were cruising so near them, whereupon they fled to places more remote and unknown.'[35]

All was not lost, however, as the buccaneers continued to cruise the islands and found several boats filled with valuable merchandise such as silks, cottons and so forth, which they brought back to Panama. They told Morgan the story of the galleon, which was confirmed by the many prisoners they'd taken while cruising the islands, and Morgan then ordered that Searle's barque and the three other ships he'd captured were to go out again and search for this galleon. They used Taboga as their main base and while they were out searching for this large ship they captured a ship from Peru with an unremarkable cargo of 'cloth, soap, sugar and biscuit', but it did have 20,000 pieces of eight, which the buccaneers took and brought back with them to Panama. They'd been gone for eight days.

Meanwhile, the slow excavation of the charred rubble of what was left of the city was beginning to bring in results. The buccaneers searched in wells and cisterns of rainwater where the Spanish had hastily hidden their valuables. Gradually the amount piled up. Not just gold, but jewels as well.

Esquemeling also tells us that Morgan had sent out a party of 150 men to Chagres Castle to tell them of the victory at Panama.

> Those he had left in the castle of Chagres had sent for two boats to cruise. These met with a Spanish ship, which they chased within sight of the castle. This being perceived by the pirates in the castle, they put forth Spanish colours, to deceive the ship that fled before the boats; and the poor Spaniards, thinking to take refuge under the castle were caught and made prisoners.[36]

The cargo was not one of riches, however, but of provisions, which was more important, for the buccaneers were in need of food. Hearing this, Morgan decided to stay longer and ordered more parties to go out into the outlying country and gather 'much riches and many prisoners'.

Finally, Morgan decided it was time to leave. Pope tells us that there had been some heavy rain while the buccaneers had been at Panama and the river was now open all the way from Chagres to Venta de Cruz, and the boats that Morgan had ordered to be left behind had made their way upriver to that town, where they now waited.

Esquemeling tells us that the buccaneers left Panama on 24 February 1671, while Pope states that it was the 14th.[37] Morgan states that the date he left Panama was the 14th and that they stopped in Venta de Cruz until the 24th. We can be reasonably sure that somewhere between the 14th and the 24th the buccaneers finally vacated the ruins of Panama.

> 14 February. Began their march to Venta Cruse with all their prisoners, where they stayed and refreshed till 24th, and on 26th came to Changraw, where the plunder (amounting to about 30,000 pounds) was divided and the castle fired and the guns spiked. 6 March. Began their voyage for Jamaica, where some are arrived and the rest daily expected. Had it from the prisoners that the reason there was no more wealth was because they had two months' notice, and laded two great ships of 350 and 700 tons with money, plate, gold, and jewels.[38]

So the buccaneers left Panama and returned the way they'd come. This time, however, they had with them 175 pack animals that Morgan had ordered be gathered up for carrying their loot back to Venta de Cruz, where it would be loaded onto boats. Esquemeling says that Morgan left from 'the place where the city of Panama stood; of the spoils whereof he carried with him 175 beasts of carriage, laden with silver, gold, and other precious things, beside about 600 prisoners, men, women, children and slaves.'[39]

Morgan wanted to ensure that he could get as much ransom for his prisoners as possible so he gave orders for the march to stop at Venta de Cruz for several days while the prisoners did their best to raise the ransom money. Again, we have only Esquemeling's word that Morgan at this point commanded the prisoners 'that within three days everyone should bring in their ransom, under penalty of being transported to Jamaica.' Some of the prisoners paid their ransom while some could not, and they remained prisoners. The march back to Chagres began again on 5 March and at small town between Venta de Cruz and Chagres, Morgan decided it was time to search everyone to ensure that no one had absconded with any of the loot. To do this he ordered all the buccaneers to muster and swear an oath that they had nothing hidden 'even not to the value of sixpence', wrote Esquemeling. Morgan knew that the buccaneers would not necessarily stick to their oath (as told to us by Esquemeling) and so ordered that everyone be searched.

He commanded everyone to be searched very strictly, both in their clothes and satchels and elsewhere. Yea, that his order might not be ill taken by his companions, he permitted himself to be searched, even to his very shoes.[40]

Morgan had about 1,500 men with him at this time for he had picked up the men who had been at Venta de Cruz with the boats, making it difficult indeed for him to cheat anyone, even under the scrutiny of so many pairs of eyes.

With that task out of the way they continued upriver to Chagres, where they arrived, according to Esquemeling, on 9 March. Here they divided all the booty that had been collected, which some say was as high as 400,000 pieces of eight, while other historians say it was closer to 140,000. Indeed, one buccaneer wrote that 'the party got but 101 per man in money and plate, besides negroes.'[41]

Finally, Morgan decided it was time to leave Chagres and he ordered the cannon of the castle to be carried onto the ships for use at Port Royal. The remaining prisoners were released and the castle was demolished, 'the edifices to be burnt, and as many other things ruined as could be done in a short time,' says Esquemeling.

It's at this point in the story of Morgan that Esquemeling's true dislike of the man comes to the fore because he accuses him of heaping great cruelty upon a beautiful Spanish woman who was married to a wealthy merchant, and he also accuses him of cheating his fellow buccaneers by loading up his ship with as much of the loot as he could carry and stealthily slipping away from Chagres Castle.

Esquemeling devotes several paragraphs to the way that Morgan treated this woman. He had her set apart from the rest of the prisoners in a room alone and gave her a female slave for company. He gave her food and drink from his own table, he chatted with her every day in Spanish until, Esquemeling states, 'he sent a message asking her to consent to her own dishonour, and afterwards made a similar demand directly, in person, giving her at the same time several precious jewels.' Once she refused, Morgan allegedly had all those kindnesses taken away, including her clothes, to the point that she was almost starving.

However, while Esquemeling was a surgeon, he was not the chief surgeon. Richard Browne was and he was likely in more of a position to observe Morgan's actions than Esquemeling ever was. Indeed, Browne stated that:

> the report from England is very high, and great deal worse than it was; what was in fight and heat of blood in pursuit of a flying enemy, I presume is pardonable; as to their women, I know or ever heard of anything offered beyond their wills; something I know was cruelly executed by Capt Collier in killing a friar in the field after quarter given; but for the Admiral, he was noble enough to the vanquished enemy.[42]

Then there is the question of whether Morgan cheated his men. It must be remembered that most of the buccaneers lived in Port Royal and if Morgan had cheated them they would come looking for him. He owned a plantation; he had a wife and cousins, nephews and nieces. Would he really put all of that in jeopardy for a few jewels and other trinkets?

First we need to consider that at the time at the Castle at Chagres there were upwards of 1,500 buccaneers so slipping away without being seen would have been very difficult for Morgan. Stephen Talty puts it even more succinctly when he states, 'The Admiral would have been taking his life in his hands; on the slightest evidence of double-dealing, his men would have slashed his throat.'

Esquemeling also states that the buccaneers tortured and committed other atrocities on the prisoners and people they'd found. Whether this is true or not is not backed up by other reports and, as we have seen, Browne, who would have been close by to treat wounded men, did not hear of such tortures.

One last allegation from Esquemeling is that there were a large number of men who wanted to leave Morgan and turn pirate to go cruising in the South Sea for rich Spanish galleons and raid towns up and down the coast. He states that Morgan put a stop to this by having all the masts of the boats in Panama cut down. There is no evidence outside of Esquemeling's account to support this.

One thing that most sources agree on is that Morgan left in a hurry, with only four ships, although the reason for this was not because he'd cheated the buccaneers but because he'd heard from two ships that had arrived at Chagres that the peace treaty between England and Spain had been signed and privateering commissions were not being handed out any more. Worse yet was that the buccaneers might now need to be punished for their actions against the Spanish.[43]

The impact of this information must not have been lost on Morgan and his captains. Port Royal had moved on and many of his captains decided that instead of returning as heroes to Port Royal, they would continue to cruise the coasts of Nicaragua and Honduras, attacking coastal vessels and raiding towns.

Morgan, on the other hand, had more to lose. He had his family, his plantation and his reputation in Port Royal, which all needed to be protected. While we can never know what Morgan was thinking it is highly probable he was realizing that his life as a privateer was over. He had a lot to protect and to do that he needed to set the record straight in Port Royal, and that meant getting home fast. It is for this reason, say Talty and Pope, that Morgan left Chagres so quickly.

The rest of the buccaneers dispersed in different directions. The French went to Tortuga and Esquemeling's ship sailed on to Costa Rica.

Perhaps it is fitting to end this account of the sack of Panama with a Spanish perspective from the governor of Panama, Don Juan Perez de Guzman, who with the city in ruins tried desperately to raise an army.

After this misfortune, I gave order to all the People I met, that they should wait for me at Nata for there I intended to form the Body of an Army once more to encounter the English. But when I came to that City I found not one Soul therein, for all were fled to the Mountains.

The same happened to me at the Town from whence I dispatched a Vessel to Peru with the sad News of our misfortune, as I had done by Land to Guatemala, Mexico and Puerto Belo.

And although I afterwards attempted several times to form an Army, yet I could not do any good of it because no Man would be persuaded to follow me. So that I remained utterly destitute of any Guard, till such time as the English marched back to the Castle of Chagres to make his Voyage for Jamaica.

This Sir has been a Challenge from Heaven, and the same might have happened to that great Captain Fernando de Cordova, as did to me if his Men had deserted him, for one Man alone can do little.[44]

Part II

The Politician

Chapter 20

Prisoner of the State

As Morgan sailed into the harbour at Port Royal he had no idea of the changes that were about to befall him. Nor did he realize that Panama would be his last expedition, although he may have had an inkling. Although Modyford was still in place as governor a new lieutenant governor, Thomas Lynch, had been appointed in London and by April 1671 he had not yet sailed for Jamaica.

The peace treaty that had been signed between England and Spain made matters worse. Modyford had not officially been told about it but he had heard about it through his son, Charles, who wrote to him from London.

The first that anyone in London was aware of the Panama expedition was in late February to early March when a newsletter was published that said Admiral Morgan had sailed in command of a fleet of thirty English and French ships with the express purpose of sacking Panama.[1]

Meanwhile, Port Royal once again went wild when Morgan arrived in the *Mayflower*, accompanied by the *Pearl*, the *Dolphin* and the *Mary*. These four ships carried about 500 buccaneers, less than two-thirds of the force that had attacked Panama. But for the merchants, brothels and tavern-keepers of Port Royal the arrival of these buccaneers was a godsend and they would soon be helping the men to spend their cut of the booty.

Almost from the moment he arrived, criticism and rumour were laid at Morgan's door. The French had accused him of cheating and these rumours spread like wildfire through Port Royal and Jamaica. His critics pointed to the fact that he'd lost the *Satisfaction*, that each of the buccaneers had received a low share of the booty and that the *La Santísima Trinidad* had been allowed to get away with all the riches of the city of Panama.

But hadn't he taken the men across the isthmus, down to the South Sea and attacked Panama? He'd done more than just attack the city; he'd occupied it for twenty-eight days and taken as much treasure out of it that had been left. The *La Santísima Trinidad* had escaped his clutches because his orders had not been carried out. The men had been too drunk on wine to recognize the ship and what it meant. The reason why each man's share was so low was because there were so many buccaneers on the expedition. Few people listened to the critics because Morgan had done what no one else had. In a little more than two years, he had brought into Port Royal almost £950,000 pieces of eight – £50,000 from the raid on Puerto del Príncipe, £250,000 from the attack on Portobello, another £250,000 from Maracaibo and Gibraltar, and £400,000 from Panama.[2]

Once he was reunited with his wife, Elizabeth, at their plantation, Lawrencefield, Morgan sat down to write his report.

In London, the recently married Sir Thomas Lynch sailed with his new wife for Jamaica just a few days after Morgan completed his report and handed it to Modyford. With Lynch came his instructions as the new lieutenant governor of Jamaica:

> Instructions for Sir Thomas Lynch, Lieut Governor of Jamaica. (1.) With these instructions he will receive His Majesty's Commission as Lieut Governor of Jamaica, a revocation of Sir Thos Modyford's Commission of 15 February 1664, and a letter to said Sir Thos (2.) To deliver to Sir Thos said letter and revocation, assemble the present Council and principal persons and officers, and publish said revocation together with his own commission.[3]

Not only was he to revoke Modyford's commission, he was to send him back home to London as a prisoner. He was also ordered to reign in the activities of the buccaneers and publish the articles of the treaty signed in Madrid within eight months of October 1670 after agreeing with the local Spanish governors on the day:

> for the better encouragement of all belonging to the privateer ships to come in, immediately after the publication of said peace to proclaim a general pardon to all that shall submit to His Majesty within reasonable time and betake themselves to planting or merchandising, of all offences committed from June 1660 to the said publication, and assure them that they shall enjoy all such goods as they shall be possessed of at the time of said publication, except the 10ths and 15ths, and that if they will plant they shall have 35 acres by the head; that if they will employ their ships in trade, they shall be admitted to trade in them with the same freedom as if they were English-built; and that if any will serve on His Majesty's ships of war, they shall be received into his service and pay.[4]

In addition, Lynch was to keep the council members as they were and send back the accounts of Thomas Modyford for perusal in London. He was to make laws and raise taxes in the same way they were done in England, according to English law, among many other instructions.

However, while Lynch was on his way to Jamaica, Modyford had still not heard officially about the treaty, even though he knew about it through his son, Charles, as well as from other sources. The first official notice he had of the signing of the peace treaty came from a letter written by the governor of Puerto Rico to Modyford that was dated 30 April. This letter essentially said that the treaty had been sent to all Spanish governors in the region who would then have to contact the governors of the English colonies to agree a suitable date for the simultaneous publication of the treaty. This letter now confirmed the anecdotal evidence that Modyford had received through his son about the signing of the peace treaty.

In May, Modyford wrote to the governor of San Dominigo in Hispaniola, stating that he had:

> received last night by Don Francisco Calderon His Excellency's despatch of the 6/16 current, with the Articles of Peace between the crowns of Great Britain and Spain, and his desire that the same be published by them both on the same day. Has not yet received any orders from his [Modyford's] master, but is in hourly expectation thereof, and if they come soon enough, will cause the treaty to be published on St John's Day as the Governor of Porto Rico desires. All his master's subjects under his command rejoice much in this peace, and will contend with the Spaniards in all points of civility and friendship.[5]

After reading Morgan's account and the letter from the governor of Puerto Rico, on the 7 June Modyford began drafting a report that outlined his reasons for giving the buccaneers commissions to attack the Spanish.

Entitled 'Considerations from Sir Thomas Modyford which moved him to give his consent for fitting the privateers of Jamaica against the Spaniard', the document went into great detail on the events leading up to Modyford providing commissions to the buccaneers:

1. The peaceable state they were under, having in May 1669 called in all commissions, and never intending to give more, till in July 1670 they were enforced by the Queen of Spain's Scaedula of 20 April 1669, commanding war against them, which arrived in June 1670.
2. The execution of this war by the violences of Rivera Pardal, who, after burning their houses, took two vessels, and would have taken all vessels from England.

3. The constant advices of more vessels preparing to come to him, 'every little success setting that easily heightened nation a tiptoes.'
4. His Majesty's instructions empowering the governor on extraordinary cases by the Council's advice to use extraordinary remedies.
5. The unanimous consent of the Council and their fear of the ruin of the country.
6. The complaints of the merchants, fishermen and sailors, fears of the planters, cries of the women and children, and the danger of the governor's person and reputation should he have denied to take arms on so general an importunity.
7. The certain increase of the enemy's courage and pride, 'if it were possible,' and the debasing of ours, 'which is the next to beating.'
8. The fatal consequences of the foregoing evils.
9. Lord Arlington's letter of 11 June 1670, which arrived in August, commanding him to keep the privateers in the posture that letter should find them in.
10. The commission to Morgan being solely to revenge these affronts and prevent more.
11. The commission to private captains being only to execute Morgan's orders, whereby it is evident nothing was in design but His Majesty's service.
12. And whereas it may be objected that the fleet might have been called in after the coast had been secured, and so the mischief at Panama prevented; it must be considered that, the privateers finding ships, arms, ammunition, and provisions on their own charge, would not have obeyed such orders, expecting 'as the late Lord General, that great master of war, adviseth, the soldier to look on the enemy as the surest pay.'[6]

On 25 June 1671, the lookouts at Fort Charles spotted two frigates heading for the harbour at Port Royal. Once it was realized that the frigates were flying British colours a runner was sent to notify Modyford.

This was a special occasion for it had been some time since an English frigate had arrived in Port Royal. Now it was doubly special, with the arrival of two of them – the *Assistance* and the *Welcome*. These two ships heralded the arrival of Sir Thomas Lynch, the new lieutenant governor, with a new set of instructions from the king, as we have already seen. Modyford, of course, knew nothing about the instructions.

Lynch had been away from Jamaica for several years. In addition to his instructions he brought with him his new wife and a painful attack of gout that would keep him bedridden for a number of days. He was only thirty-eight.

Once the ships had anchored in the harbour and the passengers disembarked, Lynch and his wife met with Modyford. Lynch showed Modyford his commission as the new lieutenant governor of Jamaica and also provided him with the official news of the signing of the peace treaty with Madrid and the instructions for publishing the treaty.

However, he did not tell Modyford that he was to replace him, nor did he tell him at that time that Modyford was to be arrested and taken back to London as a prisoner and imprisoned in the Tower of London. Since the death of old Colonel Edward Morgan, Modyford had been a governor without a lieutenant governor and now it appeared that Lynch was the new replacement. For the first few weeks this is how Lynch played his part. Since there was no official residence for a lieutenant governor Modyford invited Lynch and his wife to stay with him in his official governor's residence as his guests until a new house could either be built or found for the Lynches.

In the first seven days of his arrival Lynch was in bed for four of them, as he wrote in his first letter to Secretary of State Lord Arlington:

> Has kept his bed four out of the seven days he has been here, and now writes this on it. Was very sick all the way from Barbados, and such a fit of the gout has taken him as he never had before. But no time has been lost, for he must have a house and know how to get victuals, give commissions to officers, and appear at the head of the several regiments before he can embark him [Sir Thomas Modyford]. Feared nobody but this regiment, which made him divide it into two. Does not see but on a dispute he would have more adherents than Modyford, for people love novelty, are displeased about privateering, and the quantity of land given out. The truth is, 'there is not in him or any the least appearance of any disposition to resist the King's authority,' however, shall not till well established put him on board, nor is there any ship fitted or a farthing in the treasury to fit one, so thinks of putting him on board a good merchant's frigate that will sail about six weeks hence; or else to send the *Welcome*, which will save the King a great deal of money; she is an old vessel, and if taken in any distress of weather would be lost and all her men, but the *Assistance* with a catch would be sufficient to awe the privateers ...[7]

We can see that in this first letter to Arlington, Lynch was already working out a way to arrest Modyford and get him on board a vessel with as little fuss or public outcry as possible. He also made no bones about the fact that both Modyford and Morgan were disliked in London.

The rumours about how Morgan and his captains cheated the buccaneers who went with them on the Panama raid spread through Port Royal as more and more of the privateers returned with little in their pockets and began grumbling about their hardships. Lynch reported these rumours in his letter when he stated that 'this voyage has mightily lessened and humbled them, and they would take it for a great compliment to be severe with Morgan, whom they rail on horribly for starving, cheating, and deserting them.'

However, the first item of business for both Lynch and Modyford was to ensure the treaty was published by the Spanish governors in the West Indies on the date prescribed by the governor of Puerto Rico, so they decided to send the two frigates to Cartagena with the treaty and bring away any English prisoners. However, on the voyage out, Captain Hubbard, who was commanding the *Assistance*, died.

In the meantime, Surgeon Browne reported to Joseph Williamson:

> Sir Thos Lynch arrived about twelve days since, and was very well received by the old Governor and people: he has been much troubled with the gout; the old Governor visits him very often, and they have agreed to suffer ships to fetch logwood out of the Bay of Campeachy. Is informed there are about forty ships cutting logwood: certainly the Spaniards cannot suffer it, but may take some of them, which will occasion a new war. About six weeks since Spaniards landed from a small bark, burnt a house and carried a prisoner to Cuba. The *Assistance* frigate, and the *Welcome* are to go to Carthagena and Cuba with the articles of peace.

While both of those vessels were away, Morgan became ill with fever. As he lay on his sickbed the rumours about how he and Collier and the other captains had cheated the buccaneers grew. In late August, surgeon Browne entered the fray when he wrote to Williamson that:

> there have been very great complaints by the wronged seamen in Sir Thos Modyford's time against Admiral Morgan, Collier, and other commanders, but nothing could be done, but since Sir Thos Lynch's arrival they are left to the law. The commanders dare but seldom appear, the widows, orphans, and injured inhabitants, who have so freely advanced upon hopes of a glorious design, being now ruined through fitting out the privateers.[8]

Why Browne suddenly decided to turn against Morgan is unclear. In his letter he blatantly accuses the commanders of the Panama expedition of cheating 'the soldiers of a very vast sum, each man having but £10 a share, and the whole number not being above 1,800.' Browne then says of the commanders at Chagres:

they gave what they pleased, 'for which ... we must be content or else clapped in irons, &c.,' and after staying there a week the Admiral and four or five more stood for Jamaica, being like to starve in that ten days' run, and the rest for want of provisions were forced to leeward, where hundreds were lost, starved, which is half the undoing of this island. At their going out on this unfortunate voyage they had thirty-seven sail of men-of-war, and knows of nineteen cast away and not above ten have ever yet returned.[9]

This letter is important because it puts the raids by Morgan into context. Essentially, Browne asks why such a massive force was put together in response to the pitiful action by Rivera of burning four houses and taking a few hogs.

Cannot tell what infatuated 'our Grandees' to send forth such a fleet on so slender an account; can 'find no other cause but a pitiful small Spanish man-of-war of eight guns, which came vapouring upon these coasts with a commission from the Queen of Spain ... took one small vessel ... burnt four or five houses, and took away about thirty live hogs ... and he himself was taken with his ship.' We do the Spaniards more mischief in one hour than they can do us in seven years; it is incredible what loss they received by us at Panama.[10]

In his next sentence Browne puts this action down to Spanish gold and silver rather than revenge as being the main motivation.

In a letter dated 20 August 1671, Lynch talked about the return of the *Assistance* and the *Welcome* from Cartagena where, he states, that 'they were treated infinitely well by the governor and the city, of which His Lordship has here a narrative by Major Beeston, and "all the autos and formalities of it in Spanish from the governor", and likewise the governor's letter, the publication of the Peace, and a letter about the sweepstakes.'[11]

This lengthy letter is essentially providing Lord Arlington with an update on how well Lynch had put the king's instructions into action. He had established the government, with him as the new governor. However, of the privateers or buccaneers he states that for the most part they were divided or had become planters or logwood traders. Logwood from Hispaniola was a thriving business for Jamaica. Lynch goes on to say that he had sent proclamations to all the buccaneers' haunts promising them a pardon if they came in within six months. He claimed in his letter that he was taking their side against their commanders, 'of which they have cheated them, which has contributed mightily to the bringing them in and reducing them.'[12]

However, a large part of his letter is taken up with his arrest and detaining of Modyford. Lynch had been waiting for the return of the two frigates before he carried out his orders from the king about arresting Modyford. Those instructions came in the form of a private letter from the king that ordered him to seize Modyford and send him to London under 'safe passage'. Once this was done, the instructions ordered him to take 'quiet possession of the government'. Modyford was held in high esteem by many people in Jamaica so there was always the possibility that there might be resistance at his arrest – something that Lynch clearly wanted to avoid, as his deferring of these instructions indicates. If there had been resistance Lynch was to use the two frigates to assist him in keeping order 'by annoying in all ways the island, and particularly by burning, sinking and destroying the privateers that shall assist the island in such opposition to His Majesty's commands.'

What of Modyford's arrest? That took place on 15 August, and for a detailed account we shall turn once again the letter Lynch wrote to Arlington five days later that recounts the whole sordid affair:

But the sending home Sir Thos Modyford a prisoner according to the King's order troubled him most; he was prepared to come home when told 'by the by' lest I should too much exasperate his friends and surprise him that the King expected him. But twelve days since came news by a Bristol man, which by great luck and art he suppressed, that Mr [Chas] Modyford was secured in the Tower, which made Lynch mortally apprehend Sir Thomas' escape. To prevent which watched himself divers[e] nights. Set guards or rather spies on the boats and at the ports, and last Friday week having ordered Lieutenant Colonel Freeman to come armed, letting none know the reason, Major General Banister and some others very luckily coming to town, he invited them to accompany the Lieutenant Governor to the sea side. In the morning went to Sir Thos Modyford and prayed him to go with them, and that the Lieutenant Governor's wife should return with him. Modyford excused it, but told him he must enter the boat and go on board the *Assistance*, where Lynch had something to communicate to him from the King. Called those of the Council into the boat, and being come on board acquainted Modyford with the King's orders to send him home prisoner. Both he and they were much surprised and troubled. To lessen it, said all he could to him which His Lordship had bid Lynch say, that his life and fortune were in no danger, and that the Lieutenant Governor had orders to pardon all which was a mark Sir Thos Modyford was not such a capital offender, but there was a necessity of the King's making this resentment for such an unreasonable irruption. Wrote to the same purpose to his son and to Admiral Morgan, who were sick, and to some of the Council in the town, fearing the surprise or fear might occasion some rash actions; but, God be thanked, all remained quiet.[13]

There are other sources that provide a different perspective. Major General James Bannister, former governor of Surinam, wrote to Lord Arlington on 15 August that 'Sir Thos Lynch received from him [Modyford] as honourable a reception as could be, which he has ever since continued, being also very forward with his best advice for the good of this island till the very time of his restraint.'[14]

Surgeon Browne reported that he felt the way in which Lynch handled the affair of making Modyford a prisoner was prudent, especially publishing a proclamation so quickly after the event, which he believed 'gave good satisfaction to the people who before were much startled.'[15]

In London, Charles Modyford had been taken prisoner and put in the Tower of London as surety for his father's good behaviour. This was something that Lynch was not aware of.

With Modyford a prisoner on the *Assistance*, Lynch was now in charge and he immediately called a council meeting where he showed the members his orders from the king, which were not to be disputed. He did, however, suggest that his 'manner of carrying out his orders might privately be censured.'

Not only did the king's orders stop any attempt by the council to rebel but Lynch's explanation of why he had Modyford imprisoned the way he did helped as well:

Told them there were but three ways of doing what he was commanded, viz, either by taking Modyford's oath and security to render himself a true prisoner, which he could not do with one whom the King had charged with such crimes; or to have made him a prisoner at town, which was impossible, his own servants being sick, the townsmen partial, and any of Modyford's desperate friends might have murdered him, and has since heard that two have sworn that had they known Lynch's intentions they would have cut his throat. But the third and the way taken was the safest. Shows he could not be charged with ingratitude, and that his arguments seemed to satisfy all, and immediately the cause of his imprisonment was published and the King's pardon, he allowed the Council to confirm the Act by which Morgan was commissioned, which Modyford carries home with him, and gave him a letter certifying that he found in him or the people no disposition to rebel. Has likewise visited him every day aboard and carried him to take the air, and showed him all the civilities imaginable, both to palliate his misfortunes, for two days after his restraint came public news of his son's imprisonment, and 'to set myself with those friends of his that might think I was the cause and not the instrument of his misfortunes.' Before letting him go aboard the *Jamaica Merchant* that is to bring him home, swore the Captain, Joseph Knapman, with all his crew, and put aboard twelve of the *Assistance's* men under Lieutenant Bucke and Mr Fogge, with commission to guard him, if possible right into the Thames; so hopes it will appear he has served the King with all the duty and punctuality imaginable, and that they may blush who have reproached His Lordship for preferring him to this occasion. Did they but know the risks run and the money expended, and the little advantage he is like to have by it, they would pity rather than envy him.[16]

Lynch had Modyford moved to a merchant vessel, the *Jamaica Merchant*, which sailed for London on 25 August.

In Europe the political scene had become even more precarious. Within days of the peace treaty signed with Spain in Madrid, Britain had signed a treaty with the Dutch along similar lines but despite this treaty, relations between the two countries were at a low ebb. The prospect was that another war with the Dutch was looming.

On the Spanish throne was the sickly young new King Charles II of the Habsburgs, who was twisted and warped in both body and mind. It was unlikely that this king would produce an heir and Louis XIV of France wanted the Spanish throne. He was waiting for the poor young king to die but to seize the throne he needed an ally. He turned to Britain to support his ambitions and as relations between the French and the Dutch were also unravelling, war was threatening. In secret, King Charles II of Britain signed a treaty with Louis XIV supporting his claim to the Spanish throne and to support France in their war with the Dutch in return for a large payout. Charles could not afford to upset the French or the Spanish; he and his ministers were doing their best to ensure their new allies were placated.

Into this political arena came the news of the raid on Panama and as the details came in of the devastation and cruelties meted out by the buccaneers the Spanish ambassador's protests in London grew. The fact that Modyford had been arrested was, as far as the Spanish ambassador and the Spanish government were concerned, not good enough. Spain was so incensed at the destruction of Panama that it was considering war.

Fresh orders from Arlington were sent to Lynch for the arrest of Henry Morgan and his immediate transportation back to London. It was hoped that the Spanish might cool down a bit if they knew the architects of the Panama raid were both imprisoned in the Tower of London.

Back in Jamaica Morgan remained in his sickbed and for the first time since arriving, Lynch faced a similar crisis to the one that Modyford had faced more than a year earlier. News coming in from London, Spain and Holland to the merchants in Port Royal talked of an impending attack on Jamaica by the Spanish:

The Church and Grandees of Spain have undertaken to reduce this island with thirty-six sail and 5,000 men. Only fear the port; the island, in probability, is as safe as England. Has had a general council of war, and resolved to defend that place to the last man, and on his own credit, the King or public having no money, is fitting the fort the best they can.[17]

Because there was no money in the treasury, Lynch was forced to use his own to purchase the stores needed to build the defences of the island, such as buying the material to build fireships. He did not believe the stories and rumours of war were true. After all, why would the Spanish break the peace? He told Arlington that he could not 'think it is for the Spaniards' interest to break it, lest we should bring the war again into their quarters.' He went on to ensure Arlington knew that Lynch would not do anything without explicit direction and since no one from London had sent him any information about war with Spain, Lynch believed that there was little danger, 'but will be glad to know whether such an invasion would not give them liberty to offend the enemy, without further order from His Lordship.'

However, the council of war did not take such a lackadaisical view as Lynch did of what could be impending war. Instead, the council ordered among other things that 'a regimental court martial, and put in execution the Act of Militia, ordain places of rendezvous, and times of exercise, and in case of invasion publish and put in execution all the Articles of War, and in fine order within the precincts of the regiment what shall be for His Majesty's service, and the safety of the island.'[18]

Shortly after the council of war had met, the instructions for Lynch to arrest Morgan and have him sent back as a prisoner to London arrived. Lynch was taking a defensive posture and not many of the influential people in Jamaica supported it because, in the past, Modyford had taken the offensive posture along with Morgan, taking the fight to the Spanish, which had always been successful. Also, should war come, Lynch was beginning to realize that he might need the privateers to help defend the island.

Just as Modyford had been before, Lynch found himself in a dilemma. While he denounced the lifestyle of the buccaneers, he also realized he needed them. First he gave command of the island's militia to Major Beeston:

a gentleman of good estate, parts and conduct, for whom the whole island will answer. Has made Prynce [sic] one of the most famous of the privateers, one of his lieutenants, that the Spaniards should see they were willing to serve His Majesty; and was afraid the sending home Morgan might make all the privateers apprehend they should be so dealt with, notwithstanding the King's proclamation of pardon.[19]

As for Morgan, Lynch stated that he was unable to send him home because he was still sick. 'However shall send him home so as he shall not be much disgusted, yet the order obeyed, and the Spaniards satisfied.'

Instead he hoped that Morgan would be ready to sail in six weeks on the *Welcome*. 'To speak the truth of him, he's an honest brave fellow, and had both Sir T. M. and the Council's commission and instructions, which they thought he obeyed and followed so well that they gave him public thanks, which is recorded in the Council books.'[20]

In November the banns were called for the youngest of Colonel Edward's daughters, and Johanna Wilhelmina married Colonel Henry Archbold. By this time Robert Byndloss and his wife, Anna Petronilla, another of Colonel Edward Morgan's daughters, had produced two sons, Thomas and Charles, who would one day inherit from the estates of Robert Byndloss and Henry Morgan respectively.[21] The three men now being brothers-in-law, Morgan, Archbold and Byndloss had a significant amount of power among the most politically active planters.

By the end of 1671 Lynch had made a change that would affect most people, Morgan included. He had called for elections for a house of assembly, something Modyford had not done for six years. Morgan signed an affidavit so he could be involved in the proceedings. The first Assembly sat in the early part of February 1672 and refused to reimburse Lynch for the money he'd spent building up the island's defences, declaring that was the responsibility of the Crown.

But by the end of March 1672, Morgan, still a sick man, had been arrested and was on his way to London, a prisoner aboard the *Welcome* per the instructions from Arlington. Lynch had instructed the captain, John Keane, commanding the *Welcome*, to immediately sail 'for England, taking under convoy the *Lyon* of Bristoll, the ketch *Golden Hind*, and the pink *Providence* of London, and the doggerboat *Johanna*: to touch at the first port of England, put ashore the letters and advise Lord Arlington of his arrival: to receive on board Col Henry Morgan as His Majesty's prisoner.'[22]

On 6 April the *Welcome* sailed, with Morgan a prisoner in its leaky and damp hold. In this difficult time for Morgan he did have a friend in Major James Bannister, who wrote to Lord Arlington on 30 March that:

Admiral Henry Morgan is sent home confined in the *Welcome* frigate, to appear, as it is suspected, on account of his proceedings against the Spaniard. Knows not what approbation he may find there, but he received here 'a very high and honourable applause for his noble service therein', both from Sir Thos Modyford and the Council that commissioned him. Hopes without offence he may say 'he is a very well-deserving person, and one of great courage and conduct, who may, with His Majesty's pleasure, perform good public service at home or be very advantageous to this island if war should again break forth with the Spaniard.[23]

Chapter 21

Toast of the Town

But fears all may be lost if they have not a frigate or two to defend the island. It is impossible to raise privateers against the Dutch that have neither country nor merchants to take, and one caper of thirty or forty guns might exceedingly harass them, because our best settlements are all round the island along the coasts.[1]

On 4 July 1672, the *Welcome* anchored off Spithead and Captain Keane immediately sent word that the ship had arrived and that his two prisoners, pirate Captain Francis Witherborn, who was condemned to death, and Admiral Henry Morgan, were very ill. Indeed, Morgan had been getting sicker by the day as they drew closer to England. Morgan was used to high tropical temperatures and the weather dropped by a degree with each passing day. To make matters worse, the *Welcome* was a damp, leaky vessel so for Morgan there was nowhere on the ship for him to stay warm.

Back in Jamaica Lynch was alarmed at the news of war with the Dutch and he wrote, on 6 July, to the king asking for help. Instead of walking the fine line that Modyford had done with the buccaneers, keeping them close but with some degree of control during peace so that he had them there for war, Lynch had sentenced those privateers he could and executed them. Indeed, many hung from gibbets along the coast. Lynch believed that trading with the Spanish and appeasing them was in the best interests of Jamaica and that the buccaneers were the main obstacle to achieving that end.

Lynch had been in Jamaica a year and within the first few days of his arrival he'd written in his first letter that there was no money in the treasury, the sugar cane and cocoa crops were poor, and two Royal Navy vessels would cow the buccaneers. Yet by November 1671 his letters to Lord Arlington were more urgent, saying that he had declared martial law and was funding preparations to fend off a Spanish invasion. He called his first assembly in January 1672 and by February wrote to Lord Arlington that the assembly had refused to pay for rebuilding fortifications on the island. The following month he wrote to Arlington stating that he felt the people were content. Then in July 1672 came the letter that included the quote that begins this chapter, with Lynch begging for a couple of frigates to defend the island, otherwise 'all would be lost.'

To make matters worse, a hurricane hit Jamaica in September 1672 and by November Lynch had received word from London that attacks on Jamaica from the Dutch fleet were imminent.[2]

In London, Modyford remained in the Tower, where prisoners had been tortured and murdered since the jail had been built. Yet Modyford was a prisoner without a charge and though he was not mistreated, he remained in this cold, damp, stone prison.

Morgan, on the other hand, had the freedom of London, where he had to pay for his own lodgings, food and clothing. He was free because of a change in the political winds. The war against the Dutch Protestants had not progressed as well as had been planned. Indeed, the French had advanced rapidly up the coast towards the Scheldt and the Dutch rallied; using guerrilla tactics they opened the dykes to flood their countryside, halting the French advance in its tracks. The battle of Sole Bay between the English and the Dutch fleets was a costly stalemate, with both sides claiming victory. With the war going badly, 'the English commoners were growing weary of battle, and with weariness came irritation. Why was the nation expending its money and the lives of its youth on fighting good Dutch Protestants?'[3]

England was essentially a Protestant nation and the Dutch should have been their natural allies against Catholic France and Catholic Spain but it was the other way round and as the war dragged on the old hatred of Catholicism and France began to rear its head. King Charles II had taken a Catholic mistress and others in the court had converted.

'Jailing Morgan would only have incensed Charles's anti-Catholic critics, and so he stayed out of prison.'[4]

Also, this was not the England he'd left as a young man. This was the Restoration and London was buzzing in a similar way that Port Royal did when the buccaneers came back from an expedition with their pockets full of riches. There was hard drinking, open displays of wealth, extravagant and colourful dress and loose morals; to Morgan it must have seemed very familiar except that it was 30 degrees colder than Jamaica.

Because of the alliance with France, London fashion and fetishes were towards everything Catholic and French. London's wealthy wore French wigs, spoke in French, read Catholic novels and patronized French and Spanish theatre. This was the environment that Morgan found himself in upon leaving the *Welcome* when he'd been released pending a trial.

Yet, though he was free, Morgan was not free of the fever and while he waited for his case to be decided he spent 'his time being feted in London taverns and coffee houses, gambling and going to the races and theatre, and also visited his relatives in Wales.'[5]

Morgan's victories were the only real successes that England had against their enemies during this time so he was hugely popular. Perhaps because of his popularity many people wanted to help him, including William Morgan, a relative. William Morgan was the lieutenant deputy to Lord Monmouth and he wrote to the Privy Council to plead Morgan's case:

> I have a very good character of him, and in the management of the late business to Panama he behaved with as much prudence, fidelity and resolution as could be reasonably expected ... and all good men would be troubled if a person of his loyalty and consideration as to His Majesty's affairs in those parts should fall for want of friends to assist him.[6]

Help also came from another very powerful individual Morgan met during the round of dinners, drinking and socializing. It came from the young Christopher Monck, Duke of Albemarle, son of General Monck and one of Modyford's relatives. The general, the old duke, had helped to restore Charles to the throne and became one of the most influential and richest men in England. Now, Christopher, the second Duke of Albemarle, inherited his father's wealth, influence and power. Because of his father's very close ties with the king, the young duke, in his late teens, also had the same closeness as his father had with the king. Morgan was thirty-seven and the young Albemarle only nineteen when they met.[7]

Albemarle was a Member of Parliament, on the Privy Council and one of the Lords of Trade and Plantations who had the ear of the king. He had worked hard to have his relative Modyford released from the Tower, which took place in 1673. He had also promised to help Morgan, who was a frequent guest at Albemarle House, regaling attentive listeners with the stories of his expeditions – how the governor of Panama had, in a vain attempt to save his city, forced out hundreds of cattle to try to stop the advancing buccaneers, or how he had managed to sail past the Spanish at Maracaibo without fighting them. 'These were stories that won Morgan the hearts of ladies and the envy of other men.'[8] Why? The stories Morgan told impressed his audiences because they were true; these events had happened and he had been the one that had made them happen. As Dudley Pope states, they were accounts of expeditions that had been 'well planned'.[9]

In the fashionable drawing rooms of London and at Albemarle House, Morgan told his eager listeners how, with 10,000 men, the whole of the

West Indies could be conquered. The young duke of course made sure that everything Morgan said about the West Indies went directly back to the king.

By August of 1673 the war with the Dutch was still going badly. The Dutch could sail out of Curaçao at any time and threaten British colonies in the West Indies. 'The unappeased Spanish were still a threat; even the French could not be trusted. But with Morgan thousands of miles away, the privateers could not be called on to defend the island, as Lynch had so alienated the Brethren that they would not come to the country's defence.'[10]

With the changes in the threats facing the West Indies, the king and Secretary of State Lord Arlington were forced into a reversal of the earlier policy where they had, to appease the Spanish, arrested Modyford and put him in the Tower, brought Morgan home as a prisoner and put Lynch, an appeaser, in charge in Jamaica. From his letters begging for more frigates, it was clear Lynch was not up to the job. He had alienated the privateers whereas Modyford had shrewdly kept them close by as Jamaica's private army and navy, led by Henry Morgan.

In July 1673, the king, through Lord Arlington, asked Morgan to draw up a memorandum on his ideas for the defence of Jamaica. He'd heard of Morgan's exploits through Albemarle and now the king seemed to be interested in what Morgan had to say. Topping Morgan's list were twenty large iron guns and ammunition to supply the batteries at Port Royal and a fifth-rate frigate to take him back to Jamaica. Morgan was called into to see the king and they went over his points. 'The meeting went so well that he was later presented with a snuff box bearing the king's profile done in small diamonds.'[11]

In his book *Admiral Sir Henry Morgan: The Greatest Buccaneer of Them All*, Terry Breverton states that Morgan wanted to clear his name and that he complained to the king that he had not had a chance to put his case forward. His wishes were fulfilled and he had an informal hearing where he and others gave evidence in front of the Lords of Trade and Plantations. Breverton tells us that the king personally saw the evidence, which was, at best, inconclusive. 'Modyford could prove that he had sent a messenger to the Isle des Vaches [Île à Vache] to tell Morgan that there was a truce with Spain. Morgan could prove that the messages were returned with their seals unbroken.'[12] No one who had been on the expedition was called during the hearing to testify to Morgan's whereabouts when these messages allegedly arrived. He was then obliged to meet with the king and provide his personal account and answer a few questions.

The complaints against him were largely about the sharing of the booty from the Panama expedition. In Morgan's defence he had the letter from William Morgan testifying to his good character, the letter from Major

Bannister who had written about Morgan's noble service. Albemarle too had been lobbying for Morgan's name to be cleared.

However, the Spanish ambassador claimed that even if Morgan had not known about the signing of the Treaty of Madrid the commission he'd been given from Modyford did not permit him to undertake land campaigns against the Spanish. Morgan replied that there was a phrase within the commission that gave him the authority to do whatever necessary in order to ensure his men were paid from the booty they'd plundered.

Then a ministerial secretary suggested that 'by marching and giving battle in military formation had not the accused arrogated the privileges of His Majesty's Army and thus made an official act of war?'

Morgan replied that it 'was a war to end a war'. As he saw it he had to continue the work he'd done at Portobello and Maracaibo. 'That pestiferous nest of Panama had to be wiped out to stop Spanish aggression.'

'Why did you not believe the Spanish when they told you that there was peace between our two nations?' came the next question.

Morgan casually answered that he couldn't remember if he'd been told that. 'I would have disbelieved it anyway because my experience shows that the Spanish are liars.'

King Charles II, according to Breverton, was said to explode with laughter after Morgan's last remark, which ended the hearing.[13]

Morgan's expeditions had brought riches for the king as well as for his brother, the Duke of York, also the Admiral of the Fleet. Both men had gained financially from Morgan's successes. The verdict from the hearings came from the closest advisors to the king, the so-called Cabal, consisting of Lords Arlington, Ashley, Buckingham, Clifford and Lauderdale, and the result was – *not proven*. Morgan was free and the complaints against him now gone.[14]

Charles and his inner circle realized they needed Morgan back in Jamaica, that they needed a strong firm hand on the rudder to ensure Jamaica's success.

On 6 November, few days after the hearing, Morgan heard that he was to be deputy governor of Jamaica and later the same month he was knighted. The official announcement of his commission as deputy governor of Jamaica came on 23 January, when Lord Arlington, addressing the Council of Trade and Plantations, announced that the new governor of Jamaica would be the Earl of Carlisle and that Sir Henry Morgan would be his deputy.

Chapter 22

The New Governor

Morgan remained in London while he waited for his commission to be drawn up. Initially, Lord Carlisle was named as the new governor of Jamaica but he turned the post down and on 3 April 1674 it was given to Lord Vaughan, a man who, at thirty-four, was five years younger than Morgan. Both men were complete opposites. Vaughan was a patron of the arts and himself a poet. He knew nothing of fighting in the way that Morgan did and Vaughan took an instant dislike to his deputy governor.

A month earlier, on 19 February, peace between Holland and Britain had been established with the signing of a formal treaty.

However, that same month, the Spanish government had agreed that commissions could be granted to Spanish privateers from governors in the West Indies. The French had been busy attacking the Spanish in the West Indies and the governors wanted to defend themselves. After Morgan's destruction of the Spanish fleet at Maracaibo the governors had no other choice but to turn to privateers.

The Spanish government had also heard from their ambassador in London that Henry Morgan was not a prisoner, he was not in the Tower, but he now had the ear of the king! With the way open for commissions to be granted to Spanish privateers many flocked to the ports of Cuba, Hispaniola and Puerto Rico. These men were known as Biscayners because they were stationed in ports along the Biscay coast. It wasn't long before they began raiding.

In his last sent copies of the orders and instructions of the Queen of Spain for encouraging privateers to take the French and English pirates that rob on their coasts and cut logwood, which will not be executed by their own nation, but by English renegados, and they have news of one of their merchantmen taken in the bay by one of their revolted privateers with Spanish commission. If the Queen gives orders to punish as pirates all that take wood on the coast, and they persist in it, they will infallibly break with the Spaniards, and hazard this island, if not the peace in Europe.[1]

As Modyford before him had discovered that he was being replaced through personal letters and gossip, so too did Lynch. No official word arrived for some time so, thoroughly frustrated and angry, he sat down on 20 November 1674 and penned a letter to Sir Joseph Williamson. Lynch expressed his concerns in this letter over the safety of Jamaica with the news that the Spanish were issuing commissions:

> The Spaniards they expect the galleons in two or three months, with twenty Biscaniers, Ostenders and Flushingers, which are likely to clear the Indies of all that infest them. One of the reasons of their coming is the noise of Admiral Morgan's favour at Court and return to the Indies, which much alarmed the Spaniards, and caused the King to be at vast charge in fortifying in the South Sea.

He later states how he feels about the impending arrival of the new governor and his deputy governor:

> Wonders he has not been made acquainted with Lord Vaughan's coming that he might have done all that is possible for his reception, for provision is not suddenly made, and Admiral Morgan's letters have long since declared first Lord Carlisle, then himself, for Governor; others, Lord Vaughan, or Sir Rd Ford.[2]

The issuing of commissions to Lord Vaughan and Morgan had been held up because of complaints that Vaughan had about the appointment of Morgan as his deputy. His complaints were to the king and the Privy Council. In essence he complained that Morgan should not be called deputy governor but lieutenant governor. Also, he did not like the way that the responsibilities of the two offices had been drawn up.[3]

While these complaints had been going on, neither man could leave London. On 3 November the commission that gave Lynch the title of lieutenant governor was revoked and new commissions were subsequently written for Vaughan and Morgan reflecting changes that were a result of Vaughan's complaints. Three days later, Morgan attended the king for the ceremony that made him a knight of the realm – Sir Henry Morgan.

In any historical biography there are, more often than not, discrepancies with dates and Morgan's story is no exception. For example, we have Dudley Pope saying that Morgan and Vaughan left England in their respective ships, the *Jamaica Merchant* for Morgan and the *Foresight* for Vaughan, in January

1676. Terry Breverton, in his book *Admiral Sir Henry Morgan: The Greatest Buccaneer of Them All*, states that they left England in January 1675.

However, from the minutes of the council meeting in Jamaica dated 7 March 1675, Morgan is listed as being present at that meeting. Indeed, it is this meeting where the council 'being constituted Lieutenant governor under His Majesty's Sign Manual, was, by a clause in said revocation under the Great Seal, sufficiently invested with authority to assume the Government.'

So from these minutes we know he arrived in Jamaica in March 1675 and so he must have left England in January of the same year. We can only assume that 1676 was a misprint in Pope's book.

Under the terms of the commission Morgan could act as governor in Vaughan's absence, so the governor decided to give Morgan written instructions that during the voyage he should ensure both ships remained within sight of each other. This did not happen. Morgan either ignored Vaughan's instructions or, as he stated in his letter, 'their anchor was so fast in the ground, His Excellency in the frigate was got about the Foreland and they could not see him afterwards.'[4]

From that point onwards it became a race as to who would arrive in Jamaica first. Morgan's crossing took six weeks. *Jamaica Merchant* was under the command of Captain Knapman, who, once out from England, sailed with Sir Roger Strickland's fleet, which was heading south. Knapman then steered for the Leeward Islands and by the end of February he was sailing down the coast of Hispaniola, with Jamaica only 200 miles away. At this point, the ship ran aground off Cow Island (Île à Vache). As this was Morgan's old rendezvous point for his buccaneers he knew the area well. Why they were sailing so close to the coast has not been explained, although there is much speculation about it.

Most of the crew were saved, but the brass cannon that Morgan had been given for the batteries at Port Royal sank to the bottom, along with ammunition and powder. Even Captain Knapman wasn't entirely sure why the ship ran aground when he wrote:

Doubts not he has had an account of the unfortunate loss of the *Jamaica Merchant* on 25 February on the east side of the Isle of Ash on the south side of Hispaniola, within twenty-four hours sail of this port. Knows not what evil genius led him there, and never was any man more surprised considering the course they steered. Saved all the people, and five or six days after, one, Capt Tho Rogers, a Jamaica privateer now sailing under the French, carried Sir Henry Morgan and all the passengers for Jamaica, but he and his men stayed behind to save, if possible, His Majesty's stores and the ship's furniture, and he was obliged to offer them one-third of what they could save, or could get them to do nothing. Were a month ere they got to Port Royal, in which time they saved a great part of His Majesty's stores, and some of the ships, for which he will be accountable. With difficulty saved Mr Alderman and his son's gold, for he was forced to swim with it on his back. Left a small sloop to keep possession of the ship for the King, and Lord Vaughan has since sent up two great sloops to save what may be saved.[5]

Talty tells us that the 'evil genius' was Morgan himself because he had taken command of the ship from Knapman and 'that Morgan himself whipped the crew on to leave Vaughan in his wake.'[6]

Another possibility is that Morgan 'wanted to meet someone at his favourite rendezvous', speculates Breverton in his book. Some theories suggest that Morgan and Modyford (which means Modyford was on the ship as well) wanted to collect some buried treasure on the island while other theories claim that 'Modyford wanted the ship wrecked to claim insurance upon it.'[7]

The wreck delayed Morgan's arrival until 6 March, when he sailed into Port Royal. The following day the Council of Jamaica met and power of the island was transferred to Morgan.

On reading the revocation of Sir Thomas Lynch's Commission, it was the opinion that Sir Henry Morgan, being constituted Lieutenant Governor under His Majesty's Sign Manual, was, by a clause in said revocation under the Great Seal, sufficiently invested with authority to assume the Government; whereupon Sir Thos Lynch made a demission of the Government to him, and it was ordered, that a proclamation immediately issue to continue all persons in their employments, military and civil, till further order.[8]

Morgan immediately set about rebuilding the island's defences, which under Lynch's administration had crumbled into disrepair. The militia had been idle as well and there were few ships available to mount a defence of the island should it be required. Lynch's programme of appeasement with the Spanish and his arguments with the Assembly had ensured that the defences fell into ruin.

However, Morgan had little time to do much before Vaughan arrived on 13 March. The day before, the island lookout spotted the *Foresight* on its approach to Port Royal and Morgan pulled out all the stops for greeting Vaughan. The guns at Fort Charles were cleaned and primed and flags flew on every flagpole. Morgan and the council members greeted Vaughan as he arrived on land, the guns blasting out their welcome.

On 17 March the Council of Jamaica met, with Vaughan in attendance. Vaughan was sworn in as governor, as the minutes state:

His Excellency's Instrument of government under the Great Seal read, wherein His Majesty's Council were likewise appointed. The Oaths of Allegiance and Supremacy administered to him by five of the Council according to His Majesty's command, also the oath as Captain General and Governor-in-Chief of this Island.[9]

It would not be long, however, before Vaughan was writing back to the Secretary of State about his dislike of Morgan. Initially, Vaughan had a quarrel with Lynch over the fact that his accounts were not prepared and not ready. Morgan had written to the Secretary of State in London that:

His Majesty's stores so exhausted, that there was found in all the stores but fourteen Barrells of powder, which on occasion would not last three hours. Nevertheless that shall not daunt him, for before he will lose His Majesty's fortifications, he will lose himself and a great many brave men more, that will stand and fall by him in His Majesty's service.[10]

The year before, Lynch had chartered a vessel with a commission against the Dutch and sent this ship to sea. The ship, *Thomas and Francis*, under the command of George Gallop, returned with a Dutch prize. This prize carried several hundred slaves, which were sold in Port Royal, reported Lynch in a letter to London. However, he failed to record in his accounts the king's and the Duke of York's share of this sale.

Nevertheless, this quarrel between Vaughan and Lynch was patched up within a month and the money somehow found so that Lynch's accounts were put right. 'Sends this by their friend Sir Thos Lynch, for he shall now always call him so, being very well satisfied with his prudent government and conduct of affairs.'[11]

Modyford was also back in Jamaica and was soon made Chief Justice by Vaughan. Many of Morgan's friends were on the council and because of this, Pope tells us, Morgan became a little careless. Vaughan was watching him and his friends for any sign of indiscretion that he may refer back to the Secretary of State and the Lords of Trade and Plantations.

He didn't have long to wait. Many of the buccaneers had left Port Royal for Tortuga, where they could obtain French commissions against the Spanish. But with Morgan back in Jamaica, as a knight and as deputy governor, some of his old buccaneering friends began inquiring about the safety of returning to Port Royal. At this time, Morgan had a secretary, Charles Barré, through whom his response to the privateers of Tortuga were written. Indeed, his response to the requests from some of his old friends such as Captain John Edmunds who had sailed with him on many expeditions was that they (the buccaneers) would 'be very welcome in any harbour' and would have as much 'privilege as he can in reason expect'.

While the buccaneers stayed away from Port Royal they used other smaller and quieter harbours along the Jamaican coast for unloading and selling their goods. These goods would appear in the merchant shops of Port Royal. By doing this, the buccaneers avoided paying a share of their profits to the French governor of Tortuga even though they were sailing under French commissions. Many of the ships with French commissions were owned in Port Royal.

Robert Byndloss, Morgan's brother-in-law, was also a target for Vaughan. The French governor of Tortuga wrote to Byndloss asking him to collect his shares from the privateers landing and selling their goods in Jamaica and he gave Byndloss power of attorney. This letter also ended up in Vaughan's hands.

Vaughan's displeasure with Morgan is evident in the letter he wrote to Williamson first on 18 May 1675, where he stated that he had:

> so tired of him that he is perfectly weary of him, and frankly tells Williamson that he thinks it for His Majesty's service he should be removed, and the charge of so useless an officer saved. What he strove for in England was not so much for Sir Henry as against the dividing of the Commissions, which he considered would cause disputes. What he has further discoursed to Sir Thos Lynch he will communicate. Has written all the Ministers the truth of this miscarriage, and believes His Majesty and His Royal Highness will much resent it. Should the King make this alteration that in the absence or approaching death of the Governor he should have power to appoint a fitting deputy.[12]

And again, in September, Vaughan wrote:

> Is every day more convinced of his imprudence and unfitness to have anything to do in the Civil Government, and of what hazards the Island may run by so dangerous a succession. Sir Henry has made himself and his authority so cheap at the Port, drinking and gaming in the taverns, that Lord Vaughan intends to remove thither speedily himself, for the reputation of the Island and security of that place, though he pretends it is only to change the air, having lately had a fever.[13]

Morgan's two plantations – one at Lawrencefield and the other in Morgan Valley – were doing well so at this time he decided to look around for another plantation and purchased 4,000 acres in the parish of St Elizabeth.

In the meantime, Vaughan was putting together evidence that he hoped would bring down Morgan and give him the ammunition he needed to remove him from power. To make matters worse, the Assembly had voted to give Morgan £600 'for his good services to the country during his Lieutenant Governorship, but none to his successors.'[14]

The capital of Jamaica was St Jago de la Vega, where Vaughan occupied the king's House, the official governor's residence. Morgan, on the other hand, stayed mostly in Port Royal, which added to Vaughan's mistrust of Morgan, as he 'saw him as being head of a "de facto" second capital of the island.'[15]

To make matters worse, the Spanish were up to their old tricks again, as the Secretary to the Council of Jamaica wrote to Lord Williamson:

> My Lord [Vaughan's] great trouble is to carry himself even with the Spaniards, for they are daily taking all ships they can master, and are very high, for when His Lordship sent to demand satisfaction they answered they would look upon us as enemies, and take all they came up with; and truly, were not the French from Tortuga daily galling them with their privateers, should conclude ourselves in some danger, though if they had war would not question by carrying it to their doors, we should sufficiently defend our own. The French would prove very ill neighbours in war, and much more dangerous than the Spaniards.[16]

More incidents took place that infuriated Vaughan. An admiralty court had been set up, which consisted of Henry Morgan, Major Beeston and Robert Byndloss, with Vaughan as the Chief Judge. In early 1676 a ship arrived in Port Royal carrying more than 300 slaves from West Africa. It had been seized at sea and brought into port, where it was discovered that the master and crew of the ship did not have the appropriate licence from the Royal African Company. Vaughan ordered the ship to be condemned as a prize and the case was heard by the admiralty court with Morgan presiding, who after hearing the evidence dismissed the case. This action infuriated Vaughan so much that he ordered a new trial.

In addition there was the case of Captain John Deane, commanding the *St David*, a privateer who sailed into Port Royal. Vaughan had him arrested and charged with piracy. Deane came before the admiralty court but this time it was Vaughan who tried him, found him guilty and sentenced him to death. However, this backfired on Vaughan and added to his dislike of both Morgan and Bydnloss. Because the outcry against his decision was so loud from the merchants, planters and shopkeepers across Port Royal, Vaughan believed that this opposition had been stirred up by his two enemies rather than realizing he was wrong in his sentencing of Deane.

All the documentation regarding Deane was sent to the Lords of Trade and Plantations for their verdict and while Deane cooled his heels in jail, Vaughan began the finishing touches on his evidence against Morgan. A letter dated 28 July 1676 from the Lords of Trade and Plantations later gave Vaughan his answer regarding the Deane case. They found that the trial that Vaughan had carried out and the proceedings were 'not warranted by the laws of this Kingdom, it not appearing that pirates were de facto tried by the civil law.'

During his time as governor, Vaughan behaved as if he was the king of Jamaica. He believed that the government should reflect the government of England. It had an assembly, a council and the governor, the king's representative in Jamaica, and that made him king of the island, in his eyes. So it galled him that there were Jamaican ships owned in Port Royal flying French flags. This was a flagrant disregard for the law and Vaughan was sure that Morgan was either behind it or involved in it in some way. In fact, he believed he had evidence to prove it.

In July 1676 he choose a regular council meeting to present his evidence and have Morgan removed. During the previous December, Morgan had been sworn in as a member of the council, which also galled Vaughan. After complaining about Morgan, Vaughan had been told to patch up the quarrel by Williamson and put Morgan on the council.

Now here he was, six months later, about to present evidence that he hoped would get Morgan off the council and removed from his position as lieutenant governor. He wrote to Williamson complaining about Morgan:

What I most resent is, and which I consider as part of my duty to lay before Your Honour, that I find Sir Henry, contrary to his duty and trust, endeavours to set up privateering, and has obstructed all my designs and purposes for the reducing of those that do use that curse of life. Had by several proclamations declared he would not permit those rapines and spoils, and that he would proceed against the offenders as pirates if they came into any of our ports. They went to Tortugas and took French commissions, and Sir Henry recommended some of our English privateers to the French Government for commissions, was himself concerned in their vessels, and put a deputation into his brother Byndloss's hands to receive the tenths for the King of France, and has ever since corresponded with them.[17]

At the council meeting Vaughan laid his documents, mostly copies of letters, before the council. He claimed that Morgan had been in contact with the privateers and was using his, Vaughan's, name as governor:

> Sir Henry was called in and His Excellency proceeded to examine him on certain interrogatories in reference to his dealings with the privateers in 1675 which follow with his answers to same. Then His Excellency exhibited certain articles against Sir H. Morgan with the several proofs to each of them, the 1st Article being that Morgan in March 1675 presumptuously made use of His Excellency's name and authority without his orders in divers[e] letters he wrote to the privateers, to which are added Morgan's answers to each Article. Then follow the Articles exhibited against Robert Byndloss with his answers to each of them, which have also reference to Byndloss's dealings with the privateers, especially his correspondence with M. Ogeron, Governor of Tortugas, about the recovery of certain tenths due to the French Admiral by captains of privateers who touched at Jamaica. Ordered that the examinations, articles, and answers aforesaid, with all the letters, depositions, and proofs, be kept upon the Council file and entered upon the records, fairly copied, and transmitted to His Majesty under the hand of the Clerk of the Council and the seal of His Excellency.[18]

The council meeting was essentially a trial, where Vaughan claimed that Morgan had written to privateers – Captains Thomas Rogers, John Barnett, Edward Neville and others – saying that he had the backing and power of the governor's office that all privateers, including the French, would be allowed to visit Port Royal in safety and freedom. In addition, Vaughan claimed that Barré, Morgan's secretary, had done business on Morgan's behalf with the privateers; a fact that Barré denied.[19]

Once Vaughan had made his accusations to the council it was time for Morgan to be brought in and questioned. He did not have a defence but answered the questions. His defence would be in the form of depositions and letters to the Lords of Trade and Plantations. However, on the charges of dealing with the privateers Morgan answered that he was carrying out diplomatic relations. 'If relations with the French were forbidden, where was the written order? Were there any minutes or documents to prove this?' He also claimed that any dealings he had directly with French privateers was because he wanted to be sure 'the French were not issuing commissions to buccaneers.'[20]

Vaughan then turned his attention to Robert Byndloss and began questioning him over his acting for the governor of Tortuga. When Vaughan asked Byndloss for a written answer to the charge, Byndloss initially refused until threatened with arrest, when he gave in and handed Vaughan a written statement.

Breverton states that at this point in the trial the council 'were sensing a sea-change in the relative positions of authority of Lord Vaughan and Admiral Morgan.' Indeed, it is Breverton who tells us that the council 'had seen that there was effectively no case to answer, and while the status quo reigned until Whitehall came to a decision, they knew that Vaughan had lost the running battle.'[21]

The defence that Morgan and Byndloss prepared included a deposition from Morgan's secretary, Charles Barré. In the questioning from Vaughan, Barré had told only part of the story. The deposition he signed, witnessed by a magistrate, for Morgan's defence added that the letters Morgan asked him to draft to the privateer captains had been given to Vaughan before being sent for his approval. Vaughan did not send the letters but held them as evidence. However, these were not the finished letters and as such they were only drafts, so were therefore not official. Barré's deposition was sent to the new secretary of the Lords of Trade and Plantations, Sir Henry Coventry.

Deposition of Charles Barré, Secretary to Sir Henry Morgan, Lieutenant General of Jamaica. That about March 1675 he did copy by Sir Henry's orders two letters Sir Henry had written with design to have sent them to the captains of several privateers, to advise to come to Jamaica with prizes and they should be well received, but understood Sir Henry wrote said letters by consent of Lord Vaughan and sent him copies of each letter to underwrite his approbation, which the Governor deferring Sir Henry refused to send said letters. Confesses accepting Captain Smith's offer to go a trading voyage with him, but positively denies he was sent by Sir Henry to treat or act any business with the French or English privateers neither did Sir Henry. Also touching Lord Vaughan's examination of this deponent after his return from his said voyage.[22]

Vaughan also put his accusations in writing to bolster his position with London. In early August he wrote that he told Morgan that he 'should not use his name nor should he have written any such letters to the Privateers without acquainting the governor.' In his long letter he continued to accuse Morgan and Byndloss of acting with the privateers. 'But afterwards, taking notice how little he regarded what I said to him, and that his brother Byndloss and he were only continuing to act by themselves, and privately set up a privateer faction, I thought it my duty to lay the whole matter before his Honour in December last.'[23]

In his defence Morgan wrote a letter to Secretary Coventry in November that:

If His Majesty should be deaf to all and these things should give His Majesty occasion to put me out that he will be graciously pleased to order that I may be tried here at his Court of King's Bench where the witnesses are … and if ever I err in one title, then let me ever be condemned for the greatest villain in the world, and as God is my judge and witness I have never entertained a thought in my life but what hath been really devoted to His Majesty's service and interest nor never will.

With the letter were the documents primarily from the privateer captains and from his secretary that detailed his actions in the matter. He stated, 'I sucked the milk of loyalty and if I would have sold one little part of it I might have been richer than my enemies ever will be.' As for his brother-in-law, he stated that he knew:

nothing of crime in him, but his being related to Sir Henry, for he lives 20 miles from Port Royal, has a wife and five or six children and one of the best estates in this island, therefore he is an understanding man and would not venture that hazard and estate against nothing. His unhappiness is he serves a superior here that is jealous of all his actions and put himself to study Sir Henry's ruin for what reason knows not.[24]

The end of the year saw the closure of this incident. The power had shifted to Morgan, although there was nothing official, but as Breverton tells us, Morgan had more sway in London than Vaughan did. 'Morgan's lobby was far closer to the locus of power than Vaughan's.' But they would have to wait for an official answer from Whitehall.

Chapter 23

Loggerheads

The situation in Jamaica at the beginning of the 1677 New Year was uncertain. More and more English ships were being taken by Spanish privateers on the open seas and prisoners were being taken back to Havana, where they were held. Reports were regularly coming in of Spanish attacks on British ships commissioned by the governor of Havana and it was becoming clear that Lynch's policy of appeasement at any cost was not working. Indeed, this policy had opened the door for the Spanish to harass British ships as they saw fit, with the British unable to do anything about it.

The only frigate available was the *Foresight*, which was all Vaughan had for the protection of the island. He was still trying to suppress the privateers and hang any pirates that sailed into his clutches while also trying to be friends with the Spanish. The reports he sent showed how difficult this was.

> Encloses depositions of some English who have made their escape from the Havana, and of others whom a Spanish ship robbed in the open sea. Orders should be sent to the governor from Spain to observe the peace. Divers[e] of His Majesty's subjects at the Havanna [*sic*] kept as slaves, no justification for the Governor's barbarous usage of His Majesty's subjects and his continuing to take all our ships. The people here full of discontent, seeing their hands are tied while others are at liberty to commit any robberies upon them.[1]

At this point, Vaughan had still not officially heard from the Lords of Trade and Plantations regarding the charges against Morgan and Byndloss. While he continued to follow Lynch's policy, the people of Jamaica had lost faith in his ability to protect the island.

The affair over Captain John Deane had severely damaged his relationship with the Assembly and the people. He discounted the protests from the planters as being part of Morgan's faction but he could not ignore the constant stream of letters and petitions signed by the people of Port Royal and Spanish Town demanding the release of Deane. Realizing he had little choice in the face of the public outcry, he granted the pardon and shortly afterwards received the letter from Secretary Coventry that said Deane's trial was unwarranted.

In London, the reports from Vaughan, merchants and ship owners of the Spanish attacks on British vessels were slowly having an effect on the Privy Council. The final straw that galvanized the king and Privy Council to action was the taking of the Liverpool ship, *Diligence*, by Spanish privateers. This vessel had been bound for the Bay of Campeachy with a cargo of logwood. After unloading and taking on another cargo the ship was attacked on the high seas. The Spanish took the cargo, stripped the rigging and took all the provisions – a clear breach of the treaty. The king and his council immediately ordered the British ambassador in Madrid to lodge a formal protest and then demanded an explanation from the Spanish ambassador in London.[2]

In the presence of Sir Joseph Williamson, Secretary of State, the indignant ambassador in response said, what about the Spanish ship that was captured by Captain John Barnett off Hispaniola where 46,000 pieces of eight had been taken?

Williamson knew nothing of this affair and asked Lynch, now in London, if he had details of the incident. He reported that it had been a 'French ship with a French crew, flying the French flag and with a French commission'. The Spanish prize was sold in a French port and the spoils were divided amongst the French crew and backers, so it had nothing to do with England, or especially with Jamaica.[3]

The Earl of Carlisle, who was originally offered the governorship of the island instead of Vaughan, had received letters and reports from the merchants in Jamaica imploring him to accept the position and come to Jamaica. One letter from a planter told Carlisle that Morgan and Byndloss were the men who had the protection of the island at heart and could be the two men most able to carry it out. The writer warned Carlisle of a large French fleet in the West Indies and that 'should Panama fall into French hands, the manufacturers of France would supply the South Sea, and all the world would be theirs.'[4] Carlisle passed on these letters to the king and Privy Council, which added to the change in attitude.

In Jamaica, Vaughan realized he needed to call a new assembly as the laws that had been passed two years previously had not been ratified by the Lords of Trade and Plantations despite his various letters. A new assembly needed to be called for the laws to be passed again. The new assembly sat on 9 April and were immediately at loggerheads with Vaughan over procedure.

Refers to the laws he transmitted in 1675, mostly the same as were made by Sir Thomas Lynch. Had reason to surmise trouble in the next Assembly, and describes how he discovered and prevented what was in agitation – obstruction of the Council to the Act of the Militia. Complains of his having no positive power without them, and not being able to 'suspend any on misbehaviour or unfaithfulness without their consents'. Seven of the eleven Councillors 'voted it quite out' and openly asserted His Majesty's Commission was no law to them.[5]

Exasperated, Vaughan wanted to suspend members of the council but, as the above quote shows, he was unable to do so without their agreement. Something that was unlikely to happen. 'Since the Council are so wholly interested here, and have no dependence in England, it should be in the governor's power to suspend them.'

Vaughan was also having problems with the privateers. He considered that he had little power to stop them.

Let him send what orders he will about privateering, there are almost none to execute them but who are one or the other interested. These practices so long settled it is no easy matter to suppress them. Both Council and Assembly alike interested, so nothing left but the Governor's negative voice to deny what they demand, and so little power in the Governor, and so much given to the people that when they will they may do what they please.[6]

Yet here is a man who took on the roles of judge, jury and potential executioner in Deane's case, and then governor for providing the pardon for Deane, something that even the king could not do in England. He treated the Assembly and the council with contempt so there is little wonder that he ran into continuous difficulty.

These difficulties came to a head when Vaughan heard that a privateer, Captain James Brown, had attacked a Dutch ship, *Golden Sun*, and taken 150 slaves from that ship that he then sold to merchants and planters in Jamaica.

The Commander was a Scotchman named Brown, most of his men English, the rest French and Dutch; that they left Jamaica about eight months since for Carthagena, where they met with this Dutch vessel trading on the coast and killed the Dutch captain and several of his men. Sent out the frigate and seized 100 negroes concealed in several planters' hands. Intends to have them condemned in the Admiralty as goods piratically taken, and to be restored to the right owners.[7]

The planters immediately protested Vaughan's action of ordering the seizure of the slaves so they could be returned to their owners. They protested because they had paid for them. At the same time, French privateers had raided a small town north of Cartagena, Santa Marta, on the Spanish Main, taken hostage a bishop and demanded ransom. When a Spanish fleet arrived with hundreds of soldiers the privateers battled their way back to their ships and sailed for Port Royal. These were privateers with French commissions sailing under French flags.

The arrival of the French privateers in Jamaica alarmed the Assembly so much that they hurriedly drafted a law prohibiting anyone from Jamaica serving under a foreign flag against any nation that England was at peace with. Naturally, the penalty for anyone disobeying the law was death. However, the law called for a three-month amnesty period where privateers could come into Jamaica and claim a pardon. This grace period meant that many of the old English privateers returned from Tortuga, where they had been operating with French commissions.

The significance of this new law is that Brown, who along with eight of his crew had been arrested and charged with piracy, should have now been able to claim a pardon. Brown had sailed into Port Royal so he could do just that. Brown and his eight men were found guilty and sentenced to death. They immediately appealed to the Assembly, which was in session for clemency under the new law. The Assembly requested a stay of execution from Vaughan, who flatly refused. However, Vaughan did grant the eight crewmen a pardon, but not Brown.

> At least 300 come in since the passing of the Act against serving under a foreign prince. Men will not venture their lives to serve the French, it being death by said Act to do so. Several Spanish towns taken by the French of late at the taking of St Martha, they had about 100 English, who have all since come in upon the Act.[8]

Realizing that Vaughan's intransigence could jeopardize the security of the island by forcing the privateers who had come in to leave Port Royal and even turn on Jamaica, the Assembly passed a resolution that ordered Brown's execution be delayed. Writing later of the affair, Sir Thomas Lynch provided the final details:

> Relates the circumstances of the taking of a Dutch Negro ship by one Brown, a Scotchman, who had a commission from Mons Ogeron, Governor of Tortugas, who has been dead above a year; the trial and condemnation of Brown and his Company for piracy, Brown was ordered to be executed, his men being pardoned, but he petitioned the Assembly that he might have the benefit of their Act, who petitioned the Governor for a reprieve, but he sent orders for

immediate execution 'whereupon the fellow was hanged.' Half an hour after the Marshal came with an order signed by the Speaker to observe the Chief Justice's writ of *habeas corpus* which had been granted, but superseded by the Governor's order. My Lord resented this proceeding and immediately sent for the Assembly, which after reproving he dissolved.[9]

Vaughan had no power to do what he did. His running battle with the Assembly had come to the attention of the Lords of Trade and Plantations as well as the Privy Council in London and the decision was that he needed to be replaced.

To make matters worse for Vaughan he received word from London regarding their official response to the charges he'd laid against Morgan and Byndloss.

The business of Sir Henry Morgan and Colonel Byndloss as they stand accused by Lord Vaughan for corresponding with privateers taken into consideration. Abstract of the articles against them read, and their Lordships do not come to any resolution until they have proceeded to a further examination of the whole matter.[10]

As the year came to a close tensions between the English and the French flared and came to a head when the French refitted and prepared a fleet to sail to the West Indies. The Lords of Trade and Plantations sent warnings to the governors of Antigua, Nevis, St Kitts, Montserrat, Jamaica and Bermuda of the French fleet.

In London, Lord Carlisle had been appointed the new governor of Jamaica and his commission was signed on 1 March 1678.

Prior to that, Vaughan, who must have heard that he was being replaced, cut Morgan's salary of £600 a year in half. On 14 March 1678, Lord Vaughan left Jamaica forever. He was the largest landowner at the time. Perhaps it was the realization that he had lost control of his government, or that realizing he'd exceeded his powers and he knew he was going to be replaced, that was the cause of his sudden decision to leave. We can only speculate.

The King's warrant to Charles, Earl of Carlisle, Captain General of Jamaica. To cause drums to be beat about the city of London for raising 200 men for His Majesty's service in Jamaica.

Commission to Charles, Earl of Carlisle, Captain General and Governor-in-Chief of Jamaica and the territories depending thereon, to be Captain of a company of Foot, consisting of 100 men besides officers, to be raised for His Majesty's service in Jamaica.

A like Commission to Sir Henry Morgan, Lieutenant Governor of Jamaica, to be Captain of a company of 100 men besides officers, Also Commissions to Ralph Fetheronhaugh to be Lieutenant, to Sir Henry Morgan; Elias Markham to be Ensign to the Earl of Carlisle, John Tolderoy to be Lieutenant to the Earl of Carlisle, and Usher Tyrell, gent, to be Ensign to Sir Henry Morgan.[11]

Chapter 24

Morgan's Second Term

This day Sir Henry Morgan took the oath of Commander-in-Chief, and the councillors also took their oaths to be true to him. No persons to have a ticket to leave the island except such as are necessary for sailing vessels. Upon apprehensions of a foreign enemy ordered that a council of war be called to consider the best means for securing this island, and that notice be given to the several field officers.[1]

With Vaughan gone Morgan was now acting governor of Jamaica and within three weeks of this taking place he received word from the Lords of Trade and Plantation to prepare for an imminent French attack. That warning arrived late on 1 April. Morgan called a council meeting and on 3 April was sworn in as commander-in-chief. Two days later, the first council of war met and ordered that martial law be declared, the militia companies be exercised and that they be 'well provided with arms and ammunition, and make a return to the commander-in-chief.' The council ordered the captain of the forts to make an inventory of the arms and ammunition held by the merchants of Port Royal and that no vessel land at Port Royal after ten at night till sunrise. 'The orders to be observed in case of a general alarm. Ordered, that the tenth Negro of all Negroes in the island be employed on the fortifications, all of which are specified in the several parishes.'[2]

Two new forts were to be built, the Rupert, named after the king's cousin, and another later named Carlisle. Port Royal was a peninsula with a thin strip of land running parallel to the coast, which then widened out to a larger area of land at its tip. This larger area was where Port Royal had been built. Fort Morgan and Fort Charles were situated on Morgan's Lines, facing seaward, while Fort James was on the inside tip covering the entrance to the harbour. (Morgan's Lines sometimes refers to the line of guns along the seaward wall of Fort Morgan where twenty-six guns were mounted in order to cover the vulnerable coastline. This included trenches for snipers and sharpshooters and trenches along the wall below the guns.) Fort Rupert was to be placed at the beginning of the thin strip of land covering the coastal approaches should the French land along the coast and try to attack Port Royal that way. Fort Carlisle was to be situated further along the peninsula on the approach to Port Royal in case any enemy vessel managed to get past the batteries on Fort Charles.

The council of war had ordered that one in ten slaves from each plantation be used for building the two new forts. News that London was expecting war with France arrived eight days later and Morgan called his second council of war to extend martial law until 10 June. The ship that brought the news of imminent war also brought news that Lord Carlisle was on his way to Jamaica.

The threat of attack by the French was real. The French fleet was under the command of Count d'Estrées and consisted of eight ships of the line, eight frigates, three transports and more than a dozen French privateers who had joined the fleet in France. The transports carried hundreds of guns with enough powder and shot for each gun. D'Estrées's flagship was the seventy-gun *Terrible* and this fleet was on its way to attack Dutch and British colonies in the West Indies. Its first target was Curaçao.[3]

Morgan sent the sloop *Advice*, commanded by Captain Thomas Wigfall, to Hispaniola to find out more about the French fleet. On 31 May, Morgan called his third council of war, where it was decided that 'no ship be permitted to sail for Europe until a fortnight hence, when a good fleet of merchantmen would be ready, whereby they might in some measure secure themselves.'[4]

The very same day, the *Advice* returned with some startling news. Just after docking, Captain Wigfall immediately went to Morgan to brief him on what had happened to the French fleet. He stated:

That upon 3 or 4 May last, as Count d'Estrées was sailing with his whole fleet to Curaçao, about eight at night, he ran upon the shores of the Isle of Aves, who, with two frigates finding themselves aground, fired three guns apiece, but the rest mistaking it for the signal of a council of war crowded in, and there perished with near 500 men, 250 brass, and 300 iron guns. All had run the same fate but for a small privateer who gave notice of the danger. Count d'Estrées's ship 'burst' all at once, who was saved with difficulty, but most of his men lost. The Count stayed off Petit Guavos until 28 May, and then sailed with seven ships, all that remained, to France, but was forced to leave 500 of the Old France men behind.[5]

With the French fleet wrecked the threat of attack and invasion had gone for the time being. Morgan had hurried the construction of the two forts and the refitting of the existing forts so that they were ready for the next threat, whatever that would be.

This harbour much strengthened by two new batteries, the Rupert and the Carlisle, by the diligence of Sir Henry Morgan since Lord Vaughan left. On expectation of war with France many privateers under French Commissions coming in; employing them will be a difficulty unless the trade of logwood be adjusted with the Spaniard.[6]

Morgan, now forty-three, was once again able to enjoy life as one of the largest and influential landowners on the island. All that he had on the horizon to worry about was the arrival of the new governor.

Lord Carlisle arrived in the frigate *Jersey* on 17 July. The crossing had been bad for his gout but, fortunately, he and Morgan got on well together. Both men spoke well of each other and Carlisle had read a confidential report that detailed Morgan's importance to the security of Jamaica. But Carlisle brought with him trouble. Because of the feuds that both Lynch and Vaughan had created with their respective councils and assemblies London had decided that all laws for Jamaica would be made in Westminster and it was Carlisle's job to see that Jamaica would lose its ability to make its own laws.

Morgan and Carlisle were friends and it may have been out of friendship that Morgan stayed out of the political wrangling that took place between Lord Carlisle, the Assembly and his council. In London, Carlisle had been given instructions from the king that he was to synchronize Jamaican law with English law and that the Assembly were not to pass laws of their own but ratify the laws from Whitehall. Nor were the Assembly of Jamaica allowed to reject any legislation from Whitehall.

Of course this went down very badly with the Assembly and the council. Indeed, the council agreed to send two members to London to plead their case with the king and the Privy Council.

On 2 September the wrangling began with the first day of the new assembly. Wisely, Morgan busied himself with continuing to build up the island's defences while the political battle intensified.

Some of the Council much dissatisfied at the alterations in the laws and the manner of passing them, particularly at a clause in the Militia Bill which they are jealous of lest that thereby they make it legal to execute all instructions that are or shall be sent to Carlisle or any succeeding Governor, which scruple might easily be avoided, but that the Great Seal being affixed to the laws I have no power to make any alteration which I might have done both to their satisfaction and the preservation of the King's right.[7]

Carlisle, with advice from Morgan, sent the frigate *Jersey* to go back to the point where the *Jamaica Merchant* sank three years before to salvage the guns and ammunition from the wreck that lay off Cow Island near Hispaniola. The 200 soldiers who came on the *Jersey* with Carlisle were split between Spanish Town, under Carlisle's command, and Port Royal, under Morgan's command.

For five long weeks Carlisle argued with the Assembly about the new constitution that stripped it of its ability to pass its own acts of law. Finally, the argument turned into a bitter quarrel as the Assembly refused to accept the acts brought by Carlisle as legal and the new governor dissolved the Assembly. In mid-September, Carlisle wrote again to Secretary Coventry concerning the Assembly. 'The Assembly met on the 2nd instant, and are so dissatisfied with the alterations in the Government that the governor questions whether they will pass any of these laws,' he wrote. 'They object to the Act for revenue, and are nettled at the expression in the preamble that the revenue was raised by the governor and Council.'[8]

By late October, Carlisle's frustration with the new system of government he had tried to impose upon the Assembly could be seen in his letter to Sir Joseph Williamson when we wrote that 'the proceedings of the Assembly have been so cross-grained that they have thrown out all the Bills he brought under the Great Seal. The disgust to the new frame of Government occasioned it. Some of the laws were faulty themselves.' Stating that he had foreseen this would happen when he was in England he continued quite bluntly, saying that:

> it rests now with the King and those about him to consider whether you will gratify the people in reverting to the former way. The dilatoriness of passing laws in a new Colony is a sting he shall beg may be altered. Has taken more pains than ever he did in any business in his life to make the Assembly sensible of the hurt they did themselves and the island, but all to no purpose; they will not consent to lose their deliberative power.[9]

Carlisle wrote again on 15 November to the Lords of Trade and Plantations recommending that the 'present form appointed for making and passing laws very impracticable besides very distasteful to the sense of the people here. Begs His Majesty's instruction to call another assembly and re-enact and make what laws are fit for this place.'[10]

Chapter 25

Lord Carlisle

In January 1679 Carlisle wrote to Secretary Coventry stating that the security of the logwood trade in the Bay of Campeachy should be of great importance for the security and prosperity of Jamaica. He stated that he needed agreement for an 'early arrangement with the Spaniard' if the logwood trade was to prosper. He warned that if no arrangement was made the men whose sole income was the logwood trade would very likely turn to piracy and attack the Spanish.

Over the next two months, Carlisle kept up a steady stream of letters, writing about the Indian uprising in Dutch-held Surinam and how the English and Dutch had to take refuge in the castle while the Indians burnt their plantations, houses and furniture and destroyed as much as they could.

He wrote about French privateers sacking Spanish towns and taking their booty back to Hispaniola. He told Sir Henry Coventry how five men from the frigate *Jersey* were accused and tried for sodomy and sentenced to death. Three of the men Carlisle pardoned, but the fourth he executed.

The reasons why the Assembly had rejected the laws Carlisle had brought over under the Great Seal of government reached the Lords of Trade and Plantations. They prepared a report in May 1679 that went to the king in council. Here they stated that:

The Assembly has no right to meet but by the Governor's permission, and that temporary and for probation. It is therefore surprising that they should regard as a right what was granted as a favour, thus discouraging future Royal favours of the same kind, and treat all temporary and experimental constitutions as a resignation and devolution to them of the Royal authority. Since, therefore, it is evident that the Assembly of Jamaica rejects the King's favours, and that the King's resolution is likely to be the measure of their respect and obedience, we recommend that the Governor be empowered to call another Assembly, and represent to it the expediency of accepting the laws transmitted by the King; and that in case of refusal the Governor be furnished with such powers as were formerly given to Colonel Doyley, the first Governor of Jamaica, and to other

Governors since, whereby Lord Carlisle may be enabled to govern according to the laws of England.[1]

However, it appears that this report did not reach Carlisle as a month later he wrote to their Lordships as plainly as he could about the political and legal situation in Jamaica:

> I find the inhabitants of this Island dissatisfied with having the deliberative part of making laws and power to alter and amend Bills transferred hither under the Great Seal of England taken from them. They will never be induced to accept the system, for they judge it unreasonable because of the distance of Jamaica from England. I therefore beg of your Lordships to prevent further loss of time, nor leave this Island 'languishing for want of necessary laws'.[2]

In the meantime a peace treaty between France and Holland had been signed and in Holland the first edition of Esquemeling's book, *The Buccaneers of America*, was published. The author, Alexander Oliver Oexmelin, wrote his book in three parts. The first of was his own life, in Tortuga and Hispaniola, the second was about the daring and brutal raids of the French privateer Francois L'Ollanais, and the last part, the most important for us, was the descriptions of Morgan's expeditions. As we have seen in earlier chapters, the details of these expeditions make it clear that Esquemeling was there and his descriptions of the battles matches the reports from the Spanish of the same events.

However, Pope tells us that the Spanish, realizing that if they manipulated the translation of the book, they would have evidence of the atrocities committed by the buccaneers – Henry Morgan especially. The Spanish version of Esquemeling's books was 'an amazing story of rape and robbery, treachery and treason, pillage by land and sea, and (because the translator knew what was required of him) in which every foreigner was a scoundrel and nearly always an English one.' Of course, every Spanish person in the book was above reproach, devout, the women were beautiful and chaste and the Spanish governors heroes, virtuous, brave and courageous.[3]

In July the threat of a French attack returned when two French ships sailed into Port Royal. They were both hit by cannon balls fired from the batteries that Morgan had refurbished. In return, the French fired a volley of seven shots into the town and then quickly sailed away. However, that did not end the matter. Morgan met up with Carlisle and they waited for another French attack. A week later, in late evening, the alarm was raised as Carlisle wrote:

The Point was alarmed by the appearance of eight French men-of-war in the offing. The Point fired guns to give the alarm to leeward. I received it myself at Guanaboa, 22 miles from The Point, took horse, and was in with the forces at their arms before day. Being got early to The Point in a good condition of defending itself, I met there Count d'Erveaux, a Knight of Malta, with some other French officers, who pretended to come from Count d'Estrees to ask leave to wood and water at Blewfield's Bay, or Point Negril, one of the most leewardly ports of this Island. The reason given was that they were bound first for Carthagena to demand thence all French prisoners, but, being driven to this coast by violent breezes, were now bound to Havanna to make the like demand; that they were unwilling to trust to Spanish courtesy for wood and water, which they intended to demand, but believed that the denial thereof by the Spaniards would lead to quarrel, they expecting the same privilege in the West Indies as in the Mediterranean. They told us they came from France fourteen sail, but had left seven at Lisbon to attend Count Schomberg. To what end these French are come here we cannot possibly learn; they say, against the Spaniards, but the people distrust their speech.[4]

The arrival of the French caused such a panic within the inhabitants of Port Royal that they:

removed their goods and families for fear of a French descent; and several sloops coming in with advice that the French fleet was standing off to windward, this so increased their jealousies that I called a Council to The Point. It was agreed that a council of war should be held and martial law proclaimed for thirty days, which was done accordingly. The whole of the inhabitants, soldiers and slaves were set to work to increase the fortifications, I being very glad of the opportunity of carrying on work which would otherwise have gone forward very slowly. Still, in my opinion, the French aim rather at Havanna than Jamaica, and if they get possession of this, the key of the West Indies, as they certainly may unless obstructed by England, they will command the treasure of this part of the world more to the prejudice of England than the Spaniards.

Carlisle ended his lengthy report by stating that the 'occurrence has done us more good than harm, but the generality of people will not give up their opinion that the French fleet when reinforced is designed against this Island.'[5]

Carlisle received a letter from Barbados that outlined the intention of the French to take Jamaica and with feelings running high, Carlisle recalled the Assembly. A committee was then set up by the Assembly and council to determine what was required for extra defences and put into the hands of Sir Henry Morgan to oversee.

He wrote a report that made 'seven recommendations for strengthening the breastwork, arming the new works, providing four fireships'. He recommended extra trenches should be dug for snipers and sharp shooters, new gun platforms be set up and a new fort built. That fort was to be called Fort Morgan.[6]

In August Carlisle told the Assembly he had received a letter from the Council of Trade and Plantations that they believed the system of government should be of the type where the laws are made in England and essentially imposed on Jamaica. Carlisle told the Assembly on 20 August that 'he proposed that the Act of Revenue should be continued for eighteen months, for he had sent Sir Francis Watson to England to negotiate the ancient system of making laws, and intended if Sir Francis failed, to go himself next March.'

The threat from the French gradually died down but the inhabitants were still very much on edge. However, the Spanish privateers began increasing their activities, taking more British ships in retaliation for the attacks on them by the same French fleet that had sent boats into Port Royal to ask for wood and water. From 30 August, Carlisle spent 'three days at The Point, and on Friday morning went with Sir Henry Morgan to Three Rivers, some 12 miles from The Point, and thence round the Cod of the Great Harbour to the Rocks, where we observed the properest passes to secure both The Point and Liquania in case of attack by land.'[7]

On 1 September Sir Thomas Modyford died and his son, also named Thomas, died shortly afterwards. A few days earlier the Attorney General, Mr Wright, also died.

In the autumn of 1679, many of the logwood cutters in the Bay of Campeachy, angry at the lack of security from Jamaica, turned to piracy. Once such pirate was Captain Peter Harris, who captured a twenty-eight-gun Dutch vessel. Carlisle immediately ordered the frigate *Success* to go out and get Harris and bring him back for trial. During the ensuing chase, *Success* hit a reef and was lost while Harris sailed away through the South Keys.[8]

In October, Carlisle again presented the laws he'd brought over from England under the Great Seal to the newly called Assembly for their ratification. Again, the Assembly rejected the laws.

Morgan's first libel case took place around this time but it had begun back in July when Captain Francis Mingham, upon arriving in Port Royal in his ship the *Francis*, was accused by the port customs of not declaring some of his cargo: two butts of brandy and twenty casks of cherry brandy. They said this was a deliberate move on Mingham's part and so seized the vessel and the cargo, then sent the case to be heard before the admiralty court, presided over by Morgan. He sided with customs and ruled that the *Francis* should be condemned. Mingham was furious and decided to travel to London, where he petitioned the Privy Council to have his case reheard.

> The matter came to a trial in the Court of Admiralty, and his ship was condemned for making a false entry. Notwithstanding my kindness, whereby he was prevented of being sold according to the condemnation, he is still dissatisfied, and I believe will incense his owners to attempt your ears to inform the King.[9]

Mingham was so secure in his case that he managed to secure summons for both Morgan and the Receiver General of Jamaica, Thomas Martin, for a hearing to be held in London on 1 May 1680 and travelled to Jamaica to serve the summons personally. In February 1680 Carlisle wrote to Secretary Coventry about the whole incident, stating that 'in the main I am well satisfied. Mingham is a very ill man. He took upon him (though there was no mention of me either in the petition or the order) to serve me too, as he had served Sir H. Morgan and Mr Martin, as if I had been concerned in what he so falsely and maliciously charged them with.' In his letter Carlisle points out to Coventry that Mingham wasn't entirely truthful by saying that his ship was sold for £300 but in the petition Mingham stated it had been sold for £800. He accused Morgan and Martin of dividing the money between them, writing:

> I do not believe that they turned a penny of it to their own use. Sir Henry as Judge of the Admiralty Court has not yet received even his fees, and Mr Martin has given his share for the building of an Exchange in Port Royal for the encouragement of trade. They are now engaged in a trial with Mingham before the Grand Court, the result of which shall be reported to you as speedily as possible.[10]

As soon as Morgan received his summons he sued Mingham for libel, starting a course of action where lawyers on both sides would have to prepare their cases. Carlisle tried to persuade Morgan not to continue with his libel action if Mingham provided a written statement that his petition was 'false and scandalous'. Morgan refused to do so and 'resolved to put it on the country, and the jury has given him £2,000 damages. Whereby your Lordships may see how easy it is for us at this distance to be reproachfully and scandalously traduced to you, till we are made happy in an opportunity of vindication,' Carlisle reported.[11]

Before the verdict came through, Morgan put pen to paper outlining the incident and including documents to substantiate his claim:

> With the papers and depositions will, I doubt not, prove to your Lordships that the petition of Francis Mingham is false and scandalous, except in the one fact that the ship was condemned. The petition says that she was condemned for two casks of brandy; but it was in reality for two butts of brandy and twenty casks of black cherry brandy which were plainly kept on board to defraud the customs. Other statements are equally false. It is plain that Mingham makes no conscience of swearing falsely, for he exhibited a bill in the High Court of Justice denying on oath that he had ever delivered the petition or served me with a copy of your Lordships' order, and a little later another bill in part confessing it. There was no malice on my part or Mr Martin's in the trial before the Admiralty Court as Mingham falsely asserts, nor did covetousness enter into the matter. The office of Judge Admiral was not given me for my understanding of the business better than others, nor for the profitableness thereof, for 'I left the schools too young to be a great proficient in either that or other laws, and have been much more used to the pike than the book; and as for the profit there is no porter in this town but can get more money in the time than I got by this trial. But I was truly put in to maintain the honour of the Court for His Majesty's service,' without which the Acts of Navigation cannot be enforced for it is hard to find unbiased juries in the Plantations for such cases.[12]

Mingham, however, was unable to pay the damages and so was put in debtor's prison. His wife sent a petition against Morgan to the Privy Council in London complaining of his imprisonment. It was decided that Mingham could be freed if he put up a deposit for the damages he owed Morgan. So late in 1680, Morgan discharged Mingham and the entry in the Minutes of the Council of Jamaica stated that 'Francis Mingham's troubles in Jamaica were due more to his own imprudence and malicious desire for revenge than to any purpose of Sir Henry Morgan to oppress him.'[13]

But this was a sideshow compared to the real problems of governing the island. The Assembly still refused to accept the laws that Carlisle had brought with him. The Assembly had sent representatives, Chief Justice Samuel Long, the chief architect of the Assembly's objections to the new system of government and who had been dismissed by Carlisle from the council for his total intransigence, along with Major Beeston to argue the case for allowing Jamaica to make its own laws.

Carlisle also realized that he could argue the case better in London than he could in Jamaica so he too left, and with him gone, Morgan's enemies in London could plot anew knowing there was no one there to protect him.

Chapter 26

Last Years

Morgan was now forty-five and drinking heavily. Even so, he was at the pinnacle of his success. Carlisle left in May of 1680 and one of his last acts was to set up a seven-man committee headed up by Morgan to analyze how merchant shipping in the area around the island and beyond could be protected. The committee drew up their report and Carlisle took it with him to London. In appreciation for his work, Carlisle gave Morgan a stipend of £600 annually from his own pocket.[1]

With Carlisle gone, Morgan was virtually in complete control of Jamaica. In his biography of Sir Henry Morgan, Dudley Pope tells us that Morgan was now Justice of the Peace, Judge of Admiralty Court, Vice Admiral, Colonel/Commandant of the Port Royal Regiment and the Lieutenant General of Jamaica, as well as acting governor.[2]

Still tall and lean, the heavy drinking was beginning to take a toll on Morgan. But the drinking was not that of a sad man or a man that drank to forget; it was because he was a larger than life character who spent many of his evenings smoking and drinking, exchanging stories of wild adventures with his peers.

Morgan was still a rugged man and though he liked to live the life of a buccaneer, his life had undergone a substantial change. Since his return to Jamaica after being arrested he'd entered the political arena with a passion, having been the deputy governor to two governors. He'd made enemies of both Lynch and Vaughan, built up Jamaica's defences and added to his plantations.

However, there was one thing that set Morgan apart. While he may have caroused in the evening with old friends and relatives, he'd separated himself from his past. As a deputy governor he'd been charged with the eradication of piracy from Jamaica – a task that was almost impossible. But he set about this task with gusto, determined to do it to his best ability. 'The Admiral had seen the future, and it was trade, not pillage. Privateering had given him estates and status, but he knew that only a rational system of trade and a lasting peace could ensure his family's position for generations to come.'[3]

Morgan had done what few pirates or buccaneers could ever do: change their stripes. He'd looked to the future and realized that true power and wealth lay in trade with all the outlying colonies, indeed with his old enemy, the Spanish. As such he clamped down on piracy and privateering.

As the acting governor, in his third term in office much of Morgan's time was taken up in putting down the privateering and piracy so that he could establish peaceful trading relations with the Dutch, French and Spanish. He regularly wrote letters about his activities in this regard:

> We are not less troubled with privateers belonging to this Island. Strict orders for their arrest were issued by Lord Carlisle before his departure and by myself since, and some of their men having been taken, who are now in prison awaiting trial, the rest are alarmed, and not daring to enter any of our ports, keep on the wing until they can find some place to settle on. I much fear that this may occasion the loss of many men to this Island, but it can only be prevented by the continual attendance of some nimble small frigate in coasting round the Island and surprising the privateers.[4]

Further evidence of Morgan's change towards the privateers can be seen when he wrote to London that:

> Nothing can be more fatal to the prosperity of this Colony than the temptingly alluring boldness and success of the privateers, which draws off white servants and all men of unfortunate or desperate condition. I spare no care to put down this growing evil, having lately granted a special commission for the trial of several runaway whites who fired in a body at a party sent to apprehend them. These privateers discourage the Spaniards from private trade with us, which would otherwise be considerable.[5]

One incident illustrates this point most effectively. An unknown sloop anchored in Montego Bay but the crew remained on board and nothing was unloaded or loaded onto the vessel. Morgan was notified of this and became suspicious. It was the kind of thing that buccaneers would do if they were unsure of the reception they would get if they came ashore. Morgan sent an invitation to the seventeen men aboard the sloop to join him for dinner at the governor's mansion, King's House, in Port Royal. The food was excellent, the alcohol flowed, and the more it did, the more the men confessed that they were pirates and that they knew where the best Spanish ships were ripe for the taking. Laughter filled the evening and Morgan regaled them with stories of his adventures. Finally, they all went to their beds and in the morning as the men left they were arrested by the militia and put in prison.

When the seventeen men were brought into the admiralty court they were stunned to find Morgan staring down at them from the bench. As the Chief Judge, he was a different man from the one they'd caroused with. The trial was quick; they were sentenced to death and hung the same day.

Morgan filled the council and the top spots in the Jamaican government with his friends, family and other supporters. 'His brothers-in-law, Byndloss and Archbold, were on the council and Robert Byndloss was Chief Justice.' The Commandant of Port Royal was his third brother-in-law, Charles Byndloss, and the Attorney General was his great friend, Roger Elleston.[6]

In London, fellow Welshman Sir Leoline Jenkins became the new Secretary of State and as Morgan kept up his letters and reports to London detailing his activities in putting down piracy and increasing trade, he soon learned that both Lynch and Vaughan were plotting against him.

By the end of 1680, Morgan had also acquired another 1,200 acres near Port Maria that he called Llanrhymni, after the place where he'd been born.[7]

In February 1682, Morgan sent the writs out for elections to hold a new assembly. Yet despite Morgan's efforts a new pirate had appeared on the scene who was causing havoc. The Dutch pirate Captain Jacob Eversten had a crew of sixty-four British and six Spanish aboard his brigantine. Repeated attempts at catching the pirate at sea failed but one evening Morgan received a report that the Dutchman had anchored in Bull Bay, not far from Port Royal. Sensing his chance to catch the pirate, Morgan ordered that two dozen soldiers from the Port Royal Regiment embark on a merchant sloop with smaller coasters also carrying soldiers following. For some reason Eversten did not believe the little fleet posed a threat but by the time he realized his mistake, he and his men were quickly overwhelmed by the soldiers. In the ensuing engagement Eversten and most of his crew managed to swim to shore but they were rounded up, along with the twenty-six pirates captured during the battle. In all, sixty British pirates and some Spanish came before Morgan. The Spanish he sent to the governor of Cartagena. When the remaining men came before him he stated they:

> were tried by a special Commission of oyer and terminer in the Court of Admiralty, when they were convicted of piracy and sentenced to die. But after deliberation, and reflection that the General Assembly was to meet on the 18th following, I thought it not fit to post them to execution lest it should scare all others abroad from returning to their allegiance.[8]

Morgan's intense dislike of privateers of all nationalities can be seen in his many letters to London. In one, dated 16 February, which he sent to Lord Sunderland, Morgan stated:

> I present this complaint to your Lordship against the unchristianlike conduct and unneighbourliness of the Spaniard, who take all our ships at sea or in port. They have this year captured twenty-two sail and absolutely ruined our Bay trade. Though not ordinarily prejudicial to this Colony, this is most detrimental to the King's customs, as you will perceive from depositions which I have forwarded to Lord Carlisle. I could multiply them if I chose to countenance addresses against the Spaniards' inhumanity. We treat them on all occasions with all imaginable respect and kindness, and in return receive only ingratitude; they have many English prisoners, we not one Spanish, and why they should have credit at Whitehall and we want it I leave to your Lordship.[9]

Breverton tells us that Morgan's enemies in London were plotting his overthrow and that Lynch bribed the king – his coffers virtually bare from his wild lifestyle – with £50,000 so he could return to Jamaica as governor. The king took the money and Lynch returned in 1682, much to Morgan's surprise and chagrin.

In May of 1682, Lynch arrived in Jamaica a sick man. His earlier dismissal from his post and seeing Morgan taking up the reins of deputy governor must have rankled with him so much that he spent many years plotting Morgan's downfall. Now he was in a position to achieve some sort of triumph over Morgan, who was ten times the man that Lynch would ever be. We can't know the emotions that drove Lynch but from his subsequent actions we can guess that he was a petty man. Where Morgan was decisive, vigorous, brave, courageous, strong-willed, full of charisma and able to lead hundreds of men by his will alone, Lynch was nothing of the sort. He lodged with one of his supporters on the island, Hender Molesworth, and on 14 May he handed Morgan a letter that stripped him of his role as lieutenant governor and lieutenant general. Lynch dismissed Morgan from power but not from being a council member.

For Morgan the new state of affairs sent him into heavy drinking. He was upset at being cast aside after having done so much for Jamaica, possibly the one man who had saved Jamaica from becoming Spanish.

Lynch then turned to Morgan's friends and began wholesale dismissals. Lynch had orchestrated a condition on his returning to Jamaica, which was that he had the power to dismiss members of the council. Lynch dismissed Roger Elleston from his role as Attorney General in January 1683 for speaking out against Protestant dissenters who spoke against the king. Elleston, Morgan, Byndloss, Ballard and Watson were part of the Loyal Club, loyalists to the king and country.

Lynch's charge against Elleston was that his speech was malicious and that Morgan was behind his actions. It is strange that both Lynch and Vaughan believed that every bad thing that befell them during their time as governors was always down to Morgan. They could not see that the real reasons were their own deficiencies.

With Lynch in total control, piracy grew once again, with eighteen ships being captured off the coast of Hispaniola by just one French privateer, the *Trompeuse*. This was a loss of some £50,000 and there were several privateers – French, Spanish and Dutch – operating in the Caribbean.

The next to go from the council was Byndloss on 10 October, as well as being removed from the militia and any form of public office. The following day, Morgan's other brother-in-law, Charles Morgan, was also removed from the council and his position as Commandant of Port Royal was also taken away from him. The following day it was Morgan's turn to be booted off the council when the membership voted that he should be stripped of all his offices, commands and then suspended.

Morgan's health was deteriorating; he had swellings in his stomach and his legs, and problems with his liver were taking effect – all from his heavy drinking and the results of the fever he'd never really been able to get rid of.

By 1684, every Morgan supporter on the council had been removed by Lynch, who now filled the council with his own supporters, friends and family. Morgan sent Charles Morgan (also his cousin) to London to protest the way that Lynch had acted. As Morgan had been a few years earlier, Lynch was now in charge of Jamaica with virtually no opposition. He did not have long to enjoy this position as he died on 24 August 1684 and was succeeded by his great friend, Hender Molesworth, who took over as acting governor of the island.

Around this time two booksellers in England picked up Esquemeling's book and published an English version translated from the Spanish edition because it had done so well in Holland, France and Spain. Thomas Malthus and William Crooke, both booksellers, were hoping for the same success in England. In London, Charles Morgan saw the new English translations for sale and purchased copies of each, which he sent to Morgan in Jamaica. He also consulted a lawyer, just in case.

While the book 'painted Morgan as a bold and sometimes brilliant leader, it also painted him as a rampaging, torturing, thieving pirate.'[10] Morgan was furious. To him, respect of the family was everything. While he held the commissions from the king he was acting respectably and within the king's instructions. That meant he was not and never was a pirate. He was a privateer. The fact that the book made him out to be a criminal is what incensed him most of all. He immediately instructed his lawyer to sue the booksellers for libel.

In London, Morgan's lawyer, John Greene, began the libel suit against the two booksellers. Immediate compliance came first from Crooke, who agreed that he would put an insert about Morgan that would be very favourable to him in the second edition. To add to his compliance he also issued a pamphlet, according to Breverton, stating that Esquemeling had falsely reported several things about Morgan in his book and 'wrongfully represented and consequently are much redounding on the Disreputation and Dishonour of the Worthy Person, Sir Henry Morgan; For the Wounds of whose reputation by that Author, I have been, ever since my better information, both heartily sorrowful, and concerned in the sincerity of my mind.'[11] The libel case against Crooke was dropped.

However, Malthus was a different story and he refused to settle. The action went to court and in the end Malthus was forced to publish an apology and pay £200 damages to Morgan. This libel suit had set a precedent where money could be awarded for legal libel.

Back in Jamaica, Morgan heard news that filled him with joy. His old friend from his younger days, the Duke of Albemarle, had been made governor of Jamaica. Albemarle had fought on the side of the new king, Catholic King James II, who had succeeded Charles II, during the Duke of Monmouth rebellion. That rebellion had been put down with Albemarle's help and in return he wanted to be governor of Jamaica. In 1686, while Molesworth remained as acting governor, he was busy lining his pockets with the slave trade, as Terry Breverton tells us in his book. 'Molesworth was a factor of the Royal Africa Company, which now had a monopoly on the slave trade with Spain. He had no need for Morgan or any other local leaders – he was too busy making money.'[12]

While still in London, Albemarle asked for both Byndloss and Morgan to be reinstated on the council but his request was refused by the king.

In early 1687, Robert Byndloss died, which left Morgan to look after his old friend's wife and eight children. With the help of the king, Albemarle had sent an expedition to the West Indies in search of Spanish gold and silver from a sunken ship said to have gone down somewhere near the north–east coast of Hispaniola. His luck was in as the first of the two ships he'd sent to find it came back filled with gold bullion and other treasure and then returned to salvage more. Albemarle had frittered away the fortune he'd inherited from his father and this treasure had made him wealthy again.

Once the two ships had returned from their treasure hunting, with Albemarle's fortune intact, he set sail for Jamaica and arrived on 20 December 1687. He immediately dismissed Molesworth and gave Morgan an unofficial role as 'chief advisor to the governor', writes Breverton.

With Albemarle in Jamaica he did his best to get Morgan reinstated to the council.

> I think it will be truly necessary for the King's service to have always a considerable number of members of Council resident in the island. Sir Charles Modyford is dead, Colonel Cope is sick beyond hope of recovery, and sickness and other accidents have prevented several from attending, insomuch that once we had not members enough present to make a quorum, and the Council had to be postponed. Several times only the bare number of five has appeared, and that after long waiting. I hope that you have approved of Sir Henry Morgan and have represented him to the King as a fit man for the Council here, for the Council have recommended him to me as I have already told you.[13]

Yet, by early 1688, Morgan had still not been reinstated onto the council, which was his chief desire. By this time he was very ill with dropsy. One of the finest medical men of the time had accompanied the Duke of Albemarle to Jamaica, chiefly to look after the Duke's highly strung wife, whose mental illness was growing more and more profound. Dr Hans Sloane also attended Morgan and he provides a description of our hero in the last days of his life. He described him as lean, sallow with yellowish eyes and a prominent stomach. Morgan was complaining that he had no appetite and 'had a kicking or reach to vomit every morning and generally a small looseness attending him, and withal was much given to drinking and sitting up late which I supposed had been the cause of his present indisposition.'[14]

Morgan continued to drink, perhaps to keep the pain of his swollen stomach and legs at bay. He spent most of the time lying in his hammock, unable to move. Sloane stated that his condition did not allow for a remedy of purging and medicines that could have helped his condition that was 'threatening his life'.

Finally, in July 1688 news came that the Lords of Trade and Plantations had finally agreed to allow Morgan to be reinstated to the Council of Jamaica. The ship that brought the news from London brought happiness to Morgan and his family. Albemarle called a meeting of the council for 12 July, when Morgan was officially recalled to the council. There was a ceremony to mark the special day and the council also voted for a new assembly to be called. Morgan and his supporters – all Tories and Loyalists to king and Country

– won the majority of the seats, 'becoming the largest party', as Breverton states.

By this time his body was bloated and he found it difficult to pass water. Yet he kept on drinking. This ceremony was Morgan's last public outing. He arrived in a carriage and now used a cane to help his mobility. After the ceremony, Roger Elleston, whom Lynch had banned from practising law in Jamaica and now the speaker of the new assembly, gave a rousing and touching tribute to Morgan from his early days in Jamaica through the expeditions and everything the man had done for the independence, survival and prosperity of the island. The tables had turned and in his last few days Morgan triumphed over the small-minded, vengeful Lynch. He'd triumphed over Vaughan as well.

On 25 August, Morgan died in his Llanrhymni estate, leaving Elizabeth everything in his will.

I have admitted Sir Henry Morgan to the Council pursuant to the King's order, but I am afraid that he will not live long, being extraordinarily ill.[15]

Governor Albemarle, also quite ill, gave Morgan a proper state funeral with all the trappings of a major government official and politician. He had a horse-drawn carriage with many people in black walking beside it. Indeed, Talty tells us that Albemarle granted a twenty-four-hour amnesty for anyone who wanted to come and either pay their respects or revel over the fact that Morgan was dead. This amnesty brought in buccaneers and privateers from many different places, along with people from all walks of life, some his friends, others his enemies. Some had not forgiven Morgan for what they thought was his violation of trust during the Panama raid and yet Morgan was by far so much more than just that one expedition.[16]

Morgan was fifty-three when he died. At the time of his death his estate was worth £5,000 and it was all left to his wife, Elizabeth. Upon her death, the estate would go to his nephew, Charles Byndloss, as long as he changed his last name to Morgan so as to carry on the family name.

The Duke of Albemarle died in October of 1688, only a few months after Morgan.

Legacy

In all the histories about pirates, buccaneers or privateers that sailed the Atlantic and Caribbean there are many others whose names we know today – Blackbeard, Kidd, Rackham and Roberts. The name of Morgan is still relatively unknown. Yet this man commanded thousands of men right into the heart of the Spanish Main. He sacked Portobello, Maracaibo and Panama. He was a man of courage, determination, bravery, and oozed the charisma that every leader needs to command men. He was a planner, a brilliant military strategist and intensely loyal to the king, to England and to Jamaica.

But unlike so many of the Brethren, he was flexible and adaptable, able to see that the future for Jamaica lay not in plunder or pillage but in peaceful trade with the Spanish, Dutch and French colonies of the West Indies and Americas. He turned his back on the Brethren, indeed, hunted them down and executed some of those that were captured in order to pursue the single-minded determination to build trade.

He was responsible for building up the defences of Jamaica to repel invasion or attack. He was also an adept politician and held office longer than any of the governors of his time. He was lieutenant governor under Vaughan, Carlisle and, briefly, Lynch.

The Port Royal that Morgan thrived in was destroyed by an earthquake and subsequent tsunami on 7 June 1692. Many researchers and scholars writing about Morgan go into great detail about the destruction of Port Royal but we will leave that for another time. Suffice it to say that, during that apocalyptic day, Morgan's coffin was brought up from the heaving earth and washed out to sea – perhaps a fitting end for a man whose wealth and position gained from his expeditions began on the sea.

Sadly in the modern world it is unlikely that a man of Morgan's stature could ever achieve what he did. The Western World of the twenty-first century is too mediocre and politically correct to enable a man like Morgan to flourish. His expeditions can never be repeated and so while he was a man of his time he is still a man much larger than his time and should be forever remembered for what he accomplished. Did he commit atrocities? It is likely that some of the Brethren did commit savage acts while on his expeditions but whether he did is questionable. But Morgan's life over the centuries has become more myth than fact and his expeditions and actions larger than life. Yet, as Talty states, 'you can't attempt to do what Morgan and his men did without seeing yourselves as a prince of the New World, deserving of every wonder it possesses.'[1]

Like most men of Morgan's stature, fame and legend, his star shone brightly for a short time and then quickly dimmed, but he shall never be forgotten.

Appendix I

Modyford's Reasons for Granting Commissions

B elow is the narrative by Sir Thomas Modyford, governor of Jamaica, setting out his reasons for granting commissions to privateers against the Spanish even though he knew, though not officially, that a peace treaty had been signed between England and Spain.

His letters to Lord Arlington from Barbadoes will testify what an aversion he had for the privateers, as also his affectionate letters to the Spanish Governors after his landing in Jamaica on 4 June 1664, and his severe handling [of] those people, by imprisoning them, executing some and restoring their prizes, to the great hazard of the peace. But when he found how powerful an enemy he had made of those who were formerly the best friends to this place, and who not only knew all their ports, bays and creeks, but every path in the island, and had many correspondents on shore, and that some of them were gone to the French at Tortuga and Hispaniola, and the rest preparing to go, and could better attempt this place than we could defend it, Modyford found the fatal error he was running into, and having notice of the Dutch war by Lord Arlington's despatch of 12 November 1664, he changed his behaviour so effectually that he persuaded all in or near this harbour to undertake against the Dutch at Curaçao, giving them suitable commissions and Col Ed Morgan, his Deputy Governor, for their general; they went cheerfully without putting the King to one penny charge, and took Statia and Saba, but by the death of Col Morgan they scattered and left the rest of that service unperformed.

He sent Major Beeston to treat with them for a second voyage to Curaçao, which they promised to undertake. Meantime he advised the Duke of Albemarle of the state of this place in relation to the privateers by letters of 6 March 1665; in answer to which he had orders of 30 May 1665 to grant or not commissions against the Spaniards, as to him should seem most advantageous for His Majesty's service, and letters from Lord Arlington, that from the Lord General he should receive His Majesty's directions touching the privateers, and also letters from the Lord Chancellor to the same purpose, and from Sir James Modyford, and also his Grace's own letter in Feb 1667, confirming all the former, and that after the peace with Spain, as by the abstracts annexed may appear.

The privateers meantime were driven to leeward, and the admiral fell in with the island of Providence and without any commission took it; to which Modyford sent a Governor, which was not only approved of at home, but another Governor under the broad seal of England authorized and sent. Yet notwithstanding this full power he would not proceed to grant commissions until the council of this island unanimously affirmed it was for the good of the island and gave their reasons hereto annexed and thereupon in March 1666, there being also war with France, he granted commissions, which was approved by His Grace, his end being only to keep them from joining with the French, but they had only commissions for taking ships, and none for landing. He always reproved them for so acting, especially in the business of Puerto Bello and Maracay [Maracaibo]; to which they made their defence by writing, which he sent home, but never received any answer to.

Meantime, by reason of their numbers and not knowing the sense at home, he thought it prudential to forbear punishing them; and, receiving an intimation of His Majesty's sense in his son's letters, and also advice of the intentions of the Spaniards to attempt them, the galleons being daily expected in the Indies, and the New Spain fleet already there, in order to detain the privateers on the island, he repealed all their powers. Hears that divers[e] of them intend to set up for themselves, and only two have as yet joined the French. 'If the peace with France were immortal, or if that warlike Prince had no design this way, I should be little concerned at the lawless motions of these privateers, but well knowing the uncertainty of the former, and the assuredness of the latter, I must confess it troubles me to be driven to that saddest error of all Governments to act so imprudently as in this most active age to weaken ourselves and strengthen our enemies.' Will say something to the unreasonable rumours of the great wealth these privateers are said to get; the Puerto Bello business cleared them 60 pounds per head, and the fight with Don Alonso at Maracay 30 pounds; this the common sort spent immediately in arms, clothes and drink, and the owners of the ships in refitting, and some of the officers and civiller sort are settling plantations, and the owners of ships spend their shares in refitting, so that they are from hand to mouth and have little or nothing left. His Majesty's fifteenths he keeps to be employed in fortification, which may be about 600 pounds, and His Royal Highness's tenths he always sent home to Sir William Coventry and Mr Wren for His Royal Highness's account. To himself they gave only 20 pounds for their commission, which never exceeded 300 pounds.

Affirms this to be true touching his transactions with the privateers of this port, and challenges all the bold maligners and rash talkers against his actings in this particular, to disprove the least inconsiderable title or circumstance herein, not doubting but all sober and true Englishmen will not only absolve him but approve of his proceedings.

The John Deane Affair and Vaughan's Accusations Against Morgan

W hat follows here is a chronological list of the letters and reports around the John Deane affair, also covering what Vaughan believed to be Morgan's complicity in this case. These letters illustrate how Vaughan abused his authority while governor, which resulted in his isolation and ultimate paranoia that everything that went wrong was because of Morgan.

In the close of one Sir Joseph is pleased to take notice of the differences between Sir Henry Morgan and himself, and advises the Governor to make them up. Does not know what complaints Sir Henry might make, but in the character I am shall never represent any personal dislikes, but endeavour faithfully to do my duty and advise of all such who do not do theirs. Therefore wrote his sense of the loss of His Majesty's stores, and impartially placed the miscarriage where he is sure the fault was. Could complain of the great ingratitude and disingenuity of the same person in having written so many false and malicious stories of the Governor, though is satisfied His Honour will not suffer the Governor to be abused by them. 'What I most resent is, and which I consider as part of my duty to lay before Your Honour, that I find Sir Henry, contrary to his duty and trust, endeavours to set up privateering, and has obstructed all my designs and purposes for the reducing of those that do use that curse of life.' Had by several proclamations declared he would not permit those rapines and spoils, and that he would proceed against the offenders as pirates if they came into any of our ports.

They went to Tortugas and took French commissions, and Sir Henry recommended some of our English privateers to the French Government for commissions, was himself concerned in their vessels, and put a deputation into his brother Byndloss's hands to receive the tenths for the King of France, and has ever since corresponded with them. Relates all the circumstances concerning the seizure of John Deane's vessel [see Beckford's letter, ante No. 860], 'who had the impudence to come to town.' Doubts not, from the information and proofs sent, Secretary Coventry will be sufficiently satisfied of Sir Henry's disobedience and unfaithfulness, and of what dangerous consequence his setting up that kind of faction may prove to the island.

The above letter was written to Secretary Sir Joseph Williamson, dated 2 May 1676, and is in Calendar of State Papers Colonial, America and West Indies, Volume 9: 1675–1676. The following letter by Peter Beckford, Secretary to the Council of Jamaica, dated 2 May 1676, was also written to Secretary Williamson.

Seizure of a ship by Governor Vaughan; complaint of the master who brought her in that he had been robbed by privateers, upon which the Governor ordered Sir Henry Morgan to imprison the offenders, 'which my Lord imagines he did not act cordially in,' but on the contrary let them have advice that they might escape, and rather encouraged them, insomuch as one John Deane told the Governor he had done wrong in the seizure, so he was imprisoned, and at a Court of Admiralty, on 27 April, His Excellency sitting as Judge, was condemned of piracy, for which the multitude complain as well-wishers to piracy, but all of sense think it necessary, so that a strict peace be kept with the Spaniards.

The following day, 3 May, Lord Vaughan wrote to the Earl of Anglesea complaining of Morgan's conduct in the Deane affair and justifying his own actions:

Acknowledges his letter, and has written fully to their Lordships relating to the island and government. Has written to His Lordship upon all occasions, finding himself under a necessity of making use of his friends when so many had appeared industrious to misrepresent him. Hopes what he has written may by this time have given resolution to their removal, so that the island and himself may be in peace. Relates the whole circumstances of a case in which 'I have detected him [Sir Henry Morgan] of most gross unfaithfulness in his trust and a wilful breach and disobedience of my orders, only because they have obstructed his design of privateering.'

Sends the depositions and an exemplification of the trial that His Lordship may be satisfied that it is according to law, and agrees with all precedents in the Admiralty. Since the trial Sir Harry has been so impudent and unfaithful at the taverns and in his own house, to speak some things which seemed to reflect upon my justice, and to vindicate the pirate, but the people are more prudent than to be led away or persuaded by seditious discourses; however, has thought it his duty to lay it all before the Ministers, and that my Deputy

Governor endeavours to set up privateering, and has, with his brother Byndloss, encouraged the King's subjects to take French commissions, fitted them out to sea, and been concerned with them in their ships and prizes, and received a deputation to collect the tenths for the King of France.

Supposes the Ministers will not consider Sir Harry worthy of any character or authority who makes use of it only for his own ends. Knows his imprudence and weakness lead him a great way, but believes his necessities do more, which would prove of sad consequence to the island if there should be any devolution of the Government. It would be a great satisfaction to all reasonable people in the island if they could be once freed from those fears, all having great apprehensions of his succession. His brother Byndloss agitates him in all he does, has therefore given him no authority or any civil or military commission. He is a very turbulent fellow, some years since was surgeon of a ship, but can never be easy in any government. It would be a good thing if the Governor had a private instruction to put him out of the Council. Says nothing of this to any but His Lordship, as he knows he can depend upon his secrecy and friendship. Beseeches him to communicate the exemplification to the Duke of York.

On 28 July, the Lords of Trade and Plantations wrote back to Vaughan with their answer concerning Vaughan's trial of Deane and his sentencing him to death, even though Vaughan later commuted that sentence his overstepping his power can be seen from this letter:

Find that His Lordship's proceedings in the trial of John Deane, lately tried and condemned for piracy by His Lordship, are not warranted by the laws of this Kingdom, it not appearing that pirates were de facto tried by the civil law, though it is supposed they were so tried, but by Commission of oyer and terminer under the great seal of England, therefore their Lordships advised His Majesty that the execution of said Deane might be stopped, and a commission sent for his new trial which His Majesty approving has given directions for a Commission of Oyer and Terminer to be prepared and sent to Lord Vaughan with all speed; to the end His Lordship may cause the execution of said Deane to be stopped and proceed to a new trial.

The above letters can be found in the July 1676 Calendar of State Papers Colonial, America and West Indies, Volume 9: 1675–1676.

Morgan's Defence

T he following is the complete defence that Morgan and Byndloss used against the allegations made by Vaughan of their conduct as members of the Council of Jamaica. Dated 10 November 1677, the document details their defence, which was sent to the Lords of Trade and Plantations:

> On perusal of several papers, ordered by Lords of Trade and Plantations that a breviat [brief] be made of the particular charges and proofs brought against Sir Henry Morgan and Colonel Byndloss. Then follow the articles against Sir H. Morgan and proofs, and the articles against Lieutenant Colonel Byndloss and proofs.

List of Papers touching Sir Henry Morgan and Colonel Byndloss

1. Letter from Lord Vaughan to Secretary Coventry, dated 2 August 1676 [calendared, see No. 1006].
2. A state of the case on the examination of Sir Henry Morgan and Colonel Byndloss before His Excellency and Council. 6pp. Received from Secretary Coventry, 9 November 1676.
3. Exemplification of all the proceedings upon the citation of Sir Henry Morgan and Colonel Robert Byndloss before the Council held at Port Royal, 24 July 1676. Received from Secretary Coventry, 9 November 1676. By the St George, Captain Alford [calendared, see No. 998].
4. Sir Henry Morgan to [Secretary Coventry]: Account of his trial before the governor and Council of Jamaica. Beseeches His Majesty to suspend giving his judgment till the next ships come which will bring other depositions he hopes will clear all. 'But if His Majesty should be deaf to all and these things should give His Majesty occasion to put me out that he will be graciously pleased to order that I may be tried here at his Court of King's Bench where the witnesses are … and if ever I err in one title, then let me ever be condemned for the greatest villain in the world, and as God is my judge and witness I have never entertained a thought in my life

but what hath been really devoted to His Majesty's service and interest nor never will.' Jamaica, 2 August, 1676.

5.   Sir Henry Morgan to [Secretary Coventry]. Thanks for his abundant favours. Can only say, it being not in my power to make my Lord prove it, that I never since I came here writ a line to any of the privateers, therefore the copies sent are forged on purpose to my prejudice. Waited upon his Excellency expecting he would have warned me to appear before the Council, but he said nothing of it, but as I know it is false I will, the first Council, myself move it and desire what is laid to my charge may be proved which I know is impossible. 'I sucked the milk of loyalty and if I would have sold one little part of it I might have been richer than my enemies ever will be.' As for Colonel Byndloss, knows nothing of crime in him, but his being related to Sir Henry, for he lives 20 miles from Port Royal, has a wife and five or six children and one of the best estates in this island, therefore he is an understanding man and would not venture that hazard and estate against nothing. His unhappiness is he serves a superior here that is jealous of all his actions and put himself to study Sir Henry's ruin for what reason knows not. Received 4 September by Captain Hoskins of Bristol.

6. Captain John Bennett's Commission in French signed by Ogeron, governor of the Tortugas and the coast of San Domingo and condemnation of his prize. April 1675. Also Ogeron's letter to Attorney.

7. Sir Henry Morgan to Captain John Bennett. Is commanded by the Captain General to acquaint all the privateers, both English and French, that they shall have at all times as much liberty of this port as ever they had, and that they may with abundance of safety come hither. Will send his Lordship protection under hand and seal so that they need not be afraid of any harm although here is a king's frigate. They may assure themselves of His Excellency's favour and friendship, Jamaica, Port Royal. 25 March, 1675.

8. Sir Henry Morgan to the Privateers, Captains Rogers, Wright, Nevill, Bennett, Pryniar, and to all others acting under French Commissions as well English as French. Is commanded by the General to tell them they are welcome to this island and shall have all the privileges they ever had and Port Royal is free to them. Hopes their experience of him will give him the reputation that he intends not to betray them, Jamaica, Port Royal. 26 March 1675.

9. Colonel Robert Byndloss to [Secretary Coventry] Is advised that Lord Vaughan has charged the writer to His Honour for contracting with the French governor to receive the tenths for his Commissions. Account of

his being summoned before the Council on 24 July of the matters objected against him, and his answers. Begs him to believe he would as soon cut his own throat as do a thing willingly in the least to incur His Majesty's displeasure.

> Cannot tell how he has disobliged my Lord; thinks his fault is being allied by marriage to Sir H. Morgan, if so, is contented, and it's as great a riddle to Jamaica what Sir Harry hath done. Implores his aid that His Majesty may have a right understanding of his case. 3pp. Jamaica. 29 July 1676. Received, 11 October.

10. Articles to be exhibited against Robert Byndloss before his Excellency and the Council. 1p.
11. Answers of Colonel Byndloss to the preceding articles. Certified copy. 4pp.
12. governor Lord Vaughan's reply to the preceding answers of Colonel Byndloss. 1p. Certified copy.
13. Deposition of Robert Byndloss, aged forty years, before Colonel Thomas Fuller, one of His Majesty's Council. 1 August 1676. 2pp.
14. Order of Council for sending Colonel Byndloss to view the several forts at Port Royal. Missing.
15. Examination of Charles Barré before governor Lord Vaughan. That soon after His Excellency's arrival he copied several letters for Sir Henry Morgan, one was directed to Captain Bennett and the other to Rogers and other Privateers. Port Royal, 28 August 1676.
16. Colonel Robert Byndloss to [Secretary Coventry]. Complains of the governor's proceedings as to the charges he has brought against Byndloss. None of the papers sent home signed by the Council, for the governor saw not one man of them but would have cleared us since nothing was proved and it was plain prejudice. My Lord does all to make Byndloss a great friend to the Privateers. Is now a planter and has lived for nine years 20 miles from Port Royal, yet, notwithstanding his settled and easy condition which he so much loves, is willing to hazard his life and undergo any hardship for His Majesty's service, at whose command he will go in this frigate with a tender of six or eight guns and so deal with the privateers at sea, and in their holes bring in the chief of them to His Majesty's obedience or bring in their heads and destroy their ships. 3pp. Jamaica, 12 September 1676. Received, 9 January 1677.
17. Deposition of Charles Barré, Secretary to Sir Henry Morgan, Lieutenant General of Jamaica. That about March 1675 he did copy by Sir Henry's

orders two letters Sir Henry had written with design to have sent them to the captains of several privateers, to advise to come to Jamaica with prizes and they should be well received, but understood Sir Henry wrote said letters by consent of Lord Vaughan and sent him copies of each letter to underwrite his approbation, which the governor deferring Sir Henry refused to send said letters. Confesses accepting Captain Smith's offer to go a trading voyage with him, but positively denies he was sent by Sir Henry to treat or act any business with the French or English privateers neither did Sir Henry. Also touching Lord Vaughan's examination of this deponent after his return from his said voyage. 2pp. Port Royal, 12 September 1676.

This list of documents can be found in the 1–15 November 1676 Calendar of State Papers Colonial, America and West Indies, Volume 9: 1675–1676.

Appendix IV

The Francis Mingham Affair

The following correspondence illustrates the way in which the Francis Mingham affair was treated by Morgan and his council. As we know, Morgan sued Mingham for libel and won that case. This is some of the correspondence that built up around it. The first report is from the Minutes of the Council of Jamaica dated 5 November 1680, when Morgan was Lieutenant Governor:

The King's Order in Council of 21 July for the discharge of Francis Mingham from prison was read; and in obedience thereto the said Francis Mingham was sent for by Sir Henry Morgan and discharged. Francis Hanson, counsel to Mingham, averred to the Council that the article in Mingham's printed case alleging a writ of error to be denied him was most false, for no writ of error was to his knowledge demanded. Major Yeoman, Provost Marshal, made oath that Francis Mingham was arrested in an action upon judgment, and that he received no orders from Sir Henry Morgan as to Mingham's arrest and confinement. The gaol was too weak to allow Mingham the chance of escaping in his own pink. John Starr, clerk to the Provost Marshal, made oath that Mingham was not charged with Sir Henry Morgan's execution until many days after the fourteen days mentioned in the printed case. Robert Staley, gaoler, swore that he received no order from Sir Henry Morgan as to the confinement of Mingham, and Harry Sound, another gaoler, confirmed it. Francis Mingham owned that he was kindly treated in prison and admitted that it was not true, as stated in the printed case, that he had been charged 16 pounds; to build him a prison. By all of which circumstances and others too tedious for the Lords of Trade and Plantations the Council is well satisfied that Francis Mingham's troubles in Jamaica were due more to his own imprudence and malicious desire for revenge than to any purpose of Sir Henry Morgan to oppress him.

The next letter is dated 6 November 1680 and was from the Council of Jamaica to the Lords of Trade and Plantations:

In obedience to your Lordships' orders to inform you every six months of what we may think for the good of the Colony, we write to inform you that in obedience to the King's Order in Council we have released Francis Mingham from prison. And herein we find occasion to represent with all humility the many great inconveniences that will attend the prosecution of justice in this Island if this case should be drawn into precedent, or if writs of error or habeas corpus out of the King's Bench in England be allowed to remove any debtor in execution from this place thither, as in this case has been practised. For it must needs tend to the defeating of justice here and discouragement of trade (on which things the welfare of the Island depends), especially since it is not difficult at so great a distance to allege very fair and specious pretences which upon proof may appear to be clearly untrue. We therefore beg your Lordships to represent the foregoing to His Majesty in Council. Signed, Robert Byndloss, Hender Molesworth, John Webbe, Francis Watson, John Cope, Thomas Freeman, Charles Whitfeld, J. Fuller, Thomas Ballard.

Sir Charles Modyford, Thomas Modyford's son, took a deposition before Sir Francis Watson, then judge of the Supreme Court of Jamaica, dated 8 November 1680:

After the arrival of Francis Mingham in the pink Francis, from Jamaica, in the port of London, it was found on his delivering his accounts to his owners that there were several articles charged to their debt upon account of a seizure made of the said pink in Jamaica. Thereupon questions arose whether the seizure was legal or illegal. The majority of the owners, whereof deponent is one, thought it was legal, and therewith declined to be further concerned with Mingham's charges on this account, but out of pity gave him a bill of exchange for 100 pounds. Further, when deponent arrived in Jamaica he moved Sir Henry Morgan on behalf of Mingham, when Sir Henry frankly promised him that if Mingham would pay his costs in the affair and in acknowledgment of the injury he had done him would present his lady with such a coach and horses as deponent might think fit, then he would fully acquit and forgive him of his execution of 2,000 pounds; which offer was duly made to Francis Mingham and refused.

On 12 November 1680, Morgan wrote to the Lords of Trade and Plantations about his part in the Mingham affair:

I have duly discharged Francis Mingham from prison in obedience to your Lordships' letter of 25 July last, though I am persuaded that I could have given you good reasons for keeping him there. However, my duty pleased me more than my advantage in the 2,000 pounds; execution, and I am grateful to you in taking security for his answering the same in England. I now beg leave to present your Lordships with the true state of the case that you may see how your great goodness has been abused both by his original petition and his printed case; nor do I doubt that you will better understand, when you have read the same, how scandalously both I and the government have been slandered, and how much both must suffer unless your Lordships' deep foresight and wisdom obviate so growing an evil.

These reports and letters can be found in the November 1680 Calendar of State Papers Colonial, America and West Indies, Volume 10: 1677–1680.

Bibliography

Papers
Calendar of State Papers, Colonial, America and the West Indies, Volumes 7–12.

Books
Breverton, Terry, *The Greatest Buccaneer of Them All*, Welsh Books, Glyndwr Publishing, Cowbridge, 2005.
Cordingly, David, *Life Among the Pirates*, Little Brown, London, 1995.
Earle, Peter, *The Pirate Wars*, Methuen, York, 2004.
Esquemeling, Alexander O., *The Buccaneers of America*, translated by Alexis Brown, Dover Publications, Mineola, New York, 1969.
Esquemeling, John, *The Buccaneers of America*, Wilder Publications, Radford, Virginia, 2008.
Gosse, Philip, *The History of Piracy*, Dover Publications, Longman Greene, London, 2007.
Leslie, Charles, *A New History of Jamaica*, J Hodges, London, 1740.
Lindsay, Philip, *The Great Buccaneer: Being the Life, Death and Extraordinary Adventures of Sir Henry Morgan, Buccaneer and Lieutenant Governor of Jamaica*, Peter Nevill Limited, London, New York, 1950.
Peterson, Mendel, *The Funnel of Gold*, Little Brown, London, 1975.
Pope, Dudley, *Harry Morgan's Way*, Stratus Books, Cornwall, 2001.
Roberts, W. Adlophe, *Sir Henry Morgan, Buccaneer and Governor*, The Pioneer Press, Kingston, Jamaica, 1952.
Talty, Stephen, *Empire of Blue Water: Henry Morgan and the Pirates Who Ruled the Caribbean Waves*, Simon & Schuster, London, 2007.

Notes

Preface

1. Talty, Stephen, *Empire of Blue Water: Henry Morgan and the Pirates Who Ruled the Caribbean Waves*, Simon & Schuster, 2007, p.56.

Introduction

1. Peterson, Mendel, *The Funnel of Gold*, Little Brown, 1975, p.315.
2. Earle, Peter, *The Pirate Wars*, Methuen, 2004, pp.94–6.

Chapter 1

1. Cordingly, David, *Life Among the Pirates*, Little Brown, 1995, p.56.
2. Pope, Dudley, *Harry Morgan's Way*, Stratus, 2001, p.xvii.
3. This information from Morgan's early life about the capture of Jamaica comes from *Admiral Sir Henry Morgan: The Greatest Buccaneer of Them All*, by Terry Breverton, Welsh Books, 2005, pp.4–5.
4. The Spanish Main refers to the land around the Gulf of Mexico and the Caribbean Sea. It takes up the coasts of present-day Florida, Texas, Mexico and the north coast of South America.
5. See Breverton, p.10.
6. Ibid., p.11.
7. Ibid., p.15.
8. Ibid., p.16.

Chapter 2

1. See Breverton, p.19.
2. Sir Thomas Modyford to Lord Archingdale, Secretary to Lord Arlington, 16 November 1665, Colonial and State Papers America and West Indies, Vol. XIX, No. 127, held at National Archives Kew.
3. Ibid.
4. See Breverton, p.21.

Chapter 3

1. Sir Thomas Modyford's letter to the Duke of Albemarle, 1 March 1666, Colonial and State Papers America and West Indies, Vol. 20, 1142.
2. Talty, Stephen, *Empire of Blue Water: Henry Morgan and the Pirates Who Ruled the Caribbean Waves*, Simon & Schuster, 2007.
3. See Sir Thomas Modyford's letter to the Duke of Albemarle.
4. See Talty, *Empire of Blue Water*, p.65.
5. See Sir Thomas Modyford's letter, 1 March 1666.
6. See Talty, *Empire of Blue Water*, p.65.
7. Sir Thomas Modyford's letter to the Duke of Albemarle, 1 March 1666.
8. Ibid.
9. See Breverton.

10. Talty, *Empire of Blue Water*, p.67.
11. Sir Thomas Modyford's letter to the Duke of Albemarle, 1 March 1666. It is interesting to note that Modyford refers to himself in the third person in his letters, which can sometimes cause confusion for the reader.
12. Interestingly, Breverton suggests that Morgan was involved with this Curaçao mission but Talty, as we can see in Chapter 3, states that Morgan was in charge of the militia and so did not go on this voyage.

Chapter 4
1. Ibid. [Ibid to what?]
2. Talty, *Empire of Blue Water*, p.67.
3. Ibid., p.78.
4. Ibid., p 79
5. Sir Thomas Modyford's letter to the Duke of Albemarle, 8 June 1666, Colonial and State Papers America and the West Indies, Vol. 20, p.1213.
6. See Pope, *Harry Morgan's Way*, p.138.
7. Lindsay, Philip, *The Great Buccaneer: Being the Life, Death and Extraordinary Adventures of Sir Henry Morgan, Buccaneer and Lieutenant Governor of Jamaica*, Peter Nevill, 1950, p.44.
8. The Cartago account has many inconsistencies. For example, Pope suggests that a local Indian raised the alarm that roused the Spanish militia while Lindsay states that an Indian woman warned the buccaneers that the Spanish lay in wait for them and in a fury they decided to destroy whatever they could lay their hands on. Modyford states that they were not challenged, when both Pope and Lindsay say they were. Indeed, Pope provides the most convincing argument when he states that they landed on 8 April, the alarm was received by the Governor of Cartago on 14 April and by 20 April the buccaneers were back at their ships, exhausted, having suffered great casualties and having no plunder to show for their trouble.
9. See Lindsay, *The Great Buccaneer: Being the Life, Death and Extraordinary Adventures of Sir Henry Morgan, Buccaneer and Lieutenant Governor of Jamaica*, p.43.
10. See Breverton, p.26.
11. See Pope, *Harry Morgan's Way*, p.137.
12. See Talty, *Empire of Blue Water*, p.79.
13. Governor Sir Thos Modyford to Sec Lord Arlington, 16 June 1666, Colonial and State Papers, America and the West Indies, Vol. 20, p.1216.

Chapter 5
1. See Lindsay, p.45.
2. Sir Thomas Modyford to Lord Arlington, 16 June 1666, Colonial and State Papers America and the West Indies, Vol. 20, No. 100, p.1216.
3. Ibid.
4. See Pope, p.140.
5. In his letter to Lord Arlington, dated 21 August 1666, Modyford states that he had the power to grant commissions from a letter from the Lord Chancellor dated 1 June 1665 that gave him 'latitude to grant or not commissions against the Spaniard, as he found it for the advantage of His Majesty's service and the good of this island'.
6. Ibid.
7. See Talty, *Empire of Blue Water*, p.84.
8. See Modyford to Arlington, 21 August 1666, Colonial and State Papers America and the West Indies, Vol. 20, p.1264.
9. Sir Thomas Modyford to Lord Arlington, 21 August 1666, Colonial and State Papers America and the West Indies, Vol. 20, p.1264.
10. Deposition of Captain Henry Wasey, master of the *Concord*, 19 August 1668, Colonial and State Papers, America and the West Indies, Vol. XXIII, No. 43, p.1827.
11. See Pope, p.143.

12. Deposition of Major Samuel Smith, late governor of Old Providence, 19 August 1668, Colonial and State Papers, America and the West Indies Vol. XXIII, No. 42, p.1826.
13. Deposition of Henry Wasey, master of the *Concord*, 19 August 1668, Colonial and State Papers, America and the West Indies Vol. XXIII, No. 42, p.1827.
14. Letter by Sir Thomas Modyford to the Duke of Albemarle, 5 October 1668, Colonial Papers, Vol. XXIII, No. 60, p.1851.
15. Depositions of Robert Rawlinsone, Isaac Webber, and Richard Cree, before Sir Thos Modyford, enclosed with the letter to the Duke of Albemarle, dated 5 October 1668. Colonial Papers, Vol. XXIII, No. 60, p.1851.

Chapter 6

1. Letter from Richard Browne, arrived in Port Royal on HMS *Oxford*, to Joseph Williamson, dated 9 November 1667, Colonial Papers Vol. 23, No. 76, p.1867.
2. See Lindsay, *The Great Buccaneer*, p.49.
3. See Pope, p.149.
4. Letter dated 7 September 1668, Information of Admiral Henry Morgan and his officers, outlining the attacks on Puerto del Príncipe and Portobello, Col. Papers, Vol. XXIII, No. 53.
5. See Talty, *Empire of Blue Water*, p.85.
6. Lindsay states that some sources spell his name as Esquemelin or Esquemeling.
7. See Lindsay regarding the character of Esquemeling, p.50.
8. Ibid., p.51.
9. Esquemeling, Alexander O., *The Buccaneers of America*, translated by Alexis Brown, 1969, Dover Publications, pp.70–1.
10. Ibid., p.70.
11. Ibid., p.71.
12. See Esquemeling, *The Buccaneers of America*, p.72. Note that Esquemeling refers to the buccaneers in this passage as 'rovers'.

Chapter 7

1. See Esquemeling, pp.128–9.
2. See Morgan's letter, 7 September 1668, detailing the attacks on Puerto del Príncipe and Portobello, Col. Papers, Vol. XXIII, No. 53.
3. See Talty, *Empire of Blue Water*, p.88.
4. See Esquemeling, p.130.
5. Ibid., p.132.
6. See Morgan's letter, 7 September 1668. Of note here is that Morgan uses the number of 1,000 head of cattle while Esquemeling states that Morgan asked for 500 cattle.
7. See Pope, *Harry Morgan's Way*, p.158. Interestingly, in the Alexis Brown translation Esquemeling does not mention where the rendezvous point was except that it was 'on one of the islands'.
8. See Breverton, *Admiral Sir Henry Morgan*, p.39.

Chapter 8

1. See Pope, *Harry Morgan's Way*, p.164.
2. Breverton implies that he went back to Port Royal after the raid on Puerto del Príncipe but neither Pope nor Talty mention this and only Breverton mentions Captain Jackman as the privateer who had come from pillaging Campeche. The rest refer to Esquemeling's account as the pirate from Campeche as being anonymous.
3. See Esquemeling, p.134.
4. It is interesting to note here that both Talty and Breverton claim there were six men altogether who had been prisoners of the Spanish. However, our other sources, especially Pope, do not mention the numbers or, indeed, if they were English.
5. See Morgan's letter, 7 September 1668.

 6. Ibid.
 7. Ibid.
 8. Esquemeling, p.136.
 9. See Morgan's letter, 7 September 1668.
10. Ibid.
11. We learn the names of the castles from Dudley Pope, *Harry Morgan's Way*, pp.163–5. However, both Breverton and Talty name them differently.
12. See Pope, p.165. He cites historian Charles Leslie's account of the taking of Portobello as published in Leslie's book, *A New History of Jamaica*, originally published in 1740.
13. See Talty, p.111.
14. Ibid.
15. Talty states that there were forty-nine Spaniards defending this fort and they had virtually no food and water, making their cause a lost one.
16. See Talty, *Empire of Blue Water*, p.116.
17. Ibid., p.117.
18. See Pope, *Harry Morgan's Way*, p.168.
19. See Morgan's letter, 7 September 1668.
20. Ibid.

Chapter 9
 1. See Lindsay, Philip, *The Great Buccaneer*, p.79.
 2. Ibid., p.79.
 3. Ibid., p.80.
 4. This quote is an extract from a book by Charles Leslie, *A New History of Jamaica*, published by J. Hodges, 1740. and is cited in Lindsay's *The Great Buccaneer*, p.82.
 5. Letter from John Styles to the Principal Secretary of State Whitehall, 4 January 1670, Calendar of State Papers, America and the West Indies, Vol. 7, 1669–1674, p.138.
 6. Ibid.
 7. See Dudley Pope, *Harry Morgan's Way*, p.179. Pope does not mention that Modyford gave a commission to Morgan for this mission as Lindsay does.
 8. See Lindsay, *The Great Buccaneer*, p.84.
 9. Letter from Sir Thomas Modyford to Lord Arlington, 31 October 1668, Calendar of State Papers, America and the West Indies, Vol. 23, p.1863.
10. See Pope, *Harry Morgan's Way*, pp.179–80.
11. Letter from Dr Richard Browne aboard the *Oxford* frigate, to Joseph Williamson, secretary to Privy Council, 20 January 1669, Calendar of State Papers Colonial, America and West Indies, Vol. 9: 1675–1676 and Addenda 1574–1674, p.1207.
12. See Esquemeling, pp.77–8.
13. Ibid.
14. See Dudley Pope, *Harry Morgan's Way*, pp.181–2.

Chapter 10
 1. Ibid., pp.186–7.
 2. At the time of writing, the author had not found a detailed reference to the Maracaibo raid from Richard Browne, the surgeon who was on board the *Oxford* when it blew up. There are references to the Maracaibo raid but nothing really detailed.
 3. See Esquemeling, P.80.
 4. See Dudley Pope, *Harry Morgan's Way*, p.187.
 5. See Esquemeling, p.80.
 6. Ibid., p.188.
 7. See Talty, *Empire of Blue Water*, p.149.
 8. See Esquemeling, p.81.
 9. See Talty, *Empire of Blue Water*, p.149.

10. See Esquemeling, p.81.
11. See Talty, *Empire of Blue Water*, p.150
12. See Esquemeling, p.81.
13. Leslie, Charles, *A New History of Jamaica*, J, Hodges, 1740.
14. See Esquemeling, p.82.
15. Dudley Pope suggests this in his book, *Harry Morgan's Way*, p.90.

Chapter 11
1. In this case, as with the sources used for researching this book, interrogation does not imply torture.
2. See Leslie, p.123.
3. See Esquemeling, p.82.
4. These accounts can be found in Esquemeling, pp.82–4.
5. Talty's condemnation of the accounts of torture by the buccaneers can be found on p.156 of *Empire of Blue Water*.
6. Ibid, pp.156–7.
7. Ibid., p.155.
8. See Esquemeling, p.85.
9. Ibid.
10. Ibid.
11. Ibid.
12. Ibid., p.86.

Chapter 12
1. Ibid., p.87.
2. See Esquemeling, p.90.
3. According to Esquemeling, this information came from a pilot that had been on board *Santa Louisa* and who 'was a stranger', which presumably means he was not a Spaniard. This man gave Morgan all the background information he needed on Don Alonso and the Spanish fleet.
4. Ibid., p.87.
5. The full contents of this letter can be found in Esquemeling's account on p.87.
6. See Esquemeling, p.88.
7. Ibid.
8. A montero is a type of hunting cap, formerly worn in Spain, having a spherical crown and flaps to protect the ears and neck.
9. Ibid., p.88.
10. See Dudley Pope, *Harry Morgan's Way*, pp.196–7.
11. Esquemeling's account of the attack by Morgan using the fireship is on p.89.
12. Ibid.
13. Ibid.

Chapter 13
1. See Esquemeling, p.92.
2. Ibid.
3. Ibid., p.93.
4. Ibid.
5. Ibid.
6. See Talty, *Empire of Blue Water*, p.168.
7. Ibid., p.170.
8. Pope looks in greater detail at Don Alonso in his book *Harry Morgan's Way*, p.201.
9. See Esquemeling, p.93.
10. Talty, *Empire of Blue Water*, p.172. He cites many reasons why the Spanish had a difficult time in defeating Morgan, which includes the huge distances of the Spanish Main that made

it virtually impossible to defend far-flung cities, inadequate weapons, lack of money for new armament, reliance on militias mostly created from local people and not trained professionals, bureaucracy that stifled initiative, bickering provincial governors and many more.

Chapter 14

1. Leslie, Charles, *A New History of Jamaica*, J. Hodges, 1740, p.132.
2. Taken from the Minutes of the Council of Jamaica, 29 June 1670, which included a copy of a commission sent by Wm Beck, Governor of Curaçao, to Gov Sir Thos Modyford, Calendar of State Papers, America and the West Indies, Vol. 7, 1669–1674, p.209.
3. Extract of a letter from Sir James Modyford to Colonel Lynch, 18 March 1670, Calendar of State Papers, America and the West Indies, Vol. 7, 1669–1674, p.162.
4. See Talty, *Empire of Blue Water*, p.177.
5. Ibid., p.178.
6. Interestingly, Talty states that this proclamation was read in the streets on 24 June. There is doubt as to whether it is 1669 or 1670.
7. Letter from Sir Thomas Modyford to Lord Arlington, 23 August 1669, outlining the reasons for granting commissions against the Spaniards, Calendar of State Papers, America and the West Indies, Vol. 7, 1669–1674, p.103.
8. Ibid.
9. Deposition of Cornelius Carstens, purser of the *Mary and Jane*, Bernard Claesen Speirdyck commander, 20 April 1670, Calendar of State Papers, America and the West Indies, Vol. 7, 1669–1674, pp.172–3.
10. Depositions of Capt John Coxend and Peter Bursett, enclosed with the letter from Modyford to Arlington, 20 April 1670, Calendar of State Papers, America and the West Indies, Vol. 7, 1669–1674, pp.172–1.
11. Deposition of Nicholas Hicks, gent., enclosed with letter from Modyford to Arlington, 20 April 1670, Calendar of State Papers, America and the West Indies, Vol. 7, 1669–1674, pp.172–2.
12. Deposition of William Lane Boatswain of the *Amity*, enclosed in the letter from Modyford to Arlington, 5 May 1670, Calendar of State Papers, America and the West Indies, Vol. 7, 1669–1674, p.182, pp.182–1.
13. See Pope, Dudley, *Harry Morgan's Way*, p.214.
14. From the Minutes of the Council of Jamaica, 29 June 1670, Calendar of State Papers, America and the West Indies, Vol. 7, 1669–1674, p.209.
15. From an extract of a letter from Port Royal, 28 June 1670, Calendar of State Papers, America and the West Indies, Vol. 7, 1669–1674, p.207.
16. See Pope, *Harry Morgan's Way*, citing the King's orders that were still extant at the time of the council meeting, p.217.
17. From the Minutes of the Council of Jamaica, 29 June 1670, Calendar of State Papers, America and the West Indies, Vol. 7, 1669–1674, p.209.
18. Letter from Modyford to Arlington, 31 October 1670, Calendar of State Papers, America and the West Indies, Vol. 7, 1669–1674, p.310.
19. Commission from Sir Thomas Modyford to Admiral Henry Morgan, 2 July 1670, Calendar of State Papers, America and the West Indies, Vol. 7, 1669–1674, p.211.
20. Governor Modyford's Instructions to Admiral Henry Morgan, 2 July 1670, Calendar of State Papers, America and the West Indies, Vol. 7, 1669–1674, p.212.
21. Richard Browne to Undersecretary of State Sir Joseph Williamson, 7 August 1670, Calendar of State Papers, America and the West Indies, Vol. 7, 1669–1674, p.227.
22. Sir Thomas Modyford to Lord Ashley, 6 July 1670, Calendar of State Papers, America and the West Indies, Vol. 7, 1669–1674, p.216.
23. Letter from the Secretary of State Lord Arlington to Sir Thomas Modyford, 12 June 1670, Calendar of State Papers, America and the West Indies, Vol. 7, 1669–1674, p.194.
24. Ibid.

25. Letter from Sir Thomas Modyford to Secretary of State Lord Arlington, 20 August 1670, Calendar of State Papers, America and the West Indies, Vol. 7, 1669–1674, p.237.

Chapter 15

1. Letter from Richard Browne to Secretary Lord Arlington, 12 October 1670, when Browne was aboard the *Satisfaction*, Calendar of State Papers, America and the West Indies, Vol. 7, 1669–1674, p.293.
2. Letter from Modyford to Arlington, 31 October 1670, Calendar of State Papers, America and the West Indies, Vol. 7, 1669–1674, p.310.
3. Letter from Richard Browne to Secretary Lord Arlington, 12 October 1670, when Browne was aboard the *Satisfaction*, Calendar of State Papers, America and the West Indies, Vol. 7, 1669–1674, p.293.
4. See Talty, *Empire of Blue Water*, p.198, who goes into some detail on this very brief battle, especially his insight into Rivero's last moments.
5. See Modyford to Arlington, 31 October 1670, p.310.
6. Ibid.
7. Ibid.
8. There is an interesting discrepancy here in the timeline. Talty states that Collier finally managed to land his men on 24 February, yet by all accounts Collier sailed sometime between 12 September and 7 October 1670. According to Pope and Esquemeling, this expedition took five weeks, maximum.
9. See Talty, *Empire of Blue Water*, p.197.
10. See Esquemeling, p.98.
11. See Talty, *Empire of Blue Water*, p.197.
12. This sum is mentioned in Talty's book, *Empire of Blue Water*, but not in Pope's book. This could be because Talty used several Spanish sources for his work, which would also account for his assertion in this instance that the buccaneers did torture their prisoners. Ibid., p.197.
13. See Esquemeling, p.98.
14. See Pope, Dudley, *Harry Morgan's Way*, p.228.
15. Letter from Modyford to Arlington, 31 October 1670, Calendar of State Papers, America and the West Indies, Vol. 7, 1669–1674, p.310.
16. See Pope, Dudley, *Harry Morgan's Way*, p.230.
17. Esquemeling, p.99.
18. This information on the various ships in Morgan's fleet can be found in Dudley Pope's excellent book, *Harry Morgan's Way*, pp.230–1.
19. Ibid.
20. See Esquemeling, p.100.
21. Letter from Modyford to Arlington, 18 December 1670, Calendar of State Papers, America and the West Indies, Vol. 7, 1669–1674, p.359.

Chapter 16

1. See Pope, *Harry Morgan's Way*, p.237.
2. See Esquemeling, p.101.
3. Ibid.
4. See p.101 of Esquemeling's book for a full description.
5. Ibid., p.102.
6. Ibid.
7. See Esquemeling, p.102, for this whole section on the re-taking of Old Providence and Santa Catarina by Morgan.
8. Ibid., p.103.
9. Dudley Pope tells us that the captains involved in the further planning were Collier, Bradley and Morris, *Harry Morgan's Way*, p.240.
10. Esquemeling talks in derogatory terms about these men on p.104.

Chapter 17

1. Leslie, Charles, *A New History of Jamaica*, J. Hodges, 1740, p.133.
2. Letter from Modyford to Arlington, 18 December 1670, Calendar of State Papers, America and the West Indies, Vol. 7, 1669–1674, p.359.
3. See Pope, *Harry Morgan's Way*, p.241.
4. See Esquemeling, p.106.
5. Ibid.
6. Ibid.
7. Ibid., p.107.
8. For a full description of the fire see Esquemeling's account, p.107.
9. Account of the expedition to Panama signed by Henry Morgan, Calendar of State Papers, America and the West Indies, Vol. 7, 1669–1674, p.504.
10. See Esquemeling, p.109.
11. Interestingly, Dudley Pope states in his book, *Harry Morgan's Way*, that the number of men Morgan left to guard San Lorenzo castle was 400 and the number of men in the fleet was 140, not 150, as Esquemeling states. Both Pope and Esquemeling agree that Morgan headed for Panama with a force of 1,200 men. Pope states that Morgan left Hispaniola with 1,846 men, so, adding the 106 men killed and wounded in the battle and then subtracting 1,740, the figures add up.
12. See Esquemeling, p.109,

Chapter 18

1. See Leslie, Charles, *A New History of Jamaica*, J. Hodges, 1740, p.133.
2. Also, Esquemeling states that Morgan left Chagres on 18 August 1670 in the current edition while in another edition this date is changed to 18 January 1670. Morgan states they left on 9 January 1671 and as he was leading the expedition it is highly likely he would know the date of he led his men down the river towards Panama.
3. Pope tells us these boats were carved from single tree trunks and could be as long as 40 feet. See Pope, *Harry Morgan's Way*, p.248.
4. See Esquemeling, p.110.
5. Ibid.
6. Ibid
7. Ibid
8. See Talty, *Empire of Blue Water*, p.221. As Stephen Talty has researched the Spanish reports of this attack on Panama and Morgan's previous attacks, we can be sure that it is accurate.
9. Ibid., p.222.
10. See Esquemeling, p.111.
11. Ibid.
12. Ibid., p.112.
13. Ibid.

Chapter 19

1. Account of the expedition to Panama signed by Henry Morgan, Calendar of State Papers, America and the West Indies, Vol. 7, 1669–1674, p.504.
2. For greater detail on the description of Panama see Pope, Dudley, *Harry Morgan's Way*. He provides in-depth detail on the town that makes fascinating reading. For example, he states 'there were seven monasteries, a convent, a cathedral, several churches, and a hospital run by forty-five monks and twenty-four nuns', pp.253–4.
3. See Pope, *Harry Morgan's Way*, p.256.
4. A letter dated July 1671 written by Don Juan Perez de Guzman, President of Panama, was intercepted on its way to Spain and taken to Morgan, published in *The Voyages and Adventures of Capt Bartholomew Sharp and Others in the South Sea*, P.J. London, 1684.
5. This is from *Sharp's Voyages* and is entitled 'The True Relation of Sir Henry Morgan, his Expedition Against the Spaniards in the West-Indies, and his taking Panama', p.168.

6. See Esquemeling, p.114.
7. Ibid.
8. See *Sharp's Voyages.*
9. Ibid.
10. From Esquemeling, p.115.
11. Ibid.
12. Ibid.
13. Ibid., p.116.
14. Ibid.
15. Ibid.
16. Ibid. An arquebus was a forerunner of the rifle.
17. See Morgan's account of the expedition to Panama, Calendar of State Papers, America and the West Indies, Vol. 7, 1669–1674, p.504.
18. See *Sharp's Voyages*, Captain Bartholomew Sharp's account of the battle at Panama, 1684.
19. See *Sharp' Voyages*, the letter by Don Juan reporting on the battle and fall of Panama.
20. See Morgan's account of the expedition to Panama, Calendar of State Papers, America and the West Indies, Vol. 7, 1669–1674, p.504.
21. See *Sharp's Voyages*, Captain Bartholomew Sharp's account of the battle at Panama, 1684.
22. See Pope, *Harry Morgan's Way*, p.263.
23. See *Sharp's Voyages*, Captain Bartholomew Sharp's account of the battle at Panama, 1684.
24. See Esquemeling, p.117.
25. See *Sharp's Voyages*, Captain Bartholomew Sharp's account of the battle at Panama, 1684.
26. See *Sharp' Voyages*, the letter by Don Juan reporting on the battle and fall of Panama.
27. Ibid. Interesting the reference to Prince is Lawrence Prince, the man whom Morgan had put in command of the vanguard.
28. See Morgan's account of the expedition to Panama, Calendar of State Papers, America and the West Indies, Vol. 7, 1669–1674, p.504.
29. Esquemeling suggests on p.119 that this took place by Morgan.
30. See *Sharp's Voyages*, Captain Bartholomew Sharp's account of the battle at Panama, 1684.
31. See Pope, *Harry Morgan's Way*, p.265.
32. Taken from Morgan's own account of the expedition to Panama, Calendar of State Papers, America and the West Indies, Vol. 7, 1669–1674, p.504.
33. Taken from the letter written by Don Juan about the sacking of Panama reprinted in *Sharp's Voyages*.
34. See Pope, *Harry Morgan's Way*, p.268.
35. See Esquemeling, p.121.
36. Ibid.
37. Ibid., for this paragraph and the preceding one, where the information comes from Pope. It is worth noting that Talty agrees with Pope on the dates.
38. Taken from Morgan's own account of the expedition to Panama, Calendar of State Papers, America and the West Indies, Vol. 7, 1669–1674, p.504.
39. See Esquemeling, p.123.
40. Ibid., p.124.
41. Taken from William Fogg's account of the actions of the buccaneers at Panama, dated 4 April 1671, Calendar of State Papers, America and the West Indies, Vol. 7, 1669–1674, p.483. Interestingly, Pope states that the amount was 400,000, while Talty states there is confusion over the amount, which ranges from 140,000 to 400,000.
42. Letter from Richard Browne to Joseph Williamson, 21 August 1671, Calendar of State Papers, America and the West Indies, Vol. 7, 1669–1674, p.608.
43. See Pope, *Harry Morgan's Way*, p.270.
44. Taken from the letter written by Don Juan about the sacking of Panama reprinted in *Sharp's Voyages*.

Chapter 20

1. Dudley Pope tells us in Harry Morgan's Way that the date of publication for this newsletter was 23 Feb 1671.
2. These figures come from Pope, *Harry Morgan's Way*, p.272.
3. Instructions to Sir Thomas Lynch, Lieutenant Governor of Jamaica, 31 December 1670, 21 August 1671, Calendar of State Papers, America and the West Indies, Vol. 7, 1669–1674, p.367.
4. Ibid.
5. Sir Thomas Modyford to the Governor of San Domingo of Hispaniola, America and West Indies, May 1671, Calendar of State Papers Colonial, America and West Indies, Vol. 7, 1669–1674 (1889), pp.209–22.
6. Modyford to Lord Arlington, his report 'Considerations from Sir Thomas Modyford which moved him to give his consent for fitting the privateers of Jamaica against the Spaniard', America and West Indies, June 1671, Calendar of State Papers Colonial, America and West Indies, Vol. 7, 1669–1674 (1889), pp.223–8.
7. Sir Thomas Lynch to Secretary Lord Arlington, 2 July 1671, America and West Indies, Calendar of State Papers Colonial, America and West Indies, Vol. 7, 1669–1674 (1889), pp.238–43, p.508.
8. Richard Browne to Joseph Williamson, 21 August, America and West Indies, Calendar of State Papers Colonial, America and West Indies, Vol. 7, 1669–1674, p.608, British History Online.
9. Ibid.
10. Ibid.
11. See Sir Thomas Lynch to Lord Arlington, 20 August 1671, America and West Indies, Calendar of State Papers Colonial, America and West Indies, Vol. 7: 1669–1674, p.604.
12. Ibid.
13. See Lynch to Arlington, 20 August 1671.
14. See Major James Bannister to Lord Arlington, 15 August 1671, America and West Indies, Calendar of State Papers Colonial, America and West Indies, Vol. 7: 1669–1674, p.600. Interestingly, Bannister states that this took place on 12 of August, while Pope suggests it took place on 15 August.
15. See the letter from Browne to Arlington, 21 August 1671.
16. Ibid.
17. Sir Thomas Lynch to Secretary Lord Arlington, 29 November 1671, America and West Indies, Calendar of State Papers Colonial, America and West Indies, Vol. 7, 1669–1674, p.663, British History Online.
18. Minutes of the Council of War at Jamaica, 9 November, 1671, 'America and West Indies: November 1671', Calendar of State Papers Colonial, America and West Indies, Vol. 7, 1669–1674, p.650, British History Online.
19. Lynch to Arlington, 16 December 1671, Calendar of State Papers Colonial, America and West Indies, Vol. 7, 1669–16, p.697.
20. The two preceding quotes are from the letter dated 16 December 1671 by Sir Thomas Lynch to Secretary Lord Arlington, Calendar of State Papers Colonial, America and West Indies, Vol. 7, 1669–16, p.697.
21. See Pope, *Harry Morgan's Way*, p.283.
22. Letter dated 4 April 1672 with orders and instructions from Sir Thomas Lynch to Captain John Keane, America and West Indies: April 1672, Calendar of State Papers Colonial, America and West Indies, Vol. 7, 1669–1674 (1889), p.794.
23. Major James Bannister to Secretary Lord Arlington, 30 March 1672, America and West Indies: April 1672, Calendar of State Papers Colonial, America and West Indies, Vol. 7, 1669–1674 (1889), p.789.

Chapter 21

1. Thomas Lynch to the King, 6 July 1672, America and West Indies: April 1672, Calendar of State Papers Colonial, America and West Indies, Vol. 7: 1669–1674, p.887.

2. See Pope, *Harry Morgan's Way*, for this information, p.288.
3. See Talty, *Empire of Blue Water*, p.264.
4. Ibid., p.265.
5. See Breverton, *Admiral Sir Henry Morgan: The Greatest Buccaneer of Them All*, p.97.
6. Letter from William Morgan to the Privy Council, August 1672, Calendar of State Papers, Domestic, 451, cited in Pope, p.289.
7. The ages of the two men come from Breverton, p.98, while Pope states that he turned twenty in August 1673.
8. See Pope, *Harry Morgan's Way*, p.292.
9. Ibid.
10. Stephen Talty, *Empire of Blue Water*, p.266.
11. Ibid.
12. See Breverton, *Admiral Sir Henry Morgan: The Greatest Buccaneer of Them All*, p.100.
13. This whole exchange is paraphrased from Breverton's book on pp.100–101 in an effort to add a little life into the hearing.
14. This information is from *Breverton, Admiral Sir Henry Morgan: The Greatest Buccaneer of Them All*, pp.101–102.

Chapter 22
1. Lynch to Williamson, 20 November 1674, America and West Indies: April 1672, Calendar of State Papers Colonial, America and West Indies, Vol. 7: 1669–1674, p.1389.
2. Ibid.
3. See Pope, pp.294–5. While Pope doesn't go into detail about Vaughan's complaints, one wonders if the commissions gave greater power to Morgan or too much power to Morgan for Vaughan's liking.
4. Morgan to Secretary Williamson, 13 April 1675, Calendar of State Papers Colonial, America and West Indies: 1675–1676, p.521.
5. Joseph Knapman to Mr Alderman, 16 April 1675, Calendar of State Papers Colonial, America and West Indies: 1675–1676, p.525.
6. See Talty, *Empire of Blue Water*, p.269.
7. See Breverton, p.107.
8. Minutes of the Council of Jamaica, 7 March 1675, Calendar of State Papers Colonial, America and West Indies, Vol. 9: 1675–1676, p.458.
9. Minutes of the Council of Jamaica, 15 March 1675, Calendar of State Papers Colonial, America and West Indies, Vol. 9: 1675–1676, p.467.
10. See Morgan's letter to Williamson, 13 April 1675.
11. Governor Lord Vaughan to Secretary Sir Joseph Williamson, 18 May 1675, Calendar of State Papers Colonial, America and West Indies, Vol. 9: 1675–1676 and Addenda 1574–1674, p.566.
12. Lord Vaughan's letter to Williamson, 18 May 1675.
13. Governor Vaughan to Secretary of State Williamson, 20 September 1675, Calendar of State Papers Colonial, America and West Indies, Vol. 9: 1675–1676 and Addenda 1574–1674, p.673.
14. Cited in Breverton, p.108.
15. See Breverton, p.109.
16. Secretary Peter Beckford to Lord Williamson, 6 December 1675, Calendar of State Papers Colonial, America and West Indies, Vol. 9, 1675–1676 and Addenda 1574–1674, p.735.
17. Governor Vaughan to Secretary Williamson, 2 May 1676, Calendar of State Papers Colonial, America and West Indies, Vol. 9, 1675–1676, p.912.
18. St Jago de la Vega.998. Journal of the Council of Jamaica, 24 July, Calendar of State Papers Colonial, America and West Indies, Vol. 9, 1675–1676, p.912.
19. See Pope for full details of this transaction, pp.307–308.
20. See Breverton, p.112, for more detail on both these quotes. Interestingly, Pope does not mention this part of Morgan's defence so it could be that Breverton is using Morgan's letter to embellish or speculate on what answers Morgan gave at this trial.

21. See Breverton for both these quotes, p.112.
22. List of papers touching Sir Henry Morgan and Robert Byndloss, 10 Novmeber, Calendar of State Papers Colonial, America and West Indies, Vol. 9, 1675–1676, p.1129.
23. Governor Vaughan to Secretary Coventry, 02 August 1676, Calendar of State Papers Colonial, America and West Indies, Vol. 9, 1675–1676, p.1006.
24. List of papers touching Sir Henry Morgan and Robert Byndloss, 10 Novmeber, Calendar of State Papers Colonial, America and West Indies, Vol. 9, 1675–1676, p.1129.

Chapter 23
1. Governor Lord Vaughan to Secretary Sir Henry Coventry, 04 January 1677, Calendar of State Papers Colonial, America and West Indies, Vol. 10, 1677–1680, p.2–13.
2. See Pope, p.313.
3. See Breverton, p.113.
4. Cited in Pope, *Harry Morgan's Way*, p.314.
5. Vaughan to Secretary Coventry, 28 May 1677, Calendar of State Papers Colonial, America and West Indies, Vol. 10,1677–1680, p.270.
6. Ibid.
7. Vaughan to Williamson, 14 May 1677, Calendar of State Papers Colonial, America and West Indies, Vol. 10, 1677–1680, p.243.
8. 8.   Peter Beckford, Clerk of the Council, to Secretary Williamson, 01 August 1677, Calendar of State Papers Colonial, America and West Indies, Vol. 10, 1677–1680, p.375.
9. Sir Thomas Lynch to Williamson, 5 August 1677, Calendar of State Papers Colonial, America and West Indies, Vol. 10, 1677–1680, p.383.
10. Journal of Lords of Trade and Plantations, 29 October 1677, Calendar of State Papers Colonial, America and West Indies, Vol. 10, 1677–1680, p.461.
11. From Whitehall, 13 January 1678, America and West Indies: January 1678, Calendar of State Papers Colonial, America and West Indies, Vol. 10, 1677–1680, p.570, p.571, p.572.

Chapter 24
1. Minutes of the Council of Jamaica, 3 April 1678, Calendar of State Papers Colonial, America and West Indies, Vol. 10, 1677–1680, p.646.
2. Minutes of the Council of War, 5 April 1678, Calendar of State Papers Colonial, America and West Indies, Vol. 10, 1677–1680, p.649.
3. For more detail on this fleet and the incident that wrecked the fleet, see Pope, *Harry Morgan's Way*, pp324–5.
4. Minutes of the Council of War, Jamaica, 31 May 1678, Calendar of State Papers Colonial, America and West Indies, Vol. 10, 1677–1680, p.717.
5. Relation of Thomas Wigfall, Master of the *Advice* sloop, 1 June 1678, Calendar of State Papers Colonial, America and West Indies, Vol. 10, 1677–1680, p.718.
6. Governor Lord Carlisle to Secretary Coventry, 31 July 1678, Calendar of State Papers Colonial, America and West Indies, Vol. 10, 1677–1680, p.770.
7. Governor Lord Carlisle to Secretary Coventry, 14 August 1678, Calendar of State Papers Colonial, America and West Indies, Vol. 10, 1677–1680, p.779.
8. See Governor Lord Carlisle to Secretary Coventry, 10 September 1678, Calendar of State Papers Colonial, America and West Indies, Vol. 10, 1677–1680, p.794.
9. Letter from Carlisle to Williamson, 24 October 1678, Calendar of State Papers Colonial, America and West Indies, Vol. 10, 1677–1680, p.816.
10. Letter from Carlisle to Lords of Trade and Plantations, 15 November 1678, Calendar of State Papers Colonial, America and West Indies, Vol. 10, 1677–1680, p.827.

Chapter 25
1. Report of the Lords of Trade and Plantations to the King in Council, 28 May 1679, Calendar of State Papers Colonial, America and West Indies, Vol. 10, 1677–1680, p.1009.

2. Governor Lord Carlisle to Lords of Trade and Plantations, 20 June 1679, , Calendar of State Papers Colonial, America and West Indies, Vol. 10, 1677–1680, p.1030.
3. See Pope, *Harry Morgan's Way*, p.329.
4. Carlisle to Secretary Coventry, 10 July 1679, Calendar of State Papers Colonial, America and West Indies, Vol. 10, 1677–1680, p.1059.
5. See letter, 10 July 1679, Carlisle to Sir Henry Coventry.
6. See Breverton, p.116.
7. Carlisle to Coventry, 15 September 1679, Calendar of State Papers Colonial, America and West Indies, Vol. 10: 1677–1680, p.1118.
8. See Breverton, p.117.
9. Carlisle to Coventry, 20 March 1679, Calendar of State Papers Colonial, America and West Indies, Vol. 10: 1677–1680, p.943.
10. Carlisle to Coventry, 23 February 1680, Calendar of State Papers Colonial, America and West Indies, Vol. 10: 1677–1680, p.943.
11. Ibid.
12. Sir Henry Morgan to Lords of Trade and Plantations, 24 February 1680, Calendar of State Papers Colonial, America and West Indies, Vol. 10: 1677–1680, p.943.
13. Minutes of the Council of Jamaica, 5 November 1680, Calendar of State Papers Colonial, America and West Indies, Vol. 10: 1677–1680, p.1576.

Chapter 26

1. See Breverton, p.118.
2. See Pope, *Harry Morgan's Way*, p.341.
3. See Talty, *Empire of Blue Water*, p.272.
4. Sir Harry Morgan to Lord Sunderland, 5 July 1680, Calendar of State Papers Colonial, America and West Indies, Vol. 10: 1677–1680, p.1425.
5. Ibid.
6. See Breverton, p.118.
7. Ibid., p.119.
8. Morgan to the Lords of Trade and Plantations, 16 March 1681, Calendar of State Papers Colonial, America and West Indies, Vol. 11: 1681–1684, p.51. See also, Breverton, p.119, and a letter from Morgan to the Earl of Sunderland, 16 February, outlining the details of this action.
9. Sir Henry Morgan to the Earl of Sunderland, 1 February 1681, Calendar of State Papers Colonial, America and West Indies, Vol. 11: 1681–1684, p.16.
10. See Talty, *Empire of Blue Water*, p.274.
11. See Breverton, pp.124–6.
12. Ibid., p.127.
13. Governor the Duke of Albemarle to the Lords of Trade and Plantations, 11 February 1688, Calendar of State Papers Colonial, America and West Indies, Vol. 12: 1685–1688, p.1624.
14. This quote from Dr Hans Sloan is cited in Breverton, p.128.
15. Governor the Duke of Albemarle to the Lords of Trade and Plantations, 8 August 1688, Calendar of State Papers Colonial, America and West Indies, Vol 12: 1685–1688, p.1858.
16. See Talty, *Empire of Blue Water*, p.283.

Legacy

1. Ibid., p.305.

Index

Discover Your History

Ancestors • Heritage • Memories

Each issue of *Discover Your History* presents special features and regular articles on a huge variety of topics about our social history and heritage – such as our ancestors, childhood memories, military history, British culinary traditions, transport history, our rural and industrial past, health, houses, fashions, pastimes and leisure ... and much more.

Historic pictures show how we and our ancestors have lived and the changing shape of our towns, villages and landscape in Britain and beyond.

Special tips and links help you discover more about researching family and local history. Spotlights on fascinating museums, history blogs and history societies also offer plenty of scope to become more involved.

Keep up to date with news and events that celebrate our history, and reviews of the latest books and media releases.

Discover Your History presents aspects of the past partly through the eyes and voices of those who were there.

UK only

Discover Your History is in all good newsagents and also available on subscription for six or twelve issues. For more details on how to take out a subscription and how to choose your free book, call 01778 392013 or visit **www.discoveryourhistory.net**